THE SYMPHONY IN
BEETHOVEN'S VIENNA

An original study of the history of the symphony in Vienna during Beethoven's lifetime, this book explores the context in which the
composer worked. Based on an extensive study of the wider symphonic repertoire of the period and of the characteristics of musical
life that shaped the changing fortunes of the genre, from manuscript
and printed dissemination to concert life, David Wyn Jones provides a
multi-faceted account of the development of the symphony at one of
the most crucial periods in its history. The volume offers a wide perspective on musical development in the period, and will be of interest
to musicologists and cultural historians. As well as dealing with unfamiliar works by Czerny, Eberl, Krommer, Reicha, Anton Wranitzky,
Paul Wranitzky and others, it charts the changing reception of the
symphonies of Haydn and Mozart, and offers new insights into the
symphonic careers of Beethoven and Schubert.

DAVID WYN JONES is Reader in Music at Cardiff University and
has written extensively on music and musical life in the Classical
Period. He is the author of *The Life of Beethoven* (1998), *Beethoven:
The Pastoral Symphony* (1996) and is the editor of *Music in Eighteenth-
Century Austria* (1996), all published by Cambridge University Press.
His *Companion to Haydn* (2002) was awarded the C. B. Oldman Prize
by IAML UK. He is on the Advisory Board of the journal *Eighteenth-
Century Music*, a council member of the Royal Musical Association
and chairman of the Music Libraries Trust. He has contributed to
several programmes on BBC Radio 3 and Radio 4.

THE SYMPHONY IN BEETHOVEN'S VIENNA

DAVID WYN JONES

CAMBRIDGE
UNIVERSITY PRESS

CAMBRIDGE UNIVERSITY PRESS
Cambridge, New York, Melbourne, Madrid, Cape Town, Singapore, São Paulo

Cambridge University Press
The Edinburgh Building, Cambridge CB2 2RU, UK

Published in the United States of America by Cambridge University Press, New York

www.cambridge.org
Information on this title: www.cambridge.org/9780521862615

© David Wyn Jones 2006

First published 2006

Printed in the United Kingdom at the University Press, Cambridge

A catalogue record for this publication is available from the British Library

ISBN-13 978-0-521-86261-5 hardback
ISBN-10 0-521-86261-2 hardback

Arts & Humanities
Research Council

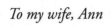

To my wife, Ann

Contents

Illustrations

Tables

Music examples

Preface

The image of Beethoven as the key figure in the history of the symphony is a fundamental one in Western culture. For over 150 years his nine symphonies have been accepted as the cornerstone of the repertoire and the foundation for the development of the genre in the nineteenth and twentieth centuries. This image has been probed and enhanced by a scholarly tradition that is almost as long, as generations of writers have sought to understand the individual works, from sketch studies to hermeneutic analysis, and to offer a view of the composer's unique creativity. But the iconic status of the composer has always tended to emphasize his individuality at the expense of the musical environment that nurtured him. While commentators have always remarked that Beethoven's symphonies build on a tradition established by Haydn and Mozart, there is no real or systematic understanding of musical life in Vienna in the composer's time and how it influenced his development as a symphonist. We understand how Beethoven moulded the future of the symphony, but not the factors that moulded Beethoven's symphonies.

Rather than making Beethoven the focus of the study, this book explores the development of the symphony in Vienna from c.1790 through to c.1830, giving attention to changing patterns of patronage, the repertoire, its musical characteristics and the perceived status of the genre. Beethoven's name figures alongside those of less familiar composers, Eberl, Hoffmeister, Krommer, Paul Wranitzky and others, while the unfolding narrative also sheds light on the early reception history of the symphonies of Haydn and Mozart, and the peculiarly self-enclosed environment in which Schubert composed his symphonies. By exploring this complex, often insecure, sometimes contradictory history the book reveals too how the modern image of the symphony in Vienna first emerged, including Beethoven's mythical status.

Ideas for this book have been simmering in my mind for several years and former undergraduate and postgraduate students at Cardiff University will recognize many of its preoccupations, even if the part they played in helping to develop and refine them may not be so apparent. Two grants from the Arts and Humanities Research Council enabled me to pursue and complete the project: a Small Grant in the Creative and Performing Arts (2001–3), and a Research Leave Award for the academic year 2004–5. During that sabbatical year the Research Committee of the School of Music, Cardiff University provided welcome supplementary financial assistance.

I am grateful to the staff of the following libraries for their assistance, either in person or by correspondence: Bibliothèque Nationale, Paris; British Library, London; Gesellschaft der Musikfreunde, Vienna (Otto Biba and Ingrid Fuchs); Henry Watson Music Library, Manchester (Ros Edwards); Ira F. Brilliant Center for Beethoven Studies, San José (Patricia Stroh); Roudnice Lobkowicz Library, Nelahozeves, Czech Republic (Laura De Barbieri and Sona Cernocka); Österreichische Nationalbibliothek, Musiksammlung; Prague Conservatoire (Miloslav Richter); and the Stadt- und Landesbibliothek, Vienna. The staff of the Music Library at Cardiff University, in particular Gill Jones and Judith Hurford, were unfailingly helpful and co-operative, even when I tested their patience (not to mention borrowing regulations) to the limit.

Numerous individuals have helped the project in various ways, from supporting grant applications, engaging in casual discussion, to answering particular queries. I am grateful for the assistance and interest of the following while relieving them of any responsibility for the use I have made of their views and expertise: Christine Barley, Derek Carew, David Charlton, Britta Constapel, Tia DeNora, Cliff Eisen, Jutta Grub, Anke Henkel, Nick Jones, Else Radant Landon, Emma Peters, Rita Steblin, John A. Rice, Rupert Ridgewell, Julian Rushton and the late Eugene Wolf. Above all, Otto Biba, the director of the archive of the Gesellschaft der Musikfreunde in Vienna, must be thanked for his support, for drawing my attention to material in the archive, sharing his profound knowledge of musical life in Vienna and patiently questioning some of my ideas. He, probably more than anyone else, will recognize the shortcomings of this volume; at the same time I hope he will regard it as a valiant attempt by a non-Viennese to get to grips with one of the most important chapters in the history of music in that city.

Finally I thank my wife Ann for her support throughout the project, in particular for reminding me of life beyond the concerns of this book.

Cardiff
September 2005

CHAPTER I

Setting the scene

BEETHOVEN PETITIONS TO BE AN OPERA COMPOSER

Late in 1807 Beethoven sent a three-page letter to the directors of the court theatres in Vienna. He had heard from one of them, Prince Lobkowitz, that they might be interested in engaging him as a house composer. Writing in the third person, Beethoven's self-belief and ambition as a composer are evident, mingled with observations on how difficult it was to realize this outlook. 'Since on the whole the aim which he has ever pursued in his career has been much less to earn his daily bread than to raise the taste of the public and to let his genius scale to greater heights and even to perfection, the undersigned has sacrificed to the Muse both material profit and his own advantage.' If the directors of the court theatres, Beethoven continues, were to engage him on a permanent basis and with a fixed income he would commit himself 'to compose every year at least one large opera' plus 'a little operetta or divertissement, choruses and incidental pieces'. Apart from a salary Beethoven made the reasonable and quite conventional requests that he should receive the proceeds of the third-night performance of any of his operas and that he be allocated at least one day a year for a benefit concert. Despite the earlier encouragement of Prince Lobkowitz Beethoven's proposal came to nothing. At a meeting on 4 December the directors noted dryly that the composer would not be engaged without further explanation of his ideas for the opera and other works.[1]

Most accounts of Beethoven's life mention this episode as part of a wider picture of the composer's troublesome life in Vienna, without exploring the motivation behind the letter and the likely implications on his career. Had Beethoven's proposal been accepted – and his demands were not, after all, extravagant ones – he would have composed one major operatic work a year

---

[1] S. Brandenburg (ed.), *Ludwig van Beethoven. Briefwechsel Gesamtausgabe* (Munich, 1996–98), vol. 1, pp. 333–5. English translation from E. Anderson (ed.), *The Letters of Beethoven* (London, 1961), vol. 3, pp. 1444–6.

to add to the existing *Leonore* and a number of other, smaller stage works, which would have allowed little time for the composition of instrumental music, the sonatas, piano trios, quartets, concertos and symphonies that had already marked him out as a composer of supreme achievement. For a brief period towards the end of 1807 the whole direction of Beethoven's career was in question and, it might be rather grandly said, the whole direction of music history. What if Beethoven's request had been accepted and he had devoted the rest of his career to stage music?

Speculation on the 'what ifs' of history are an indulgence, perhaps even an affront when the legacy of a major figure such as Beethoven is concerned, yet the thought processes that are exposed invariably clarify the nature of the historical events that did take place. In the history of the symphony to state that Beethoven's contribution to its development was a defining one is a truism of truisms. By 1807 he had composed only four symphonies and, although the intention of the requested annual benefit was to present major orchestral works, the demands of being a contracted opera composer would almost certainly have precluded the composition of further large-scale instrumental works; Beethoven himself remarked in the letter that the demands of composing and presenting a new opera 'completely excludes every other mental exertion'. At the time Beethoven was nearing the completion of the Fifth Symphony and the notional benefit concert was tied up with plans for its public premiere, as well as that of the Fourth Piano Concerto. But, while securing a position in the court theatres was partly, if impracticably, meant to yield opportunities for public concerts, the wider issue why the composer was so readily seeking to establish a stable career as an opera composer rather than a symphony composer is a tantalizing one that invites investigation.

As often in Beethoven's career a ruthless pragmatism was at work alongside the haughty idealism. A career in the employment of the court theatres offered financial security of a kind that was not possible for a composer of symphonies in Vienna in 1807. As elsewhere in Europe, opera in the major public theatres in the city, the Burgtheater, the Kärntnertortheater and, since 1801, the Theater an der Wien, was subject to fickle management, financial crises as well as changes of musical taste, from Italian to German, and from serious to comic; for all that it was a permanent presence. For any composer opera was not only fashionable and challenging but offered the prospect of financial security. The success of Beethoven's music for the ballet *Die Geschöpfe des Prometheus*, first performed at the Burgtheater in March 1801, had sown the seeds of his interest in the theatre. Shortly afterwards he was enthused by the first performances (in German translation) of operas by Cherubini and Méhul, was actually appointed composer at the Theater an der Wien in 1803 and began work on an opera, *Vestas Feuer*, before turning to *Leonore*; the first version was performed in November 1805, a revised version a few months later in March 1806. Although the composition, rehearsal and production of *Leonore* were plagued with problems, some of them of Beethoven's own making, the composer retained his enthusiasm for the theatre and the petition to the directors of the court theatres at the end of 1807 was an entirely natural development.

The part that the symphony had played in Beethoven's career up to 1807 was not as dominant as one might assume, given that he had completed four symphonies to date. The composer had first arrived in Vienna in November 1792 to receive lessons from Haydn, the acknowledged master of the genre who was preparing for his second visit to London by composing symphonies Nos. 99 and 101 ('Clock'). But there was no hint of a symphony from the young Beethoven. As his career as a pianist and composer unfolded in Vienna in the 1790s, composition of symphonies was not a priority. A symphony in C major was begun in 1795–8 but was eventually abandoned.[2] He returned to the genre in 1799 and completed his First Symphony in readiness for a benefit concert, his first, at the Burgtheater in April 1800. Encouraged by the success of this concert Beethoven formulated the plan of presenting an annual benefit concert at which he would present himself as a performer, particularly as a soloist in a piano concerto, and with a new symphony. Over-ambitious in conception the plan was continually undermined by the difficulties of securing free evenings at the court theatres for concerts. Beethoven's second benefit concert, at the Theater an der Wien, did not take place until April 1803. A further five years were to elapse before the third benefit concert took place, in December 1808, when the Fifth and Sixth Symphonies were given in public for the first time. Meanwhile Beethoven's contact with well-to-do patrons in Vienna (Prince Lobkowitz and the banker Joseph Würth) and beyond (Count Franz Joachim Oppersdorff in Silesia) had led to private performances of symphonies Nos. 3–6.

In the absence of a regular public concert series in Vienna Beethoven's symphonies were not at the centre of musical life in the city in the way that Haydn's symphonies had been in London a decade earlier and they certainly did not constitute a repertory. Part of the lure of permanent employment at the court theatres, as Beethoven's letter seeks to ensure, was that free evenings for benefit concerts and the continued presentation of symphonies, concertos and other orchestral works, as well as vocal works, could be easily secured. While Beethoven's predicament in 1807 was an

[2] B. Cooper, *Beethoven* (Oxford, 2000), p. 61, p. 64, pp. 67–70.

individual and peculiarly intense one, its governing characteristics were apparent in the creative lives of other composers of the time.

GYROWETZ, HAYDN AND VANHAL: THREE SYMPHONIC CAREERS

The career of Gyrowetz, only seven years older than Beethoven, is especially instructive. Born in Bohemia in 1763, he studied law in Prague and entered the employ of Count Franz von Fünfkirchen as a court secretary.[3] As was common practice in the Austrian territories, functionaries, from court officials to servants, were often capable musicians and Gyrowetz, who played the violin, joined his colleagues in a small court orchestra to provide regular concerts. It was for this orchestra that he wrote his first symphonies. His reputation spread quickly through the network of nobility and soon his career gravitated towards Vienna. He met Mozart who included one of his symphonies in the 1785 subscription series held in the Mehlgrube, alongside his own works and, probably, some symphonies by Michael Haydn.[4] Gyrowetz was now employed as a secretary by Prince Ruspoli who took him on a three-year journey to Italy, where he continued to compose. During a visit to Paris in 1789 he struck a valuable deal with the publisher Imbault that led to the publication of a series of his symphonies; less pleasingly he discovered that another publisher, Sieber, had issued an early symphony in G (G1) as the work of Joseph Haydn (Hob.I: G3). The uncertain circumstances following the outbreak of the French Revolution encouraged Gyrowetz to move to London, another major centre for the performance and publication of symphonies, where his career reached a notable highpoint. For the Professional Concert he composed three symphonies, subsequently published by Longman and Broderip and dedicated to the Prince of Wales (D7, F4 and C3); in addition his symphonies were regularly performed alongside those of Haydn in Salomon's concert series in 1791 and 1792.[5] The damp English climate compelled him to leave London in February 1792, armed with the proceeds of a benefit concert. By 1793 he was back in Vienna.

[3] For an account of Gyrowetz's career see J. A. Rice (ed.), *Adalbert Gyrowetz (1763–1850). Four Symphonies. The Symphony 1720–1840*, ed. in chief, B. S. Brook, B/XI (New York, 1983), pp. xiii–xviii. Gyrowetz's own autobiography, published in 1848 (two years before his death), is especially informative on his life up to the first decade of the nineteenth century. A. Einstein (ed.), *Lebensläufe deutscher Musiker von ihnen selbst erzählt. 3/4 Adalbert Gyrowetz (1763–1850)* (Leipzig, 1915).
[4] N. Zaslaw, *Mozart's Symphonies. Context, Performance Practice, Reception* (Oxford, 1989), pp. 392–6.
[5] 1 April 1791, 29 April 1791, 3 June 1791, 17 February 1792, 2 March 1792 and 1 May 1792. H. C. Robbins Landon, *Haydn: Chronicle and Works. Haydn in England 1791–1795* (London, 1976), *passim*.

At the age of thirty Gyrowetz had composed nearly thirty symphonies, widely distributed in the Austrian territories and an established part of the repertoire in Paris and London. He might reasonably have expected to continue his career in Vienna as a composer of symphonies. Over the next ten years, however, no more than half-a-dozen symphonies were composed (C4, D9, E♭6, G3, A1 and A2) as Gyrowetz turned his attention to piano music and, especially, string quartets. Only one public concert in Vienna in the 1790s included a symphony by him, Josepha Auernhammer's benefit concert at the Burgtheater on 25 March 1795.[6] His training as lawyer and his skills as a linguist (Latin, Italian, French, English and Czech as well as his native German) enabled him to acquire a post in the imperial bureaucracy, where he had special responsibility for the army archives, and for a few years he was essentially a part-time composer.

A decisive turning point occurred in 1804 when he was offered the post of Vice-Kapellmeister at the court theatres. Apart from an opera seria on a popular text by Metastasio, *Semiramis*, composed in London in 1791, Gyrowetz had not previously composed anything for the stage. His auto-biography makes no mention of this lack of experience but dwells on an even more fundamental dilemma, whether he should remain a civil servant or try his luck as an artist.[7] After considerable prevarication he accepted the position of Vice-Kapellmeister and devoted the remainder of his long life to the composition of stage works. As outlined in his autobiography his duties were not dissimilar to the ones Beethoven was to seek three years later. Gyrowetz was to compose one opera a year and one ballet (equivalent to Beethoven's 'divertissement'); but there is no mention of an evening for a benefit concert. At the age of forty-one Gyrowetz had turned his back on a career as a composer of symphonies. By the time of his death in 1850 he had become one of the most revered figures in Viennese musical life and, although much of this reverence was based on the fact that he represented a link with the Vienna of Haydn and Mozart, it did not extend to per-forming any of his symphonies. It was as an elder statesman rather than an acknowledged master of the genre that he served as one of the judges in a competition for a new symphony, held in Vienna in 1835.[8]

[6] M. S. Morrow, *Concert Life in Haydn's Vienna: Aspects of a Developing Musical and Social Institution* (Stuyvesant, NY, 1989), p. 286.

[7] Einstein (ed.), *Gyrowetz*, pp. 115–6.

[8] The prize was given to Franz Lachner (1803–90) for his *Sinfonia passionata* in C minor. M. Handlos, 'Die Wiener *Concerts spirituels* (1819–1848)', *Österreichische Musik – Musik in Österreich. Beiträge zur Musikgeschichte Mitteleuropas*, ed. E. T. Hilscher, Wiener Veröffentlichungen zur Musikwissenschaft, 34 (Tutzing, 1998), p. 310.

The last decade of the eighteenth century also witnessed the culmination of Haydn's career as a composer of symphonies. From the late 1750s he had devoted himself consistently to the genre, first as Kapellmeister at the court of Count Franz Ferdinand Morzin at Lukavec (Dolní Lukavice) in Bohemia, then as Vice-Kapellmeister, later Kapellmeister, at the court of two successive Esterházy princes, based mainly in Eisenstadt and Eszterháza with occasional visits to Vienna and Pressburg (Bratislava). His symphonies became known throughout Europe and from this esteem arose commissions for new works from London (symphonies Nos. 76–78) and from Paris (the so-called 'Paris' symphonies, Nos. 82–87, and Nos. 88–92, also written for the city), works that could be performed too at the Esterházy court. The most supportive of the Esterházy princes, Prince Nicolaus, died in September 1790, and was succeeded by his son Prince Anton who, with a keen eye on court expenditure, set in motion his plans to curtail musical life there. The resident opera company and the court orchestra were summarily dismissed with only three people retained, Haydn, Tomasini (the principal violinist) and Leopold Dichtler (singer, double bass player and occasional copyist), partly in recognition of their long-standing service, partly because they were to be responsible for engaging musicians for any occasion that might require them. If, for Haydn, this represented a rather sudden and disconsolate end to nearly thirty years of service, it also enabled him to accept an invitation to travel to London. Two visits were made, in 1791–2 and 1794–5, the principal products of which were twelve symphonies (Nos. 93–104), a glorious expansion of the genre.

One of the startling aspects of Haydn's career as a composer of symphonies is that not a single work was commissioned by an institution in Vienna and very few – Nos. 6–8, for instance, performed at the Esterházy palace in the Wallnerstrasse in 1761 – were given their first performance there. In the most circumscribed sense, Paris and London were more important than Vienna in Haydn's symphonic career. When Vienna rather than Eisenstadt and Eszterháza became the composer's principal residence in the 1790s he interacted more consistently with musical life in the city, notably for the composition and many performances of two oratorios, *The Creation* and *The Seasons*; significantly, this interaction was never to yield a new symphony.

Following each of the two visits to London Haydn organized a single concert in Vienna to present some of the London symphonies. On 15 March 1793 he gave a benefit concert at the Kleiner Redoutensaal in front of 400 to 600 people where three symphonies from the first London visit were presented.[9] As Haydn's pupil, Beethoven was almost certainly present, as also, one imagines, was Gyrowetz. A similar event in the same venue followed the second visit: on 18 December 1795 when, again, three symphonies were played.[10] These two concerts were the only ones organized by Haydn in this last stage of his life. Throughout this period, from 1795, when Haydn returned from London, to 1802, when he effectively retired from composition, there is not the merest hint that Haydn was to compose a new symphony for Vienna.

At the Esterházy court, meanwhile, a new prince, Nicolaus II, had assumed control. Gradually music came once more to assume a prominent role, without reaching the level of activity of his grandfather's time. Church music was fully supported, with a natural high point in September of every year when the name-day of Princess Marie Hermenegild was celebrated; Haydn six late masses were all, to a greater or lesser extent, associated with this occasion. In the weeks surrounding the name-day there were opera performances by visiting troupes, balls and the occasional informal concert when Haydn would accompany a vocal performance on the piano; but symphonies were noticeably absent and Nicolaus did not commission any.

By 1801 the full-time music establishment of the Esterházy court numbered eight singers and an orchestra of twenty, but their duties were to provide liturgical music and to provide Harmoniemusik.[11] Haydn seems never to have considered writing a symphony for these Esterházy forces. The virtual absence of the symphony at the Esterházy court continued when Hummel (1778–1837) was appointed Concertmeister in 1804; he willingly took on the duties of composing liturgical music and directed a regular season of opera at the court, including works of his own (*Endimione e Diana* and *Die vereitelten Raenke*, both 1806).[12] But he never composed a symphony.

One of the most prolific near contemporaries of Haydn was Johann Vanhal. Born in Bohemia in 1739, seven years after Haydn, he died in Vienna in 1813, four years after him.[13] He had moved to Vienna in 1760 or

[9] Landon, *Haydn in England*, pp. 215–6.

[10] H. C. Robbins Landon, *Haydn: Chronicle and Works. Haydn: The Years of 'The Creation' 1796–1800* (London, 1977), pp. 59–60.

[11] H. C. Robbins Landon, *Haydn: Chronicle and Works. Haydn: the Late Years* (London, 1977), pp. 63–7. R. Hellyer, 'The Wind Ensembles of the Esterházy Princes, 1761–1813', *Haydn Yearbook*, 15 (1985), pp. 32–6.

[12] M. Horányi, *The Magnificence of Eszterháza* (London, 1962), pp. 174–90.

[13] The following provides a comprehensive account of Vanhal's life and his contribution to the symphony. P. Bryan, *Johann Wanhal, Viennese Symphonist. His Life and His Musical Environment* (Stuyvesant, NY, 1997). See also D. Heartz, *Haydn, Mozart and the Viennese School 1740–1780* (New York, 1995), pp. 453–63.

1761 where, apart from a two-year visit to Italy in 1769–71, he was based for the remainder of his life. Unlike Haydn he never held a full-time post as a Kapellmeister but enjoyed the patronage of two members of the nobility on a regular basis, Baron Riesch (about whom little is known) and Count Ladislaus Erdödy (1746–86), the brother-in-law of Prince Anton Esterházy, Haydn's first patron. Active as a composer until the very last few weeks of his long life Vanhal wrote large quantities of instrumental music and sacred music. Seventy-six symphonies are safely attributed to him, mostly composed for Riesch and Erdödy and, subsequently, as in the case of Haydn, disseminated throughout the Austrian territories; for instance, the Clam Gallas and the Waldstein families in Bohemia, as well as the Esterházy family regularly acquired them. Again like those of Haydn, Vanhal's symphonies were published in Amsterdam, Berlin, London and Paris. Stylistically, the works have many parallels with those of Haydn from the 1760s and 1770s, especially the cultivation of the minor mode c.1770, the use of concertante movements and a predisposition toward monothematicism in sonata form.

Although little detail is known about when and where individual symphonies by Vanhal were composed, what is notable about his symphonic career is that is stops abruptly c.1780; for the remaining thirty years or so of his life he concentrated instead on piano music and sacred music. Not a single symphony is known to have been played in public in Vienna during this period. He had become a totally different kind of composer.

STUDYING THE SYMPHONY IN BEETHOVEN'S VIENNA

Consideration of the musical lives of three individuals, Gyrowetz, Haydn and Vanhal, who were prolific composers of symphonies for a signifi-cant part of their lives before turning away from the genre, suggests that Beethoven's contemplation of a change of emphasis in his career in 1807, towards opera and, by implication, away from the symphony, would not have been viewed as eccentric by his contemporaries.

Using the biographies of three selected composers to interpret a spec-ulative plan of a fourth, a plan, moreover, that never materialized, might appear a shaky foundation for historical enquiry; after all, Beethoven went on to complete his Fifth Symphony in a matter of weeks, followed by four further symphonies. Broadening the outlook even this far, from one composer to four, does, nevertheless, draw attention to certain insistent questions that need to be explored. Was the symphony as central to music making in Vienna and its environs c. 1800 as it had been a few decades ear-lier? Are there some common factors that explain why Gyrowetz wrote only a couple after c.1795, Haydn none after 1795, Vanhal none after c.1780, and Beethoven none until 1800? Beethoven was clearly a more tenacious and restless creative figure than Gyrowetz and Vanhal, qualities that would have almost certainly brought to an end any contract with the court theatres. What were the tensions between such creative impulses and the musical environment? Did they impact on the number of symphonies that Beethoven composed, even their nature? Are similar patterns evident in the careers of other composers?

To search for answers to these and similar questions in the biographies of individual composers is too limited an approach, axiomatically emphasizing particular circumstances at the expense of broader trends: thus Gyrowetz can be said to have lacked the creative will to explore the genre further; Haydn was too busy with the composition of the six late masses, *The Creation* and *The Seasons*; Vanhal's music had not kept pace with the times; and Beethoven was anxious to absorb the legacy of Haydn and Mozart before embarking on the symphony. Biographical information, particularly for lesser known composers, even occasionally for major figures such as Haydn and Beethoven, is limited or patchy, making it hazardous to draw conclusions; even Gyrowetz, in what is often an engagingly written autobiography, mentions only one identifiable symphony (the one that was printed and performed in Paris as the work of Haydn, G1) and says nothing about why he stopped composing symphonies in the 1790s. Finally the chronological imperative of the biography will always emphasize the new and the emergent at the expense of the old and the continuing. It is a mistake to assume that musical life in Vienna at the end of the eighteenth century and the beginning of the nineteenth century was always seeking new instrumental works. There is ample evidence that this was the time when reception history of older music began to fold into music history, with marked consequences over time for the nature and status of the symphony. Taken together the inherent liabilities of musical biography suggest that a broader, more flexible approach to the investigation of the symphony in Beethoven's Vienna is needed, one that balances repertoire, performance and reception but does not ignore creative individuality.

Keeping the focus on Vienna and its musical hinterland of Lower and Upper Austria, Bohemia, Hungary and Moravia is entirely appropriate. Instrumental music in Vienna had always been largely self-sufficient in composers and works, lacking the cosmopolitanism that characterized musical life in London and Paris. As the capital of the Holy Roman Empire until Napoleon forced its disbandment in 1806 and of the Austrian Empire from 1804 Vienna acted as a focal point for music, as it did for trade, politics and government. Gyrowetz and Vanhal were only two of many musicians from Bohemia who gravitated towards Vienna; Haydn worked for a noble family, the Esterházy family, who played a skilful mediating role between the Habsburg court and Hungary; and Beethoven in 1792 moved from Bonn, an electorate in the Holy Roman Empire ruled by Maximilian Franz, to the capital, where Maximilian's brother, Leopold, was the emperor.

Coupled with this self-sufficiency there was a commercial and economic conservatism in the imperial city that ensured that music publishing, public concert life and the musical press (in the broadest sense) were less developed than elsewhere in Europe. In the Napoleonic period self-sufficiency turned first to insularism and then virtual stagnation as the Habsburgs imposed strict censorship in order to preserve identity and to ensure survival, and the cost of the war effort unleashed rampant inflation. From the nineteenth century onwards scholarship has tended to undervalue the increasingly inward nature of the city in which Beethoven the symphonist lived and worked, preferring to view him from a European perspective, someone whose music was first published in Leipzig, London and Mainz, whose reputation was fashioned by the Leipzig *Allgemeine musikalische Zeitung* and who addressed libertarians in all countries. While Beethoven was acutely conscious and proud of his wider reputation he was also aware, sometimes painfully so, of the immediate circumstances that governed his compositional life from day to day, from month to month, and from year to year. He was, first of all, a Viennese composer, only then a European one.

Also undervalued in most discussion of musical life in Vienna is the rapid change in musical practices in the years after the end of the Napoleonic Wars. It was still a watchful city as Metternich continued to impose an iron grip on society, but there was a new ambition and a new confidence that impacted on all aspects of musical life, and it was only during this period that the symphony assumed an assured and permanent position in musical life.

CHAPTER 2

Selling symphonies

THE MUSIC DEALER, JOHANN TRAEG; THE 1799 CATALOGUE

For any musician living in Vienna at the end of the eighteenth century the inner city, still surrounded by the fortified wall first built in the Middle Ages, offered a compact working environment easily traversed on foot in ten to twelve minutes. In the south-west there were the two court theatres, the Burgtheater and the Kärntnertortheater, the home of Italian and, increasingly, German opera as well as plays and ballets, the nearby Redoutensaal (actually two rooms, large and small), and the court itself, the Hofburg. In the streets immediately surrounding the Hofburg, especially towards the north-west, were the winter palaces of the aristocracy, the Esterházy, Kinsky, Liechtenstein, Lobkowitz, Schwarzenberg families and many others. In the middle of the city lay the wider streets of the Graben and the Kohlmarkt, and the large squares of Am Hof, the Freyung and Mehlmarkt, the focus of commercial and street life. Rising above everything else and right in the geographical centre of the city was the Gothic cathedral of St Stephen with its slender spire that also served as a watchtower.

All musicians would have frequented the Singerstrasse, a street that led south-west from St Stephen's and the Graben until it hit the city wall. On this street was the shop of Johann Traeg, the principal music dealer in Vienna and a pivotal figure in its musical life for over twenty years. His career, in particular the changes in emphasis in his business, provides a revealing insight into musical life, including, crucially, the appeal of the symphony.[1]

---

[1] Information on Traeg's life is taken from the three volumes devoted to the business by Alexander Weinmann. *Die Anzeigen des Kopiaturbetriebes Johann Traeg in der Wiener Zeitung zwischen 1782 und 1805*. Wiener Archivstudien, 6 (Vienna, 1981). *Johann Traeg. Die Musikalienverzeichnisse von 1799 und 1804 (Handschrift und Sortiment)*. Beiträge zur Geschichte des Alt-Wiener Musikverlages, Reihe 2, Folge 17 (Vienna, 1973). *Verlagsverzeichnis Johann Traeg (und Sohn)*. 2nd ed. Beiträge zur Geschichte des Alt-Wiener Musikverlages, Reihe 2, Folge 16 (Vienna, 1973). Important supplementary information and interpretation are to be found in D. Edge, 'Mozart's Viennese Copyists' (PhD diss., University of Southern California, 2001), pp. 749–86.

Johann Traeg was not a native Viennese. He was born in Gochsheim in Lower Franconia in 1747 and moved with his mother, two brothers and a sister to Vienna, probably in 1779. While one brother Andreas Traeg was to pursue a career as a jobbing musician and composer (his music is represented in Johann Traeg's catalogue) and another, Johann Baptist, was to become a successful cotton manufacturer, Johann was to combine musical and commercial instincts to develop a thriving music business. He began as a music copyist, probably working for individual clients (composers, performers, churches and so on) on an *ad hoc* basis. Unlike most copyists, who were content to remain as artisans, Traeg began to build up a personal stock of manuscripts which could be used as the prime source – the mastercopy – for copies sold to the public. His first known advertisement appeared in the *Wiener Zeitung* on 10 August 1782; the music was available from his home at the time, just off the Graben.[2]

From Johann Traeg, in the Pilatisches Haus next to St Peter's on the first floor are to be had all genres of music, such as: symphonies; concertos for keyboard, violin, flute and viola; quintets, quartets, trios, duets, sonatas, etc.: oratorios and cantatas; sextets, quin- and quartets from Italian, French, and German operas. All new and select, by the best masters, cleanly and correctly written, at a cheap price. The catalogue, which describes everything in more detail, can be had at the same place.

Later advertisements in the 1780s suggest that Traeg also provided music on hire, and organized performers for private concerts (a 'fixer' in modern parlance).

Information for Music Lovers

Johann Traeg in the Pilatisches House next to St Peter's, on the first floor, has the honour to inform the most respected public that he has, encouraged by the approbation hitherto received, drawn up a plan which will be warmly welcomed by music lovers . . . There are, to wit, in this town ever more families who entertain weekly by means of large or small musical concerts. Many of these don't want to be overburdened with music parts, or, at the very least, want to listen to the items that they want to buy. Since I now possess a fine stock of the best and newest music of all kinds and am taking care daily to enlarge it, so I am offering to hire either for a week 3 symphonies, or 6 quintets, 6 quartets, 6 trios etc. against a quarterly prepayment of 3 fl. If someone wants to give concerts twice a week and accordingly needs 6 symphonies or 12 other pieces, then he can order them similarly, and pay only 5 fl per quarter. Because I must strive to serve everybody properly, so

---

[2] Edge, *Mozart's Viennese Copyists*, pp. 754–5.

nobody should have any misgiving about returning the received pieces immediately on the following day. Reflecting my extensive acquaintanceship with the best of local musicians I can also secure for large and small concerts capable musicians for a very fair price. In order best to respond to these commissions I ask that at all times the request be received before midday.

The advertisement continues with a list of items recently available, including 'the newest symphonies of Joseph Haydn'.[3]

Traeg moved several times during the 1780s, always within the confines of the city. Eventually, in 1789, the size of his music catalogue forced him to open a dedicated business in the Singerstrasse while the family moved to Wieden in the suburbs to the south of the city. Equally notable was the decision in 1794 to set himself up as a music printer and publisher, the beginning of an eleven-year period of transition that led eventually to the firm concentrating entirely on publishing.[4] Initially, Traeg was a cautious publisher, providing only two printed items in 1794, four in 1795 and 1796, and seven or eight in 1797. From the following year, however, printed music began to appear in increasing quantities, accounting for the majority of new items available from the store. His son, also Johann (1781–1831), joined the firm in 1803 and took over after the death of his father in 1805. Now organized entirely as a music publisher the firm remained in business until 1818 when the printed plates were sold to Artaria. Throughout the stewardship of the younger Traeg, there is little or no indication that the old collection of manuscript material was actively promoted. However he seems to have maintained ownership of it until 1820 when, it has been speculated, some of the music was purchased by Eduard Lannoy and Aloys Fuchs.[5]

The dispersal of the music collection of the elder Traeg is a serious loss, perhaps even greater than the disappearance of material belonging to a single patron or institution of the time. For instrumental music in general, and the symphony in particular, it represented a significant part of the repertory in the last two decades of the eighteenth century. The loss is quantified by two printed catalogues that Traeg prepared at the turn of the century, a cumulative catalogue of the stock in 1799 and a supplement in

[3] Weinmann, *Die Anzeigen*, pp. 16–17.

[4] Up to the end of the eighteenth century the word publisher (*Verleger*) was generally used in the literal sense of a person who made material available, with no distinction between manuscript and printed forms. Here, to avoid confusion, the word will be used in the later, familiar sense of a business devoted to printed material. See R. Rasch, 'Basic Concepts', *Music Publishing in Europe 1600–1900. Concepts and Issues. Bibliography*, ed. R. Rasch (Berlin, 2005), pp. 13–20.

[5] Edge, *Mozart's Viennese Copyists*, pp. 936–7.

1804.[6] As extensive, orderly lists they provide the names of composers and the titles of works which, with a little interpretation, offer clues to changes in musical fashion. In the case of the symphony the changes are especially suggestive.

The 1799 catalogue was a substantial publication of 233 numbered pages, plus a further 132 pages of indexes: *Catalogue of Old and New, likewise Manuscript and Printed Music available in the Art and Music Shop of Johann Traeg in Vienna, No. 957 Singerstrasse.*[7] The Foreword gives a clear indication of the structure and scope of the catalogue.[8]

I offer here a catalogue of a type that does not yet exist in the area of music. It is in three sections: 1) the General Catalogue according to the names of the pieces; 2) the Catalogue according to the name of the author; 3) the Catalogue according to the name of the instrument. Preceding the General Catalogue is the classification according to which it is divided. For every piece (with a few exceptions) the price is noted, also whether it is manuscript or printed; g. signifies manuscript [*geschrieben*]. In the second catalogue, or index of names, is to be found in one place all the pieces by a composer that are distributed across the General Catalogue, together with an indication of the item number and the page where they are to be found. In the third catalogue, according to the name of the instrument, is listed every piece in the General Catalogue that uses the instrument in a solo manner, again with an indication of the item number and page. Through this three-part division I believe that I have made the catalogue more useful.

Also it should be noted that amongst the old works there are many classical works [*klassische Werke*] to be found. Of the newer ones I certainly maintain that there is not a catalogue of our best masters, such as Joseph Haydn, W. A. Mozart etc., that has more material than this catalogue. From time to time supplements will follow. Every suggestion that enhances the comprehensiveness of this catalogue will be gratefully received and utilized.

The General Catalogue is divided into three areas, standard in the eighteenth century, 'Cammer-Music', 'Theatral-Music' and 'Kirchen-Music', to which is appended a miscellaneous section consisting of books on music and instruction manuals. Occupying respectively 179 pages, thirty-eight pages and eleven pages the three broad divisions of the catalogue demonstrate the particular strength of Traeg's holdings. By far the largest section, 'Cammer-Music' is subdivided into two, instrumental music and keyboard music, with further internal subdivision into genres. Of the genres the symphony is the most extensive, twenty-three pages; in fact, it is the best represented genre in the entire catalogue, followed, at some distance, by

---

[6] Produced in facsimile in Weinmann, *Johann Traeg. Die Musikalienverzeichnisse*, pp. 1–364 (1799), pp. 366–433 (1804).
[7] Ibid., p. [iv].   [8] Ibid., pp. [v–vi].

the string quartet (ten pages). It is difficult to imagine a more forceful indication of the centrality of the symphony in Viennese musical life.

Over 500 symphonies by 81 named composers are included, usually as single items, occasionally as sets of six. For each entry the instrumentation is given, followed by the key, whether the work is in manuscript or in printed parts – there are no scores – and the price. While for a prolific composer this verbal information makes it difficult to identify individual works (which symphony in D by Dittersdorf is meant?), for less prolific composers, or for works in unusual keys, or ones that have an opus number attached, identification is easier. The best represented composer is Joseph Haydn (1732–1809) with 111 works (the list includes several overtures and the Concertante in B♭ to take the tally beyond 104), over a quarter of the total number of symphonies in Traeg's catalogue and an indication of the composer's pre-eminence in the genre. Dittersdorf (1739–99) was an even more prolific composer of symphonies than Haydn – 116 extant symphonies are safely attributed to him and there are a number of lost works – but only a small proportion, 23 works, are included in Traeg's catalogue. Similarly two other prolific composers of symphonies, Michael Haydn (1737–1806) and Vanhal (1739–1813) are poorly represented, respectively 13 out of a possible 44, and 6 out of a possible 76.[9]

In his Foreword, Traeg couples Haydn and Mozart together as representatives of 'our best masters'. 19 symphonies by Mozart are included in the catalogue, a small proportion of the total it might be thought, but the material was the product of a close working relationship between Traeg and Mozart and, after the death of the composer in 1791, between Traeg and Constanze. It is likely that Traeg worked directly for the composer in his own lifetime; the copies he sold from the early 1780s onwards are textually authoritative; and he played an important role in distributing his music in general in the years immediately after the composer's death.[10] Rather than constituting a wholly random collection, the nineteen works represent the whole of Mozart's symphonic output from 1778 onwards (K297, 'Paris'; K318; K319; K338; K385, 'Haffner'; K425, 'Linz'; K504, 'Prague'; K543; K550; and K551, 'Jupiter') together with authentic arrangements of some serenades as symphonies and a few earlier works.[11] When Traeg advertized his material in the *Wiener Zeitung* he usually indicated only the composer, the work and the price. Two advertisements for the symphonies of Mozart offer

[9] B. S. Brook (ed. in chief), *The Symphony 1720–1840. Reference Volume: Contents of the Set and Collected Thematic Indexes* (New York, 1986), pp. 166–93 (Dittersdorf), pp. 295–302 (M. Haydn), pp. 540–55 (Vanhal).

[10] Edge, *Mozart's Viennese Copyists*, pp. 786–997.   [11] Ibid., Table 7.3, pp. 807–11.

comments on their perceived musical value, a small indication of his friendship with the family: K551 was advertized in October 1792 with the remark 'This symphony is one of his last works and belongs amongst his masterpieces'; and when K550 was advertized in December 1793 it was with the comment 'This is one of the last and most beautiful symphonies from this master'.[12] Plate 2.1.

One of the imponderables of the 1799 catalogue is when individual items were first acquired by Traeg. Only a small proportion were advertized in the *Wiener Zeitung* where they are often subsumed into broad descriptions such as the 'Symphonies by Wanhal, Anton Rosetti etc.' that appears in the newspaper on 21 December 1782.[13] The substantial collection of symphonies by Haydn and the particular association with the Mozart family suggest a strategic orderliness that is misleading. Traeg's instincts were primarily acquisitive and opportunistic; if, in the process, it emerged that he was also orderly and comprehensive then that was a bonus. Something of his pragmatic attitude to his collection can be inferred from the numbering system that he applied to symphonies in his catalogue.

As in other sections in the catalogue, each work (sometimes a set of six) is given a number which, like a library shelfmark or a publisher's plate number, indicated its location in the store. Extant manuscript copies associated with the firm often carry the number, written in the form of a fraction. Haydn's Symphony No. 78, for instance is 156/2 in which the divider represents the symphony section of the catalogue, the integer the item number within the section.[14] It is clear that the numbers are not the equivalent of accession numbers, applied from the beginning of Traeg's business through to 1799, since each section has a sequence that broadly follows the alphabetical order of the composers represented. In the section devoted to symphonies, the numerical sequence begins with 3, for Abel's op. 1, and culminates with 428, for a symphony in C by Zimmermann. As well as '1' and '2' there are several further missing numbers (over twenty) in the main sequence which might suggest that the numbers were applied before they were quoted in the catalogue and that the missing numbers represent stock that had been mislaid or lost in the interim. But other evidence suggests that the numbers were applied as an integral part of the process that led to the publication of the catalogue: in other words the decision to publish a catalogue prompted the ordering of the stock. A crucial entry in this regard

---

[12] Weinmann, *Die Anzeigen*, p. 35, p. 42.   [13] Ibid., p. 15.
[14] An extant source for this symphony in the Stadt- und Universitätsbibliothek, Frankfurt carries the number. See *Joseph Haydn Werke*, I/11. *Sinfonien 1782–1784*, eds. S. Gerlach and S. E. Murray (Munich, 2003), p. 270.

※ 3635 ※

Eben selbst mit 1 Cornu Concerto, Violino, 2 Viole e Violoncelle.
Die Zauberflöte in 6 und 8stimmige Harmonie.
Detti a 3 Corni Basseti.
Die Serenade von Kauer, in 6 und 8stimmige Harmonie von mir gesetzt.
Parthien Concertant von Kauer, 6 und 8stimmig.
Marche 8stimmiger.
2 Parthien auf türkische Musik.
Der Fagottist auf 8stimmige Harmonie.
Das Sonnenfest detto.
Mehrere wälsche Opern, detto.
Eine nach dem neuesten Sisteme der Tonkunst verfaßte General-Baß-Schule mit 30 bezifferten Uebungen durch alle Tonarten, von Hrn. Ferdinand Kauer.
Man kann sich auch deswegen in der obern Bäckenstrasse beym schmeckenden Wurm im Durchhause im Harbeutelgewölbe anmelden.

Neue Tanz-Musikalien
sowohl, als alle vorhergehenden von der Komposizion des Hrn. Stanislaus Osowsky, sind vom 20. Dez. an blos bey ihm selbst auf dem St. Stephansplatze beym schwarzen Berg Nr. 615 auf der Hauptstiege im 5ten Stock zu finden, wo der Anschlag-Zettel zu sehen ist.
Neue für den bevorstehenden Fasching sind:
12 Menuette, vollstimmig, 3te Lieferung, à 2 fl. fürs Klavier à 1 fl.
12 Deutsche à la Vigano, vollstimmig à 1 fl. 30 kr. fürs Klavier à 40 kr.
12 Jagddeutsche, vollstimmig 3te Lieferung, (NB auf wiederhohltes Begehren fortgesetzt) à 1 fl. 30 kr. fürs Klavier à 40 kr.
12 Menuetti à 2 Violini e Violoncello für kleine Hausbälle, die 2te Lieferung à 1 fl. 30 kr. fürs Klavier 40 kr.
12 Deutsche à deto deto für kleine Hausbälle, 2te Lieferung à 1 fl. fürs Klavier 40 kr.
12 Kontratänze dedic. au Fürst Poniatowsky mit Touren à 1 fl. 30 kr. fürs Klav. 40 k.
3 Pelonesi à tre, à 1 fl.
12 Landerische von Schmuzer à 20 kr. fürs Klavier à 40 kr.

Dann von vorigem Jahre:
12 Menuetti mit Trio und 12 Deutsche mit Trio von Mozart, übersetzt à tre 3 fl.
12 Deutsche aus der Oper: die Zauberflötte, von Mozart, 2te Lieferung, dann aus mehr anderen Opern, und von alten obigen die vorhergehenden Lieferungen um obige Preise.
Man verspricht die prompteste und von

nun an accurateste Bedienung, und erbittet sich die beliebigen Bestellungsbriefe franco.

Nachricht.
Bey Johann Träg in der Fingerstrasse Nr. 863 sind folgende neue Musikalien zu haben:
1 grosse Sinf. in G. min. von Mozart. (Diese ist eine der letzten und schönsten Sinfonien von diesem Meister).
1 detto in D. Mozart.
1 Concerto in B. arrangirt für 2 Viol. e Viola. Mozart.
1 Concertino à 2 Clar. e Fag. Zimmermann.
1 Conc. à Violino e Violonc. in A. Schlick.
1 Conc. à Violonc. Mazat.
1 Sinf. in F. Fiala.
1 Divert. à Violonc. Fag. 2 Cor. 2 Viole e Basso. Fiala.
1 Quint. à Viol. Oboe 2 Viole e Violonc. Reymann.
14 Pieces alla Camera à 2 Corni di Bassetto 2 Cor. e Fagotto, di Went.
14 detti, di Went.
1 Quint 3 Corni di Bass. e 2 Cor. Gyrowetz.
Grande Bataille imitée sur le Clav. avec accomp. Viol. Vionc. & Tambour.
12 Deutsche (des neuen Sonntagskindes) mit allen Stimmen, von Bock.
12 Menuette und 12 Deutsche, mit allen Stimmen, von Bock.
12 Deutsche mit allen Stimmen, v. Eibiska.
12 Deutsche fürs Klav. Forster.
12 ————————— Mayerhoffer.
12 ————————— Bock.
12 ————————— Eibiska.
12 (Das neue Sonntagskind) Bock.
6 Menuette und 6 Deutsche fürs Klav. Lepschy.
2 Sonatinen für die Harfe, Wiesner.
3 Sonaten, Wiesner. Der Verfasser giebt auch gründlichen Unterricht in der Harfe.

Neue Tanz-Musikalien
welche bey Meyer und Pagowsky, Buchhändlern auf dem neuen Markte zu den sieben Saulen Nr. 1110 zu haben sind, als:
12 deutsche Tänze und Coda aus dem beliebten Singspiele, das Neu-Sonntagskind, des Hrn. Müller, vollstimmig 2 fl. im Klavier 40 kr.
Ferner sind auch von einem neu-angekommenen Tonkünstler, Johann Dressler, zu haben:
12 Menuette mit 12 Trio, vollstimmig 2 fl. im Klavier 40 kr.
12 Deutsche mit 12 Trio und Coda, vollst. 2 fl. im Klav. 40 kr.

Plate 2.1 An advertisement by Johann Traeg in the *Wiener Zeitung*, 18 December 1793, p. 3635.

is the one for the symphony in F by Krommer ('Sinf. à grand Orchestr. Op. 12') allocated the number 242 within the main sequence. The work was first advertized by Traeg in the *Wiener Zeitung* on 20 December 1797[15] and refers to the publication by André of Offenbach earlier that month.[16] This is the newest identifiable symphony in the main sequence of numbers, suggesting that they were applied in December 1797–January 1798.

Having reached 428 for the symphony in C by Zimmermann, Traeg then continued the numerical sequence (though again with some missing numbers) through to 502. That number is given to a symphonie concertante in A by Pleyel (B114) published by André in July 1798,[17] a putative *terminus ante quem* for the symphony section of the catalogue. That it might, in fact, be a little later is suggested by the items in the section devoted to keyboard variations. The supplementary numerical sequence in that section includes Beethoven's variations on 'Mich brennt ein heißes Fieber' (WoO 72), issued in a printed edition by Traeg in November 1798.[18] All this implies that Traeg took about a year to compile his catalogue, from the time of the Krommer symphony to the Beethoven variations.

As well as Pleyel (1757–1831) this supplementary numbering sequence includes symphonies by other composers active in the 1790s, such as Brandl (1760–1837), Gyrowetz (1763–1850) and Paul Wranitzky (1756–1808), but it includes also works by older composers such as Monn (1717–50) and Leopold Hofmann (1738–93), plus, intriguingly, a symphony version of Mozart's serenade in D (K203). Whether these were new acquisitions in 1798 or works that had been temporarily mislaid while the main sequence of numbers was being applied cannot be determined.

The appearance of Traeg's catalogue in 1799 coincided with the increasingly evident move from selling manuscript copies to printed music. Indeed, there is a palpable feeling that the cumulative catalogue was designed to maximize sales from material that was no longer commercially viable; all the symphonies, except the most recent ones, are offered at a much reduced price, typically a third, compared with that given in earlier advertisements in the *Wiener Zeitung*.

Traeg's foreword states that the catalogue indicates whether a particular item is available in manuscript or printed format: 'g.' (*geschrieben*) is used for the former, 'st.' (*stich*, engraving) for the latter. As an alternative to 'st.' Traeg uses also a series of single letters (usually lower-, sometimes

---

[15] Weinmann, *Die Anzeigen*, p. 64.
[16] W. Matthäus, *Johann André Musikverlag zu Offenbach am Main: Verlagsgeschichte und Bibliographie 1772–1800* (Tutzing, 1973), p. 342.
[17] Ibid., p. 358. [18] Weinmann, *Verlagsverzeichnis*, p. 23.

upper-case) to indicate the place of publication. Of these the most common in the symphony section, as in the catalogue as a whole, is 'o', standing for Offenbach, that is the major firm of André. The relationship between Traeg and André is a determining one in the history of the symphony in Vienna in the 1790s and beyond.

JOHANN TRAEG AND ANDRÉ (OFFENBACH)

Table 2.1 lists the symphonies in the 1799 catalogue that derive from André. Seventy-four works are listed, approximately 15% of Traeg's total holdings in 1799. As well as the Traeg number, the name of the composer and the opus number, the table identifies the individual work according to modern scholarship, gives the date of publication as established by modern scholarship, and indicates those items that can be associated with an advertisement in the *Wiener Zeitung* placed by Traeg.

Johann André was born in Offenbach on 28 March 1741.[19] As a youth he was destined to work in the family business of silk manufacturing; gradually musical interests took over and he began to embark on a career as a composer. Business and music were united in 1772 when he began to publish music. Musical life in Offenbach, unlike that of Leipzig, London and Paris, could not sustain a major publisher and André soon developed a remarkably international outlook, publishing music by composers from throughout Europe, either through direct contact with the composer or with another major publisher. By the last decade of the century André was, without doubt, the single most important music publisher in Europe, equivalent in authority to that enjoyed a few years later by Breitkopf and Härtel, and it is a measure of the economic strength of the company that it was able to trade successfully during the disruption and strife of the Napoleonic period.

André's publications were sold on commission in Amsterdam, Augsburg, Basel, Cologne, Copenhagen, Frankfurt, Gotha, Hamburg, Munich, Rotterdam, St Gallen and Strasbourg.[20] André was also in regular contact with Traeg in Vienna.[21] The firm began advertising André prints of symphonies in 1790 and the relationship carried through to 1797, immediately before work on the catalogue was begun; indeed not more than a handful of

---

[19] For the history of the firm up to 1800 see Matthäus, *André*; for the period after 1800 see B. Constapel, *Der Musikverlag Johann André in Offenbach am Main. Studien zur Verlagstätigkeit von Johann Anton André und Verzeichnis der Musikalien von 1800 bis 1840* (Tutzing, 1998).

[20] Matthäus, pp. 56–7.   [21] Personal communication from Britta Constapel.

Table 2.1. *Symphonies published by André present in Traeg's catalogue of 1799*

Traeg number[a]	Work[b]	Reference[c]	Publication date[d]	WZ advrt[e]
J. A. André (1775–1842)				
444	op. 4		1795	
445	op. 5		1795	
446	op. 6		1795	
490	op. 7		1797	
Brandl (1760–1837)				
466	op. 12		1797	
Gyrowetz (1763–1850)				
447	op. 6 no. 1	C1	1790	1791
448	op. 6 no. 2	E♭1	1790	1791?
449	op. 8 no.1	C2	1790	1792
450	op. 8 no. 2	Q:E♭1	1792	1792
451	op. 8 no. 3	E♭2	1791	
452	op. 9 no. 1	D5	1792	
453	op. 9 no. 2	B♭1	1792	
454	op. 9 no. 3	F2	1792	1792
455	op. 12 no. 1	D6	1792	1792?
456	op. 12 no. 2	E♭3	1792	1792?
457	op. 12 no. 3	E♭4	1792	1792?
458	op. 13 no. 1	D7	1792	1792?
459	op. 13 no. 2	F4	1792	1792?
460	op. 13 no. 3	C3	1792	1792?
461	op. 14 no. 1	G2	1792	
462	op. 18	E♭5	1795	
Joseph Haydn (1732–1809)				
206	op. 66 no. 2	No. 92	1792	1792
207	op. 66 no. 1	No. 90	1792	1792
187	op. 77 no. 2	No. 96	1795	
188	op. 77 no. 1	No. 95	1795	
191	op. 83 no. 2	No. 93	1796	
193	op. 80 no. 1	No. 94	1795	
192	op. 83 no. 1	No. 97	1796	
202	op. 80 no. 2	No. 98	1796	1796
201	op. 84	Concertante	1796	
Krommer (1759–1831)				
242	op. 12	PI:1	1797	1797
Massonneau (1766–1848)				
254	op. 5		1794	1794
268	op. 3 no. 1		1792	
269	op. 3 no. 2		1792	

(cont.)

Table 2.1. (*cont.*)

Traeg number[a]	Work[b]	Reference[c]	Publication date[d]	WZ advrt[e]
Mozart (1756–91)				
280	op. 25	K250	1792	
283	op. 34	K425	1793	
286	op. 38	K551	1793	
288	op. 45	K550	1794	1796
Neubauer (1750–95)				
470	op. 1 no. 1		1791	1792
471	op. 4 no. 1		1792	
472	op. 4 no. 2		1792	
473	op. 4 no. 3		1792	
474	op. 8 no. 1		1791	1794
475	op. 8 no. 2		1791	1794
–	op. 8 no. 3		1791	1794
476	op. 12 no. 1			
477	op. 12 no. 2			
–	op. 12 no. 3			
478	op. 11		1794	
Pleyel (1757–1831)				
309	op. 30 no. 2	B124	1790	
310	op. 29 no. 2	B122	1790	
320	op. 29 no. 1	B130	1790	1791?
321	op. 21 no. 3	B138?	1788?	
322	op. 29 no. 3	B142	1790	
325	op. 33 no. 1	B145	1791	1791?
326	op. 26 no. 2	B137?	1788?	
328	op. 12 no. 2	B134	1787	1790
329	op. 27 no. 1	B139	1789	1790
331	op. 12 no. 3	B135	1788	1790
332	op. 26 no. 3	B141	1790	
379	op. 27 no. 2	B140	1790	
480	op. 38	B147	1792	1792
502	op. 57	B114	1798	
Rosetti (c.1750–92)				
481	op. 13 no. 1	A33	1794	
482	op. 13 no. 2	A49	1794	
Winter (1754–1825)				
409	Liv 2 (F)	3	1794	
410	Liv 1 (D)	2	1794	
411	Liv 3 [B♭]	4	1794	

(*cont.*)

Table 2.1. (*cont.*)

Traeg number[a]	Work[b]	Reference[c]	Publication date[d]	WZ advrt[e]
Paul Wranitzky (1756–1808)				
483	op. 17 no. 1	2	1791	1792
–	op. 11 no. 1	11	1791	1792
484	op. 11 no. 2	37	1791	1792
485	op. 11 no. 3	46	1791	
486	op. 16 no. 1	14	1791/2	
487	op. 16 no. 2	47	1792	
488	op. 25	25	1793	

[a] From A. Weinmann, *Johann Traeg. Die Musikalienverzeichnisse von 1799 und 1804 (Handschrift und Sortiment)*. Beiträge zur Geschichte des Alt-Wiener Musikverlages, Reihe 2, Folge 17 (Vienna, 1973).
[b] Ibid.
[c] B. S. Brook (ed. in chief), *The Symphony 1720–1840. Reference Volume: Contents of the Set and Collected Thematic Indexes* (New York, 1986), pp. 284–90 (Gyrowetz), pp. 587–9 (Winter). K. Padrta, *Franz Krommer (1759–1831). Thematischer Katalog seiner musikalischen Werke* (Prague, 1997). R. Benton, *Ignace Pleyel. A Thematic Catalogue of his Compositions* (New York, 1977). S. E. Murray, *The Music of Antonio Rosetti (Anton Rösler) ca. 1750–1792. A Thematic Catalog* (Michigan, 1996). M. Poštolka, 'Thematisches Verzeichnis der Sinfonien Pavel Vranickýs', *Miscellanea musicologica*, 20 (1967), pp. 101–28.
[d] From W. Matthäus, *Johann André Musikverlag zu Offenbach am Main. Verlagsgeschichte und Bibliographie 1772–1800* (Tutzing, 1973).
[e] From A. Weinmann, *Die Anzeigen des Kopiaturbetriebes Johann Traeg in der Wiener Zeitung zwischen 1782 und 1805*. Wiener Archivstudien, 6 (Vienna, 1981).

symphonies published by André in this period was not made available in Vienna.

For Traeg this source ensured a steady supply of symphonies by composers both known and unknown in Vienna. In the case of Haydn, the André connection enabled Traeg to extend his holdings up to Symphony No. 98, the final symphony of the first London visit. In Mozart's case the firm was the convenient source of printed parts of symphonies Traeg already had in manuscript; more generally, the relationship nurtured a mutual interest in the composer that led to Traeg playing a leading part in Constanze Mozart's sale of the composer's residual autographs and parts to André in 1799.[22] The two published symphonies by Rosetti, Kapellmeister at the Oettingen-Wallerstein court, brought the total by that composer up to fourteen. By 1799 Gyrowetz had been back in Vienna for six years; the André link yielded eleven out of nineteen symphonies in Traeg's catalogue,

[22] Edge, *Mozart's Viennese Copyists*, p. 997.

a symphonic presence in Vienna at a time when the composer himself had already turned his back on the genre. In complete contrast, Paul Wranitzky was the most active composer of symphonies in Vienna in the 1790s, most of which were published by André; from 1790 onwards he had acted as an unofficial agent in the city for the firm.

Pleyel in the 1790s is best described as the former Austrian composer. Having studied with Vanhal and Haydn and worked for Count Ladislaus Erdödy he left Austria more or less for good in 1781. He made two visits to Italy, worked in Strasbourg between 1783 and 1791, and renewed acquaintanceship with Haydn in London in 1792 before returning to Strasbourg. In 1795 he settled in Paris, where he became a major publisher of music and, later, a manufacturer of pianos. As is suggested by Table 2.1 the bulk of Pleyel's output of symphonies had been composed by the early 1790s and though he was a near contemporary of Wranitzky his presence in the history of the symphony in Vienna during the 1790s was not a significant one. Another near contemporary, Franz Krommer, on the other hand was to be a notable figure in the history of the symphony in Vienna through to the 1820s; op. 12 was the first of nine symphonies composed between 1797 and 1830. The remaining composers in Table 2.1 lived in the German territories and were, with the exception of Peter Winter, unknown in Vienna. Johann Anton André was the publisher's son who, a few years later, was to assume control of the business, yet managed a continuing career as a composer; Johann Brandl was the music director at the court of the Prince-bishop of Speyer and Bruchsal; Massonneau was a violinist and composer who held a series of posts in various German theatres; and Neubauer had been employed at the court of Prince Weilburg before moving to Hannover shortly before his death. Only Peter Winter was known and esteemed in Vienna. Based in Munich, his burgeoning career as an opera composer had taken him to Vienna in the 1790s for the first performances of two operas, *Das unterbrochene Opferfest* and *Das Labyrinth* (a sequel to *Zauberflöte*); despite the popularity of these two works Winter's symphonies were never to make an impact in the city.

TRAEG'S SUPPLEMENTARY CATALOGUE OF 1804

Traeg's foreword to the 1799 catalogue promised that supplementary volumes would appear from time to time. Only one supplement appeared, five years later in 1804, a year before Johann Traeg died. A clear change in the standing of the symphony is evident.

The supplement has sixty-six numbered pages plus an index of genres (two pages): unlike the 1799 catalogue there is no index of composers.[23] For the maintenance of an orderly stock as much as for the convenience of the purchaser, the catalogue follows the broad pattern of the 1799 one, three main sections with further subdivisions. Although there is some adjustment within the smallest categories the item numbers, in principle, continue the sequence established in the main catalogue and, as before, they reflect the alphabetical sequence of composers.

Table 2.2 lists the entire content of the section devoted to the symphony, a mere 30 works in total. To these are added three other symphonies, two by Clementi and one by Pleyel, that were advertized by Traeg in the *Wiener Zeitung* between 1799 and 1804. Taking the larger figure of 33, the total number of symphonies acquired in this five-year period represents an average of just over six a year, whereas the 500 or so in the 1799 catalogue represented an annual average (from 1782 to 1799) in excess of 20 per year. If this broad-brush statistic suggests that acquiring symphonies was a less obvious priority that it had been, then a glance at the number of items in other genres listed in the catalogue confirms that impression. From being the largest genre in the 'Cammer-Music' section the symphony is now one of the smallest. Those genres that are better represented reveal much about the changing nature of the instrumental repertoire at the turn of the century. Harmoniemusik (57 works) and string quartets (54 items, mainly sets of three or more works, plus 12 arrangements from contemporary operas and ballets) are well represented; more surprisingly the number of concertos for the violin (over 60) is approximately double the number of symphonies. Solo piano music had occupied a fifth of the 1799 catalogue; it is now up to a quarter.

Apart from their limited number the most striking aspect of the symphonies on offer is that, with the exception of the works by Gallus and Kreutzer, and the last three by Wranitzky, they are all printed editions from outside Vienna, mainly from André but also Breitkopf and Härtel (Leipzig), Bureau de Musique (Leipzig) and Imbault (Paris). Whereas it had been Traeg's normal practice when dealing with manuscripts to keep a mastercopy from which further copies could be made according to demand, a likely consequence of selling printed editions was that individual works would no longer be available once the last exemplar had been sold. A note

---

[23] *First Supplement to the Catalogue of Old and New, likewise Manuscript and Printed Music, which are available in the Art and Music Shop of Johann Traeg in Vienna.* Weinmann, *Johann Traeg. Die Musikalienverzeichnisse*, p. 366.

Table 2.2. *Symphonies in Traeg's supplementary catalogue of 1804*

Traeg number[a]	Work[b]	Reference[c]	Publisher and Date[d]	WZ advrt[e]
J. A. André (1775–1842)				
513	op. 11 nos. 1, 2		André, 1800	
514	op. 13		André, 1801	
Beethoven (1770–1827)				
515	op. 21	No. 1	Bureau de Musique, 1801	1802
Cannabich (1731–98)				
516	op. 8		Falter, 1795?	
Danzi (1763–1826)				
517	op. 19	No. 2	Breitkopf & Härtel, 1804	
Fischer (1773–1829)				
518	op. 5		Breitkopf & Härtel, 1803	
Fleischmann				
519	op. 5		André, 1800	
Gallus [Mederitisch-Gallus] (1752–1835)				
520	–			
Gleissner (1759/60–1818)				
521	op. 1		André, 1800	
Gyrowetz (1763–1850)				
522	op. 33	D8	André, 1797	
523	op. 47	D9	André, 1801	1801
Haydn (1732–1809)				
524	Nro. 27	No. 101	Artaria, 1799	
525	op. 91 no. 1	No. 100	Imbault, 1801	
526	op. 91 no. 2	No. 101	Imbault, 1801	
527	op. 91 no. 3 'gesch.'	No. 103	Imbault, 1801	
528	op. 98 no. 1	No. 104	André, 1801	1801
529	op. 98 no. 2	No. 102	André, 1801	1801
Kreutzer (1766–1831)				
530	Sinf. militaire a gr. Orchestre			
Krommer (1759–1831)				
531	op. 40	PI: 2	André, 1803	1804
Pleyel (1757–1831)				
532	op. 41, op. 43			1799

(*cont.*)

Table 2.2. (*cont.*)

Traeg number[a]	Work[b]	Reference[c]	Publisher and Date[d]	WZ advrt[e]
Paul Wranitzky (1756–1808)				
533	op. 33	48, 7, 34	André, 1798	1799
534	op. 36	18	André, 1800	
535	op. 37	23	André, 1800	
536	3 Berchtols-gadner Sinfon.	20 +?		

Additional works, not in catalogue: Clementi, two symphonies [op. 18], *Wiener Zeitung*, 1801; Pleyel, one symphony (B154), *Wiener Zeitung*, 1803.

[a] From A. Weinmann, *Johann Traeg. Die Musikalienverzeichnisse von 1799 und 1804 (Handschrift und Sortiment)*. Beiträge zur Geschichte des Alt-Wiener Musikverlages, Reihe 2, Folge 17 (Vienna, 1973).

[b] Ibid.

[c] B. S. Brook (ed. in chief), *The Symphony 1720–1840. Reference Volume: Contents of the Set and Collected Thematic Indexes* (New York, 1986), pp. 158–9 (Danzi), pp. 284–90 (Gyrowetz). K. Padrta, *Franz Krommer (1759–1831). Thematischer Katalog seiner musikalischen Werke* (Prague, 1997). M. Poštolka, 'Thematisches Verzeichnis der Sinfonien Pavel Vranickýs', *Miscellanea musicologica*, 20 (1967), pp. 101–28.

[d] From W. Matthäus, *Johann André Musikverlag zu Offenbach am Main. Verlagsgeschichte und Bibliographie 1772–1800* (Tutzing, 1973). G. Kinsky, *Das Werk Beethovens. Thematisch-bibliographisches Verzeichnis seiner sämtlichen vollendeten Kompositionen* (Munich, 1955). A. van Hoboken, *Joseph Haydn. Thematisch-bibliographisches Werkverzeichnis*, vol. 1 (Mainz, 1957). 'Fischer, Michael Gottherd', *Die Musik in Geschichte und Gegenwart*, 2nd edn. ed. L. Finscher (Kassel), vol. 6 (2001), cols. 1267–8.

[e] From A. Weinmann, *Die Anzeigen des Kopiaturbetriebes Johann Traeg in der Wiener Zeitung zwischen 1782 und 1805*. Wiener Archivstudien, 6 (Vienna, 1981).

next to item 527, the Imbault print of Haydn's 'Drumroll' symphony, suggests a co-existent practice: the annotation 'gesch.' (*geschrieben*) indicates, quite scrupulously, that only manuscript parts copied from this edition are now available.

With these 'English' symphonies, as Traeg terms them, the firm was able to bring its holding of Haydn symphonies nearly up to date; oddly, No. 99 is missing. The important role of Paul Wranitzky in Viennese musical life that was evident in the 1799 catalogue is again apparent, with five recent symphonies listed, though op. 35 (three works) published by André in 1800 is not offered.[24] Of other composers resident in Vienna, Krommer is represented by his second symphony, Gyrowetz by a rare recent work, Mederitisch-Gallus by an unidentifiable work and Beethoven by his First Symphony. Mozart's name is entirely absent. The remainder of the

[24] Matthäus, *André*, p. 383.

list is a random collection of works by André, Cannabich (who had died in 1798), Clementi (now more of an international businessman than a composer), Danzi (who lived in Munich), Fischer (an organist in Erfurt, north Germany), Fleischmann (in the employ of the Duke of Sachsen-Meiningen), Gleissner (a printer and composer in Munich), Kreutzer (the Parisian violinist who had visited Vienna in 1798) and Pleyel.

The transition that Traeg had made from a firm that distributed manuscript music and some printed editions through to a publishing firm and seller of printed editions from abroad was to be completed by the younger Johann Traeg when he took over the business in 1805. Printed editions of piano music dominate his catalogue (sonatas, variations, dances and arrangements); not a single symphony was published in the thirteen-year history of the successor firm.[25] In its heyday around 1790 Traeg had been at the very core of musical life in Vienna, providing the commercial energy that facilitated performance, especially of the symphony. A mere twelve to fifteen years later Vienna lacked this central commercial presence in instrumental music. Its musical life, especially opera, oratorio, church music, concertos, quartets and Harmoniemusik, as well as the occasional symphony, still relied fundamentally on professional copyists, and the names of Klumpar, Rampl, Schlemmer and Sukowaty, for instance, are ones that figure prominently in Beethoven's life; but none of these sought to emulate Traeg and become a major dealer.[26]

As regards publishing, the younger Traeg's avoidance of symphonies as well as the fact that the 1799 and 1804 catalogues contain very few symphonies that were published in Vienna point to a major characteristic of musical life in the city, the reluctance of publishers to issue symphonies.

THREE PUBLISHERS: ARTARIA, HOFFMEISTER AND THE MAGAZIN DE MUSIQUE

Music printing gained a presence in the musical life of Vienna much later in the eighteenth century than in other major European cities such as Amsterdam, Berlin, Leipzig, London and Paris; even a comparatively small town like Offenbach, with the firm of André, was a more important centre. Although there are several examples of music printed in Vienna before the 1770s it was only when the firm of Artaria expanded its activities from selling

---

[25] See Weinmann, *Verlagsverzeichnis.*

[26] J. Fojtíková and T. Volek, 'Die Beethoveniana der Lobkowitz-Musiksammlung und ihre Kopisten', *Beethoven und Böhmen. Beiträge zu Biographie und Wirkungsgeschichte Beethovens*, ed. S. Brandenburg and M. Gutiérrez-Denhoff (Bonn, 1988), pp. 291–53. A. Tyson, 'Notes on Five of Beethoven's Copyists', *Journal of the American Musicological Society*, 23 (1970), pp. 439–71.

art engravings to selling printed music from elsewhere and then, in 1778, to selling music printed under its own imprint that music publishing became a permanent feature of commercial life in the city. Located in Vienna in the main thoroughfare of the Kohlmarkt the firm had a branch in Mainz, traded regularly with firms elsewhere in Europe (especially London and Paris), absorbed the stock of some ailing local firms and, by 1800, had issued approximately 850 editions of music.[27]

The presence of symphonies in Artaria's catalogue during this time is a limited one. It was only in 1785, seven years after the business was established, that Artaria felt confident enough to challenge the traditional dominance of the manuscript trade, with three symphonies by Haydn, Nos. 79–81, the first of twenty-eight symphonies by the composer issued by the firm between 1785 and 1799, representing the total output of the composer from No. 76 onwards, with the exception of Nos. 99 and 104. As in Traeg's predominantly manuscript collection, Haydn's symphonies were the prime presence in the catalogue but, unlike Traeg's collection, no other composer was well represented. In 1785, alongside the three Haydn symphonies, two by Mozart were published, K385 ('Haffner') and K319, thereafter none. A year later a set of three symphonies by Michael Haydn (MH355, MH381 and MH390) was issued and a set of three by Antonio Rosetti (A9, A40 and A28); again, no further symphonies by either composer were forthcoming. Three extant letters by Dittersdorf, Gyrowetz and Michael Haydn that explored the possible publication of symphonies met with no success.[28] Artaria was less cautious when the opportunity arose from time to time to take over symphony publications from other firms such as Torricella (who ceased trading in 1786) and Hoffmeister. From plates prepared by the latter Artaria in 1795 issued a symphony in C by Pleyel (B128) and five by Hoffmeister himself (F7, E♭7, A1, G4 and B♭5). Other than Haydn, these were the last symphonies to be published by the firm. When, in 1799, that composer's 'Drumroll' symphony was published it was to be the last symphony by any composer to be issued by the firm, even though it remained active as a music publisher until 1858.

The longevity of the firm suggests a hard-nosed attitude to commercial success. Symphonies, like other orchestral music and, to an even greater extent, operas, oratorios and church music were expensive to produce in

---

[27] R. Ridgewell, 'Music Printing in Mozart's Vienna: the Artaria Press', *Fontes Artis Musicae*, 48 (2001), pp. 217–36. A. Weinmann, *Vollständiges Verlagsverzeichnis Artaria & Comp.* Beiträge zur Geschichte des Alt-Wiener Musikverlages, Reihe 2, Folge 2 (Vienna, 1952).

[28] See D. W. Jones, 'Why did Mozart compose his last three Symphonies? Some new Hypotheses', *Music Review*, 51 (1990), pp. 280–89.

comparison with sonatas, trios, quartets, dances and songs, and the financial returns were only to be recouped over a long period of time, if at all. At first, the firm had been wary of the traditional primacy of manuscript distribution; by the 1790s it had established a commercial principle that was to be current in Vienna throughout the next century: economic success was linked with the provision of music for the salon.

If Artaria's business outlook was pragmatic and sure-footed, Hoffmeister's may be characterized as inventive and speculative.[29] Born in Rottenburg am Neckar, near Mannheim, in 1754, Franz Anton Hoffmeister moved to Vienna to study law at the university. By the early 1780s he had established himself as one of the most fashionable composers of instrumental music of all kinds in Vienna. Since he did not have a position as a Kapellmeister and was not a gifted performer he founded his own publishing firm in 1784, at first from his home in the southern suburb of Wieden, then from a series of outlets in the centre of the city. Its prime aim was to promote Hoffmeister's own career and, at first, his compositions dominated the catalogue; later other composers feature. With enormous energy he established a branch of the firm in Linz and arranged that his publications be sold in Speyer by Bossler and in London by Bland.[30] Rather than publishing works in the traditional sets of six or three Hoffmeister issued them singly as part of a subscription series. As attractive musical plans yielded less than the expected financial return they were often modified or simply abandoned; in order to retrieve some of his losses Hoffmeister sold the plates of many editions to Artaria who issued them under his imprint. For the first few years Hoffmeister concentrated on piano music, flute music and string quartets. A solitary symphony in C by Pleyel (B128) appeared in 1786 as part of a subscription package that included a duet for violin and viola by Hoffmeister and a quartet by Vanhal; the plates of the symphony were later sold to Artaria.

On 16 March 1791 Hoffmeister placed an extraordinarily lengthy notice in the *Wiener Zeitung*, announcing a new subscription series devoted to his own symphonies.[31] He begins the announcement by noting the fate of his symphonies, forty-four of them to date. Only two have been published, the others have been distributed as manuscript copies. 'When a piece passes

[29] H. H. Hausner, 'Franz Anton Hoffmeister (1754–1812): Komponist und Verleger', *Mitteilungen der Internationalen Stiftung Mozarteum*, 38 (1990), pp. 155–62. A. Weinmann, *Die Wiener Verlagswerke von Franz Anton Hoffmeister*. Beiträge zur Geschichte des Alt-Wiener Musikverlages, Reihe 2, Folge 8 (Vienna, 1964).

[30] See I. Woodfield, 'John Bland: London Retailer of the Music of Haydn and Mozart', *Music and Letters*, 81 (2000), pp. 210–44.

[31] Weinmann, *Hoffmeister*, pp. 121–2.

through the hands of six copyists, such are the additions, omissions and falsifications of the principal notes, even of bars and phrases, that the author does not now recognize his own work any more. Moreover, I have ample evidence that some have sought to distribute spurious and wretched works under my name.' Hoffmeister then moves on to a second concern: that since many of these symphonies date from his youth they need to be revised in order to reflect modern taste. To deal with these two concerns he proposes a new publishing venture: 'Plan for a New, Improved, Complete edition of all the symphonies of Hoffmeister'. Eight features of this plan are detailed. Nos. 1–3 deserve to be quoted in full.

1. Beginning on 1 July 1791 I offer every three months, without interruption, six symphonies, that is four which have already appeared in manuscript (the two, in D and G, that are also engraved to be included in the reckoning) now entirely revised by me and two entirely new, original symphonies; so that in a course of a year 24 and, ultimately, after the end of the third year, 44 old and 28 entirely new, fully printed, appear; then the edition will be complete.
2. Each symphony will be printed alone.
3. The parts for Violin 1, Violin 2 and Basso will always be presented in duplicate, even though this increases the costs by nearly a half, in a way that has not been customary in any printed editions of symphonies, so that several players do not have to share a part, particularly at night, or the owner has to have it copied out.

The fourth clause claims that new typefaces have been prepared, new presses organized and new workers engaged for the project. The fifth clause promises that the edition will be printed on the best Venetian paper. Clauses 6 to 8 detail the rather complex arrangements for payment, inside the Austrian territories and outside them. Finally, Hoffmeister states that subscriptions will be taken in Vienna and Linz, also at Bossler's music shop in Speyer.

The unprecedented ambition of this scheme in the history of the symphony in Vienna is obvious and reveals certain attitudes that were to become standard only in the nineteenth century. Composers in Austria of all kinds of music had long lived with the fact that serial copying of music inevitably led to a deteriorating musical text. While many of them, notably Haydn and Mozart, tried to ensure the integrity of their texts by employing trusted copyists whose work was systematically checked, it was impossible to maintain this control once the work had left the working environment of the composer. Printing the musical text offered the very real prospect of permanent accuracy, the authoritative text of the composer; even the provision of multiple string parts was designed to avoid the practice of copying them.

For the composer this would imply a new sense of durability, the definitive version of a work; this, in Hoffmeister's plan, is coupled with the proposal that his earliest works should be revised. Such notions of permanence and authority had been implicit in the sonatas, quintets and songs issued by Artaria and Hoffmeister; they were now being transferred to the symphony. As the second clause states, Hoffmeister's customary practice of issuing works singly was maintained in this project and here, too, is a sense of something to come: a single individual symphony that is to be considered as an entity rather than as a work that shares characteristics with others.

Hoffmeister's Plan would have yielded a collection of seventy-two symphonies in three years, forty-eight revised works and twenty-four entirely new ones. Both for Hoffmeister the composer and Hoffmeister the businessman this was a hopelessly impractical commitment. Not surprisingly the scheme foundered after only seven symphonies had appeared. In stark contrast to the verbosity of the 1791 advertisement, Hoffmeister on 22 June 1793 in the *Wiener Zeitung* announced the end of the series: 'Entirely new music, abandoned by the press and which is to be had at fixed prices at Franz Anton Hoffmeister Music-, Art- and Bookdealers in the Wollzeile, No. 803: Hoffmeister, first instalment of the symphony edition . . .'[32]

This was only one of many setbacks that failed to dent the commercial ambitions of Hoffmeister. On a journey to Leipzig in 1799 he met the organist Ambrosius Kühnel and together they formed the new firm of Bureau de Musique which in December 1801 issued the first edition of Beethoven's Symphony No. 1. Hoffmeister retained his business in Vienna, which survived until 1806, but without issuing a single further symphony. He died in 1812.

There is no reason to doubt that in 1791 Hoffmeister's ambitions as a composer of symphonies were genuine ones. He clearly hoped that publishing his own symphonies would have nurtured his own career in the genre. Certainly without this published outlet Hoffmeister had little incentive to compose symphonies and it is significant that after the collapse of the Plan only two further works were composed, both c.1804: a symphony in D (D8) published in Leipzig by the Bureau de Musique and one in C (C8) published by Simrock in Bonn. With these two late works Hoffmeister's total output of symphonies reached forty-four, well short of the seventy-two he had envisaged in 1791.

---

[32] 'Ganz neue Musicalien, welche die Presse verlassen, und um beygesetzte Preise in der Franz Anton Hoffmeister Musik- Kunst- und Buchhandlung in der Wollzeile Nr. 803 zu haben sind: Hoffmeister, erste Lieferung der Simphonie-Ausgabe . . .'

Leopold Kozeluch (1747–1818) was another composer who turned to publishing in order to support his career.[33] Born in Velvary in Bohemia he studied law at the university in Prague. Success as a composer of ballet music led him to Vienna in 1778 where he soon acquired a position at the imperial court as a keyboard teacher. His career was firmly centred on the piano, performing and teaching, and composing over 200 works that feature the instrument in some way. Many of his earlier piano works were published by Artaria but in 1784, the same year as Hoffmeister, he established his own business, designed to consolidate and enhance his reputation as a teacher, performer and composer of piano music. When the music was his own Kozeluch indicated that it was to be had at the author's shop ('Au Magazin de l'Auteur') on the Graben; when it was the music of another composer this was amended to 'Magazin de Musique', which soon became the rather prosaic name for the publisher. The firm remained in business until 1802, concentrating to an even greater extent than Artaria and Hoffmeister on piano variations, sonatas, dances and accompanied piano trios.

Leopold Kozeluch also composed eleven symphonies, all dating from the period c.1779–1787. The last six of these were published in 1787 by the Magazin de Musique in two sets of three: symphonies in D, F and G minor in April, symphonies in C, A and G in November. These works coincide with the first publication of symphonies by Artaria, suggesting that Kozeluch, too, thought there was a market. But Kozeluch's change of mind was immediate, unequivocal and final: no more symphonies, whether by Kozeluch or anybody else, were ever issued by the Magazin de Musique.

This survey of music dissemination in Vienna at the end of the eighteenth century and into the first years of the nineteenth has revealed a number of intertwining characteristics. It was a period when the distribution of music through manuscript copies was at its most active and organized, notably through the efforts of Johann Traeg. Yet the apparently impressive efficiency of this process could not alter the fact that manuscript distribution of instrumental and orchestral music ('Cammer-Musik') was, in European terms, old-fashioned. Increasingly during the 1790s Traeg offered printed music alongside manuscript music; and, in 1794, he founded his own publishing business. When his son took over the business in 1805 this transformation was completed and the firm became a publishing house exclusively.

---

[33] A. Weinmann, *Verzeichnis der Verlagswerke des Musikalischen Magazins in Wien, 1784–1802. Leopold (und Anton) Kozeluch*. 2nd edn., Beiträge zur Geschichte des Alt-Wiener Musikverlages, Reihe 2, Folge 1a (Vienna, 1979).

In the hands of Artaria, Hoffmeister, Kozeluch (Magazin de Musique) and, later, Traeg music publishing in Vienna was economically viable only if it concentrated on smaller genres; publishing symphonies was an unusual practice, by 1800 a non-existent one. It might be thought that a division between printed editions for small-scale works and manuscript distribution of large-scale works such as symphonies, concertos, opera and oratorio would have provided a neat and durable division of labour in Vienna. But there is a new uncertainty in Traeg's attitude to the symphony c.1800 that must have encouraged his son to opt for the financial certainties of publishing. The much reduced presence of the genre in the 1804 catalogue in comparison with the 1799 catalogue, the reliance on imported editions from André, even the offering of older works in the 1799 catalogue at a reduced price, all suggest that the symphony was no longer at the core of the music trade in Vienna. It is time to turn to the people who purchased symphonies and sponsored performances.

CHAPTER 3

Performing symphonies

Alongside the sales catalogues of Johann Traeg, one of the most valuable documentary sources for musical life in Vienna at the end of the eighteenth century is the *Jahrbuch der Tonkunst von Wien und Prag* (Yearbook of Music in Vienna and Prague), compiled and probably mostly written by Johann Ferdinand von Schönfeld (1750–1821), a publisher who had lived and worked in the two cities covered by the yearbook since the early 1780s. 'Vienna and Prague' writes Schönfeld at the beginning of his Preface 'now have so many enthusiasts, friends, and admirers of music, as well as great masters and amateurs, that we have felt the need for a comprehensive catalogue.' He notes the presence of similar yearbooks for other areas of artistic and commercial life and hopes that this one, the first to be devoted to music, will be issued annually. Although Schönfeld remained active as a publisher for many more years no further music yearbooks by him followed.[1]

The 1796 yearbook is a substantial volume of 196 pages devoted almost equally to Vienna and Prague, and with a similar but not identical internal organization for the two cities. The section devoted to Vienna begins with a list of musical patrons in the city followed by the largest section, an alphabetical list of 'Virtuosos and Amateurs in Vienna'; thirteen much smaller sections are then devoted to 'dilettante academies', the Habsburg Hofkapelle, aristocratic court orchestras and windbands, amateurs who possess notable collections of music, composers (a largely redundant section that lists people treated more extensively in 'Virtuosos and Amateurs in Vienna'), violin directors, music dealers and publishers, instrument makers and organ builders, the opera orchestra of the National Theatre (Burgtheater), the orchestra of the German Theatre (Kärntnertortheater), the orchestra of the Marinelli theatre in the Leopoldstadt, the orchestra

---

[1] J. F. von Schönfeld, *Jahrbuch der Tonkunst von Wien und Prag* (Vienna, 1796); facsimile edn. (Munich, 1976). Translation of the preface and the initial three sections on Vienna are given in E. Sisman (ed.), *Haydn and His World* (Princeton, 1997), pp. 289–320.

of Schikaneder's Theater auf der Wieden, and, finally, a short, four-page outline of the present state of music in Vienna.

Given that most of the volume is in the form of a directory rather than an account of music in the city it is not surprising that there are no sections devoted specifically to an evaluation of contemporary music. The final section seems to promise one and divides its coverage into church music, concert music, military music, theatre music and dance music, but the observations are rather random, even adventitious. The shortest paragraph (nine lines) is devoted to concert music, restricting itself to noting that concerts are held outdoors during the summer and that there are numerous private concerts. There is no indication of the format or content of these concerts, let alone a discussion of major genres such as the symphony.

A careful reading of the earlier sections, however, especially the biographical ones, yields some hints on the status of the symphony. The entry on Haydn gives full emphasis to his standing but, rather surprisingly, tempers this with some reservations about his latest symphonies (probably Nos. 101–104, three of which were performed in Vienna in the autumn of 1795), remarks that may have reflected more widely held views in the city.[2]

Who in the whole of Europe has not heard of this great master in the last twenty years? However numerous his symphonies, one still longs daily, with insatiable thirst, for new ones. Yet while one has to say that his symphonies are unequalled and, as many imitators have found, inimitable, it is equally true that they are his greatest works and have added more to his immortality than all his other compositions. But there is many a man of taste who will listen to his older products of this kind with greater pleasure than to his younger ones, and it is possible that Haydn himself may secretly agree. Perhaps he has been wanting to show that he too can wear the garments of the latest musical fashion.

Elsewhere in the yearbook Hoffmeister is described as a composer who 'seems to be better known and liked abroad than in his own home town', Gyrowetz as 'a young artist who does not yet seem to have found his direction' (that is eight years before he was appointed Vice-Kapellmeister at the court theatres) and Vanhal as 'one of our oldest composers who, it seems, has fallen out of fashion'.[3]

If direct comment on the symphonic output of particular composers is rare in the yearbook, the content of the fifth section 'Aristocratic court

[2] Schönfeld, *Jahrbuch*, pp. 20–21; translation from Sisman (ed.), *Haydn*, p. 299.
[3] Schönfeld, *Jahrbuch*, p. 20, pp. 29–30, p. 64; translation from Sisman (ed.), *Haydn*, p. 299, p. 302, p. 316.

orchestras and windbands' is written with real passion and is directly relevant to the status of the genre.[4]

It was formerly the strong custom that our large princely houses possessed their own house *Kapellen* whose splendid genius was built by one person (an example of this is our great Haydn). It can only be a coldness for the love of art, a change of taste, or economy, plus other reasons, in short to the shame of art, that this laudable practice has disappeared, and one *Kapelle* after another has been extinguished, so that apart from that of Prince Schwarzenberg hardly any more exist. Amongst these one finds, especially in the wind players, excellent virtuosos. Prince Grassalkovicz has reduced his *Kapelle* to a Harmonie, of which the great clarinettist Griessbacher is the director. Herr Baron von Braun has his own Harmonie for table music [*Tafelmusik*]. Also the Court Purveyor [*Hoftracteur*] Herr Jahn has a Harmonie. This plays at the table in the Augarten during the summer. The local artillery band consists of many skilled people; the director, Herr Gromann, is a splendid oboist. This organization plays every summer evening at the lemonade huts on the Bastei, and is very good too in private concerts.

Here Schönfeld comments on an aspect of musical patronage in the Austrian territories that had been central for the best part of a century, musical retinues employed by the aristocracy and other wealthy individuals to provide music of all kinds, from church music to operas, quartets to concertos, and from music for the hunt to symphonies, a form of patronage that was, to his consternation, disappearing. He draws attention to the particular example of the Esterházy court, which under Prince Nicolaus (1714–90) had nurtured the particular talent of Haydn. Although three other aristocratic families are mentioned, Schwarzenberg, Grassalkovicz and Braun, Schönfeld's account does not even begin to give a true impression of what he himself calls the 'former strong custom'.

PRIVATE PATRONAGE ON THE WANE

In an initial survey of aristocratic dynasties in the Austrian territories that set up and disbanded musical retinues in the eighteenth century Julia Moore lists over eighty-five families; the actual number could be safely doubled.[5] While many of these dynasties, such as the Auersperg, Esterházy, Lobkowitz, Sachsen-Hildburghausen and Schwarzenberg families had their principal

---

[4] Schönfeld, *Jahrbuch*, pp. 77–8.
[5] J. Moore, 'Beethoven and musical economics' (PhD diss., University of Illinois at Urbana-Champaign, 1987), pp. 562–97. The following gives detailed information on musical retinues in Moravia, many not mentioned in Moore: J. Sehnal, 'Die adeligen Musikkapellen im 17. und 18. Jahrhundert in Mähren', *Studies in Music History presented to H. C. Robbins Landon on his seventieth birthday*, eds. O. Biba and D. W. Jones (London, 1996), pp. 195–217.

palace in Vienna and moved to the countryside in the summer months, this model has often been assumed to been the unvarying norm in the period. There were many families in Bohemia, Hungary, Moravia and Silesia who either resided most of their time in cities and towns such as Prague, Pressburg (Bratislava), Grätz (Hradec u Opavy) and Olmütz (Olomouc) or divided their time between those cities and the local countryside. The strength of the aristocratic network was that it was only partly anchored in Vienna; for many aristocrats the city was central, for others local loyalties, even indifference, meant that the city played only a small part in their lives. The composer Dittersdorf lived and worked in a number of locations in the Austrian territories and his autobiography offers a good deal of information about the characteristics of musical patronage, including its dependence on Vienna.[6]

Born in Vienna in 1739, at the age of eleven Dittersdorf entered the service of the eminent military figure Prince Josef Maria von Sachsen-Hildburghausen as a page and violinist. Sachsen-Hildburghausen lived in Vienna in winter, in the palace later known as the Auersperg palace, and had a summer palace in Schlosshof on the Hungarian border. He maintained a private *Kapelle* and during the winter gave concerts every Friday evening for invited guests. The musical retinue also accompanied the prince to his summer palace and fourteen of them, including Dittersdorf and his two brothers, even went with the prince when he commanded the imperial army during the Seven Years' War. In 1761 the prince felt obliged to move to Hildburghausen (in Thuringia) to undertake his family responsibilities as guardian to a young boy of six or seven who had just inherited the title of Duke of Sachsen-Hildburghausen. There was already an orchestra at the court – Dittersdorf does not give any details – and so the Vienna orchestra was dismissed; the prince, however, took care that Dittersdorf and most of his colleagues were taken on as players in the imperial court in Vienna.

Four years later Dittersdorf came to the attention of Adam Patachich, Bishop of Grosswardein (Oradea in present-day Rumania) who was visiting Vienna and looking for a Kapellmeister to succeed Michael Haydn. Dittersdorf accepted the post, moved to Grosswardein and set in motion four years of unprecedented musical activity at the court. Concerts were

---

[6] C. D. von Dittersdorf, *Lebensbeschreibung. Seinem Sohne in die Feder diktirt*, ed. N. Miller (Munich, 1967); English translation by A. D. Coleridge, *The Autobiography of Karl von Dittersdorf, Dictated to His Son* (London, 1896). See also W. Bein, 'Carl Ditters von Dittersdorf (1739–1799). Stationen seines Lebens zwischen Wien und Schlesien', *Carl Ditters von Dittersdorf 1739–1799. Mozarts Rivale in der Oper*, eds. H. Unverricht and W. Bein (Würzburg, 1989), pp. 13–24; and D. Heartz, *Haydn, Mozart and the Viennese School*, pp. 433–52.

held on Sundays and Tuesdays, given by a musical retinue of thirty-four, amongst whom were nine servants, a valet, a confectioner and some members of the ecclesiastical chapter. As well as concerts and church music, the court extended its activities to opera and oratorio. This rich musical life did not please everyone and, in a malicious letter to the imperial court in Vienna, a disgruntled cleric gave a misleadingly secular image of musical life at Grosswardein; Patachich felt obliged to resign and the musical retinue was summarily disbanded.

After a few months of freelance activity Dittersdorf once more became a Kapellmeister, when he entered the service of Archbishop Philipp Gotthard von Schaffgotsch in Johannisberg (Jauernig) in Silesia in the winter of 1769–70. Once again Dittersdorf embarked on building up the musical life of the court. When he arrived the orchestra consisted of ten players only, all servants; partly through the dismissal of non-musical servants and replacing them with musical servants the orchestra was gradually increased to seventeen. Money was in short supply and Dittersdorf willingly undertook the duties of forest manager (*Forstmeister*). A small theatre was built and some singers engaged so that Italian opera as well as concert music could be performed for the archbishop. Johannisberg was precariously located on the frontiers of Austrian and Prussian control and when the War of Bavarian Succession broke out in 1778 the *Kapelle* was quickly dismissed; in an ensuing battle the castle, including the theatre, suffered severe damage. After the treaty of Teschen in May 1779 the prince reoccupied his castle and re-engaged Dittersdorf and most of the other musicians, though the theatre was never rebuilt.

Dittersdorf began to visit Vienna much more regularly than previously, to the extent that he became a central figure in its musical life in the 1780s, especially as a composer of oratorio and singspiel. It was for Vienna that Dittersdorf composed his Ovid symphonies and its commercial life – music copyists, dealers and publishers – sustained not only his own career but musical life generally at Johannisberg. By the early 1790s the prince bishop, now in his mid-seventies, was becoming increasingly feeble and musical life was consequently less active, though on at least one occasion a new symphony by Dittersdorf seems to have temporarily lifted spirits. Following the death of the prince bishop in 1795 musical life at the court ceased completely; Dittersdorf's loyalty to the court was not rewarded and the last four years of his life were spent in penury.

The most striking characteristic of Dittersdorf's life as a Kapellmeister is how precarious it was. Different circumstances meant that he was made redundant three times in his life. Throughout the period court musical retinues were established, abandoned, and sometimes re-established, and while the sheer number of them in the middle decades of the century ensured that a gifted composer and performer could always find employment this became increasingly difficult in the later decades. War, lack of interest, economic retrenchment and the merging of courts on marriage were common reasons for the dismissal of musicians. Also striking is the intertwining of a professional and amateur musical culture. Although someone like Dittersdorf was a trained professional it was common practice for many of the musicians to be employed as servants too; indeed the orchestra of Count Ferdinand Philipp Harsch in Vienna consisted mainly of servants.[7] For orchestral and church musicians, a distinction between professional and amateur is not particularly helpful in this period and, indeed, well into the nineteenth century, especially if it implies a difference in musical standards. As shown repeatedly in the pages of Schönfeld's yearbook, in particular that entitled 'Virtuosos and Amateurs in Vienna', musical ability was valued regardless of economic and social status.

The size of the orchestras with which Dittersdorf worked is also typical, between ten and seventeen players. Haydn's standard orchestra at the Esterházy court in the early 1760s numbered fourteen and gradually increased to twenty-two; Count Harsch's orchestra numbered twenty-four; and that of Count Johann Nepomuk Erdödy in Pressburg rose to twenty before falling back to seventeen.[8] Symphonies in the courts of the Austrian lands were, therefore, habitually performed by much smaller orchestras than featured in the public concert life of London and Paris and at the semi-public concerts at Mannheim.[9]

Very little detailed information about the repertoire of the three court orchestras for which Dittersdorf worked is given in his autobiography; likewise the vast legacy of documents that has survived from the Esterházy court offers little detailed information about the repertoire of Haydn's orchestra. Naturally the music of the resident Kapellmeister would have featured extensively but no one composer could satisfy the need for music for performances that were held two or three times a week, even allowing for repeat performances of older works. Some idea of the size and nature of the repertoire may be gained from the library of Count Ladislaus Erdödy, for whom Ignaz Pleyel was Kapellmeister from 1777 to c.1783. In 1786,

---

[7] Moore, 'Beethoven and musical economics', p. 573.

[8] Ibid., p. 573; H. Seifert, 'Die Verbindungen der Familie Erdödy zur Musik', *Haydn Yearbook*, 10 (1978), p. 155.

[9] For representative statistics see J. Spitzer and N. Zaslaw, *The Birth of the Orchestra. History of an Institution, 1650–1815* (Oxford, 2004), pp. 306–42.

two years after the death of the count, the music collection was sold in an auction in Vienna and the proceeds given to charity; the advertisement mentions 'a few hundred symphonies, concertinos, concertos, quintets, quartets, German and Italian operas, oratorio, masses etc. by the most famous masters', an indication of a richness of repertoire that went far beyond the music of the young Pleyel.[10]

None of the three courts at which Dittersdorf worked maintained musical life after he left, or re-established it in later years; the same is true of the courts of Count Harsch, Count Ladislaus Erdödy and Count Johann Nepomuk Erdödy. Writing in the last decade of the century Schönfeld very clearly states that this once pervasive tradition had almost disappeared, a view repeated a few years later by the Viennese correspondent of the *Allgemeine musikalische Zeitung*: 'all the noble and wealthy houses that at one time had their own orchestra have disbanded them'.[11] The tradition was at its peak in the third quarter of the century.[12] By the 1790s the decline had become so marked that Schönfeld was at a loss fully to explain it and seems to be clutching at straws when he offers 'coldness for the love of art' and 'change of taste' as reasons. The former is difficult to sustain since the aristocracy retained its enthusiasm for music and remained active sponsors well into the following century; 'coldness for the love of art' better describes their attitudes at the end of the nineteenth century rather than the end of the eighteenth century. 'Change of taste' is a more promising reason and, as Schönfeld's subsequent sentences indicate, is associated with the increasing popularity of music provided by windband, the Harmonie.

The Schwarzenberg family mentioned by Schönfeld was one of the first to employ a wind ensemble rather than an orchestra. Although detailed information is not forthcoming, from at least the 1740s onwards the family had a small mixed ensemble that played in its palace in Vienna on the Mehlmarkt (now Neuer Markt) and at the summer palace in Krumau (Český Krumlov) in southern Bohemia. Ferdinand Arbesser (?1719–1794) was in charge and it is likely that the musicians were primarily servants. In 1771 a major reorganisation took place when an ensemble of two oboes, two cor anglais and two horns was established, joined three years later by two bassoons. At least one of the players, the cor anglais player Ignaz Teimer, had been a servant, but from now on the duties of the ensemble were entirely

[10] Seifert, 'Die Verbindungen', p. 152.   [11] *Allgemeine musikalische Zeitung*, 2 (1800), col. 67.
[12] E. Hanslick, *Geschichte des Concertwesens in Wien* (Vienna, 1869–70), vol. 1, p. 38; O. Biba, 'Die adelige und bürgerliche Musikkultur. Das Konzertwesen', *Joseph Haydn in seiner Zeit*, eds. Gerda Mraz, Gottfried Mraz and G. Schlag (Eisenstadt, 1982), p. 256.

musical ones. With various changes of personnel the Harmonie represented the only full-time instrumentalists at the court up to and beyond 1818. Elsewhere, ensembles with clarinets rather than oboes or cor anglais are known and from the 1770s onwards the most common formation was a sextet (pairs of oboes or clarinets, plus two horns and two bassoons) or an octet (oboes, clarinets, horns and bassoons); later, even larger Harmonie ensembles, with ten or more players, are found.[13]

By the 1780s Harmoniemusik was highly fashionable, stimulated in part, and in a way not evident in the history of the symphony, by the examples of Joseph II and his brother, Archduke Maximilian Franz, both of whom had permanently constituted ensembles. Johann Friedrich Reichardt on his first visit to Vienna in 1783 attended a concert in the Kleiner Redoutensaal. 'Tuning, articulation, everything was true and in accord; a few movements by Mozart were also wonderful. Unfortunately nothing by Haydn was given.'[14] One of the most celebrated examples was at the court of Prince Alois Liechtenstein (1759–1805). Already in existence in the early 1780s, it was formally constituted as an octet in 1789; one of the oboe players was Joseph Triebensee, a prolific and highly capable arranger of music for Harmonie. Liechtenstein went on to form a second ensemble, a 'Turkish Band' of wind instruments plus percussion instruments whose duties were more ceremonial than musical. As well as playing for the prince's own pleasure in his palace in Vienna and at Feldsberg (Valtice) in Moravia, the Harmonie played in public in Vienna in the summer months. On his death in 1805 Prince Aloys was succeeded by his brother, Johann (1760–1836) who in 1808 because of the economic difficulties caused by the Napoleonic wars dismissed the Harmonie; it was reformed in 1812 and remained in existence until 1835.[15]

Simple economics must have played a part in the fashion for Harmonie ensembles in the last decades of the eighteenth century, since an octet would incur roughly half the expenditure of a typical court orchestra of fifteen players. Such seems to have been the motive behind Prince Anton Esterházy's decision only a few weeks after the musical retinue was disbanded in September 1790 to establish a standard Harmonie of eight

[13] O. Biba, 'Beobachtungen zur Österreichischen Musikszene des 18. Jahrhunderts', *Österreichische Musik – Musik in Österreich*, pp. 215–17; A. Mysliík, 'Repertoire und Besetzung der Harmoniemusik an den Höfen Schwarzenberg, Pachta und Clam-Gallas', *Haydn Yearbook*, 10 (1978), pp. 110–20.

[14] *AmZ*, 15 (1813), cols. 667–8.

[15] H. Stekl, 'Harmoniemusik und "türkische Banda" des Fürstenhauses Liechtenstein', *Haydn Yearbook*, 10 (1978), pp. 164–75.

players, all formerly wind players in the orchestra. Although the next prince, Nicolaus II, dismissed the ensemble, a new one was formed in 1800, and the players remained in post until 1813.[16]

The Esterházy family were related to the Grassalkovicz family based in Pressburg. Following the death of Prince Nicolaus Esterházy in 1790 Haydn was offered the post of Kapellmeister by Prince Anton Grassalkovicz. At the time he employed an orchestra of twenty-four but Harmoniemusik directed by Georg Druschetzky (1745–1819) had always featured prominently in the life of the court. The approach to Haydn suggests a new focus on orchestral music; four years later, just before the death of the prince, the music retinue was, in fact, reduced to a Harmonie ensemble.[17]

As the 1799 and 1804 catalogues of Johann Traeg testify, the repertoire for these wind ensembles was an extensive one. Original works were plentiful, but equally characteristic were arrangements of extracts from contemporary operas and oratorios, even, ironically, ones of complete symphonies. The Liechtenstein Harmonie, for example, played arrangements of operas by Caldara, Cherubini, Dittersdorf, Gluck, Mozart and Salieri, plus arrangements of symphonies by Gyrowetz, Haydn and Mozart.

It will be recalled that the presence of symphonies in Traeg's catalogues changed noticeably between 1799 and 1804 and that Harmoniemusik, in particular, is much more evident in the 1804 catalogue, with the actual number of works, forty-eight, being larger than that for symphonies. Taken with the evidence about the replacement of court orchestras with wind ensembles, the conclusion is unavoidable: many patrons and listeners in Vienna and its environs at the turn of the century had come to prefer the sound of Harmoniemusik to that of small orchestras.

Despite the essential truth of Schönfeld's remark concerning the decline of court orchestras, there were still a few families that maintained court orchestras into the nineteenth century, enabling the performance and composition of symphonies as before. In Olmütz Archbishop Colloredo-Waldsee employed a small orchestra and ordered a wide variety of orchestral music until his death in 1811; in Namiest (Náměšť nad Oslavou) Count Heinrich Wilhelm Haugwitz organized concerts in his palace as well as performances of operas and oratorios up to the 1840s;[18] and further north, in Oberglogau (Głogów), Count Franz Joachim Oppersdorff sustained the old tradition of his servants forming a resident orchestra up to his

---

[16] Hellyer, 'Wind Ensembles of the Esterházy Princes', pp. 16–76.
[17] Moore, 'Beethoven and musical economics', p. 572.
[18] Sehnal, 'Die adeligen Musikkapellen', p. 200, p. 209.

death in 1818.[19] None of these individuals is mentioned in Schönfeld's yearbook since they lay outside his geographical coverage but one other figure is briefly mentioned, Prince Franz Joseph Maximilian Lobkowitz, then a young man of twenty-five; a short entry in the section 'Virtuosos and Amateurs in Vienna' describes him as 'a great lover of music, who also plays the violin very agreeably'.[20] Had Schönfeld ever provided further yearbooks there is no doubt that Lobkowitz would have figured extensively for, along with Nicolaus Esterházy, he must be counted one of the most enthusiastic and indulgent of musical patrons in the Viennese tradition. His story was also, ultimately, a tragic one that led to bankruptcy and to an early death.[21]

He was born on 7 December 1772 in Vienna where he spent most of his youth. A knee deformity that gradually led to a misalignment of his hip meant that he used crutches all his life. For this reason the traditional career in the army or the diplomatic service would have been difficult and Lobkowitz instead focused his energies on the arts, especially music. He spoke German, French, Czech, Italian and some English, became a proficient violinist and, as an adult, had a pleasing bass voice. From 1790 onwards he was taught the violin by Anton Wranitzky (1761–1820) who gradually assumed the role of informal Kapellmeister for the prince, arranging private concerts and composing works especially for him. In 1792, at the age of nineteen, Prince Lobkowitz married Maria Carolina, sister of Prince Schwarzenberg and also a great lover of music.

It was in 1797, when he reached the age of majority, that Lobkowitz was able to begin spending significant sums of money on his favoured recreation. In a manner that went contrary to prevailing practice he formed a court ensemble of five instrumentalists, led by Anton Wranitzky; among them was the cellist Anton Kraft who had served at the Esterházy court until its orchestra was dissolved and then at that of Prince Grassalkovicz until it, too, was dissolved. A year later the ensemble numbered seven players who could form a string section of three violinists, two viola players and two cellists. One of the viola players, Valentin Kolbe was also an oboist and one of the violinists, Anton Cartellieri, was employed as a singing teacher; in 1800 Cartellieri was named second Kapellmeister responsible

---

[19] O. Pulkert and H.-W. Küthen (eds.), *Ludwig van Beethoven im Herzen Europas* (Prague, 2000), p. 560.
[20] Schönfeld, *Jahrbuch*, p. 41.
[21] For an account of Lobkowitz's life see J. Macek, 'Franz Joseph Maximilian Lobkowitz. Musikfreund und Kunstmäzen', *Beethoven und Böhmen*, pp. 147–202. A revised form of the essay appears as 'Die Musik bei den Lobkowitz', *Ludwig van Beethoven im Herzen Europas*, pp. 171–216.

for opera and oratorio, allowing Wranitzky to concentrate on instrumental and church music. With this basic ensemble Lobkowitz travelled on a fixed annual pattern between his many palaces; typically, the court was in Vienna from late autumn to May; between May and autumn it moved to Prague, then the two country houses of Eisenberg (Jezeří) and Raudnitz (Roudnice), back to Prague, and from there to Vienna once more. In each of these places musical entertainment of all kinds was organized with little apparent regard for cost. As well as concerts, balls and church music, oratorio and opera were regularly given, for which new theatres were built at Eisenberg and Raudnitz. While the core personnel could provide performances of chamber music, additional players and singers had to be hired for orchestral works, oratorios and operas. In Vienna there was a ready supply of performers who sometimes then travelled with the retinue to the country; performers were engaged also from Prague and from the court of Count Pachta at Liboch (Liběchov); finally, local amateurs, especially schoolteachers, were hired. For large-scale works such as the oratorios of Haydn and the operas of Cherubini, Mozart and Paer, the orchestra could number as many as forty-two. Lobkowitz also established a separate Harmonie of seven players, subsequently increased to ten. As well as the stipends of the permanent musicians, the fees of the hired performers and the expenses of both, Lobkowitz purchased new instruments, paid for special instruction and gave regular gifts to his performers. One indication of the sheer quantity of administrative duties that were necessary to maintain the schedule of performances was the appointment of a third Kapellmeister in 1805, Joseph Rössler (1771–1813), recruited from Prague; his contract required him to direct operas and concerts as required, and 'with passion' (*Eifer*); he also had special responsibility for teaching the Lobkowitz children.

Large quantities of music of all kinds were ordered from copyists and publishers in Vienna, from marches to symphonies, and songs to operas. Indeed there was something manic about Lobkowitz's acquisitiveness, purchasing material from van Swieten's estate (including the original score of Mozart's arrangement of Handel's *Messiah*) and the entire music library of Paul Wranitzky after his death in 1808.

In Vienna performances took place at two palaces, the main one in a square (now the Lobkowitzplatz) between the Kärntnertortheater and the Burgtheater and a second one in the Ungargasse to the east of the city. It was at the former that Reichardt witnessed several performances in the winter of 1808–9, including his own opera *Bradamante*, and provided the following summary: '[a] veritable seat and academy of music . . . At any hour one can organize rehearsals as one pleases in the best and most favourable of circumstances; often several rehearsals and practice sessions are held at the same time in different rooms.'[22]

Lobkowitz's patronage of Beethoven was central;[23] he acquired his music on a systematic basis, organized the first private performances of the *Eroica*, and probably of the Fifth and the *Pastoral* Symphony too. In return Beethoven dedicated the op. 18 quartets, the Triple Concerto and the three mentioned symphonies to the prince. But if Beethoven was pre-eminent he was not alone; Eberl (1765–1807), Haydn (1732–1809), Hummel (1778–1837), Kanne (1778–1833), Krommer (1759–1831), Paer (1771–1839), Reicha (1770–1836), Reichardt (1752–1814), Spohr (1784–1859), Weigl (1766–1846) and Paul Wranitzky (1756–1808) were only a few who received support from the prince.

Lobkowitz's extravagant spending on music began to strain the family exchequer in the early 1800s when he arranged to borrow money from Count Palffy-Dunn; further loans followed from other members of the nobility. None of these prompted a review of expenditure as Lobkowitz became ever more indulgent. Ostentation and taste reached their high point in 1811 when the three weeks of celebration that accompanied the wedding of the prince's daughter, Maria Gabriella, was rumoured to have cost one million gulden; Anton Wranitzky's salary, a reasonably generous one, was 1200 gulden. Retrenchment began in the following year when the number of court employees was reduced; Joseph Rössler, for instance, returned to Prague, and the salaries of many of the musicians were summarily reduced by about a third. By the end of 1813 concerts in Vienna had come to an end and the music ensemble had ceased to exist. Aggravated by unprecedented inflation, the debts became so unmanageable that Lobkowitz's affairs were placed in administration. The prince withdrew from Viennese society and spent most of his time in Bohemia. Shame and embarrassment were followed by tragedy when his wife died in January 1816. On the following 15 December Lobkowitz too died, aged only forty-four. He was buried in the family vault in Raudnitz.

Since 1998 the music library of the Lobkowitz family has been housed at one of their palaces, Nelahozeves (Mühlhausen in Habsburg times) to the north of Prague, having previously been located in the National Library. The music collection had been catalogued in 1893 by the family librarian Joseph Dvořák and it is now, once more, laid out according to Dvořák's

---

[22] J. F. Reichardt, *Vertraute Briefe geschrieben auf einer Reise nach Wien und den Österreichischen Staaten zu Ende des Jahres 1808 und zu Anfang 1809*, ed. G. Gugitz (Munich, 1915), vol. 2, pp. 39–40.

[23] See T. Volek and J. Macek, 'Beethoven und Fürst Lobkowitz', *Beethoven und Böhmen*, pp. 203–17.

shelfmarks. There are 147 items identified as symphonies, but it is clear that this represents only a portion of the library as it existed in its heyday in the first decades of the eighteenth century; for instance there are no manuscript parts for the *Eroica* symphony and the *Pastoral* symphony, both of which are known to have been copied for the court, and sources for Beethoven's First, Seventh and Eighth Symphonies are entirely absent. Nevertheless the extant symphonies provide a clear guide to the repertoire.

Kapellmeister Anton Wranitzky is represented by fifteen symphonies, and third Kapellmeister Rössler by three symphonies, in C, E♭ and D. An extant document shows that the manuscript parts of the Rössler symphonies, like many other works, were prepared by the firm of Sukowaty in Vienna, in this case in 1806–7.[24] The parts describe Rössler as being the 'Maestro di Cappella' for 'il Principe di Lobkowitz, Duca di Raudnitz'. There are twenty-one parts for each of the symphonies: three first violins, three second violins, two violas and three for 'Violoncello e Basso'. Assuming two players per part this makes a string section of six first violins, six second violins, four violas, and, probably, four cellos and two double basses. To this are added one flute, two oboes (two clarinets in the Symphony in E♭), two bassoons, two horns, two trumpets and timpani. In total this points to an orchestra of thirty-two players, which may be taken as the norm for the symphonic repertoire at the court, large by the standards of the earlier court orchestras of Dittersdorf, Haydn and others, and itself an indication of the unsparing nature of Lobkowitz's patronage.

Other contemporary composers of symphonies whose works survive in the Lobkowitz library include Eberl (Symphony in E♭), Krommer (Symphony in F, op. 12) and Paul Wranitzky (twelve symphonies in total). From an earlier period Haydn (some fifty works) and Mozart (thirteen works) figure prominently, but Dittersdorf (three of the Ovid symphonies), Gyrowetz (the three symphonies of op. 23) and Pleyel (seven works) are all comparatively under-represented.[25] This may be taken as an indication of discriminating musical taste in the first decade of the nineteenth century: new symphonies by Beethoven, Eberl, Krommer, the Wranitzky brothers and others were *à la mode*; older ones by Haydn and Mozart were already acquiring an air of distinction.

---

[24] Macek, 'Die Musik bei den Lobkowitz', p. 194; Fojtíková and Volek, 'Die Beethoveniana der Lobkowitz-Musiksammlung und ihre Kopisten', *Beethoven und Böhmen*, pp. 227–9.

[25] The Haydn symphonies are listed in G. Feder, 'Drei Publikationen zur Haydn-Forschung', *Die Musikforschung*, 17 (1964), p. 66. The Mozart symphonies are K181, K204 (symphony version), K250 (symphony version), K297, K318, K319, K320 (symphony version), K338, K425, K504, K543, K550 and K551.

Before Lobkowitz assumed his commanding position in Vienna as a patron of music one of the most significant figures in the private concert life of the city had been Franz Bernhard Kees (1720–95) about whom, in comparison with Lobkowitz, very little is known.[26] He pursued a career in the legal department of the Lower Austrian government, was ennobled in 1764, and eventually assumed the title of Vice President of the Legal System of Lower Austria; his son, too, was a legal official. He seems to have started promoting concerts in the 1760s and, certainly, by the 1780s he was a major figure in Viennese musical life, presenting concerts twice a week. It is likely that the orchestra that performed in these concerts was not a permanent one but was engaged for each concert (or series of concerts); as elsewhere, it mingled professional and amateur players. Kees amassed a large library of music of all kinds, with symphonies being well represented, particularly the symphonies of Haydn which formed the core of the repertoire, ninety-four works in total. In 1791 he prepared a thematic catalogue of this Haydn collection, keeping one copy himself and giving the composer the other. The Kees catalogue of symphonies has always been a valuable documentary source for Haydn scholars[27] who have not found it necessary to speculate why such a specialist catalogue was compiled in the first place; after all Haydn's symphonies represented only a portion of Kees's library and it would have been more typical for any librarian to have included them as part of a larger catalogue of symphonies or of instrumental music generally. As Eybl suggests,[28] it is likely that it was linked with a special concert of Haydn's music that took place in 1792 at Kees's palace on the Bauernmarkt, behind St Peter's church on the Graben. The only known reference to this event is a report that found its way into the London newspaper, the *Public Advertiser*, on 6 February 1792.[29]

HAYDN. At Vienna a Grand Concert has lately been given in honour of this favourite Composer, at which were present the Princes, the principal Nobility, and all the great masters and amateurs; two symphonies composed last winter [Nos. 95 and 96], for Salomon's Concert were performed, at the end of each an eulogium, written in praise of this extraordinary genius was spoken. The whole was received with a thunder of applause. Mr. Haydn's picture illuminated, was exhibited in the Concert-room, and over the door of entrance were written in the German language, 'Profound Silence'.

[26] M. Eybl, 'Franz Bernhard Ritter von Keeß – Sammler, Mäzen und Organisator', *Österreichische Musik – Musik in Österreich*, pp. 239–50.

[27] Facsimile edn.: *Three Haydn Catalogues*, 2nd edn., ed. J. P. Larsen (New York, 1979), pp. 37–49.

[28] Eybl, 'Franz Bernhard Ritter von Keeß', p. 245.

[29] Quoted in Landon, *Haydn in England*, p. 124.

Haydn himself was in London, anticipating the second·season of Salomon concerts, and the report would have appealed to English readers for whom the composer was already a celebrity. While the veneration for the creative artist that is shown in the report was an accepted part of cultural life in England, it was unusual in Vienna at this time. Not only was a Kapellmeister being made a figure of honour but his music, specifically his symphonies, were to be listened to with rapt attention. Haydn was approaching his sixtieth birthday. Maybe this concert was in the form of a tribute and perhaps the catalogue of symphonies was specially prepared by Kees as a gift.

It should be stressed that Lobkowitz's extravagant musical patronage, including the sponsorship of new symphonies through performances at his many palaces, was exceptional in musical Austria at the turn of the century. But, as the formation of Harmonie ensembles suggests, the aristocracy had not lost its enthusiasm for music. As an alternative to a Harmonie, some members of the nobility who might have previously supported a small orchestra instead sponsored quartet ensembles. Thus Count Johann Nepomuk Erdödy's son, Joseph, employed a quartet[30] and Prince Carl Lichnowsky, Beethoven's principal aristocratic patron before Lobkowitz, subsidized a youth quartet (*Knabenquartett*) from 1794 to 1806.[31]

One of the most idiosyncratic aspects of musical patronage in Vienna in the second half of the eighteenth century and into the nineteenth century is the rather detached role of the imperial family, reflected in the fact that they are not even mentioned in Schönfeld's yearbook. The two principal theatres, the Burgtheater and the Kärntnertortheater were still court theatres but their management was at arm's length; the court had never played a prominent role in the development of the quartet, concerto, symphony and other instrumental music; and, by the end of the century, the principal function of its musical retinue was to provide music for the Catholic liturgy. Like several of his ancestors, though none of his successors, Emperor Franz II (I) was a capable musician, who played the violin and piano; indeed his principal recreation was to lead a quartet ensemble but symphonies were almost entirely absent from the repertory.[32] His second wife, Marie Therese, was an ardent music lover. As the daughter of Ferdinand IV and

[30] Seifert, 'Die Verbindungen', p. 29.
[31] K. Boženek, 'Beethoven und das Adelsgeschlecht Lichnowsky', *Ludwig van Beethoven im Herzen Europas*, p. 126.
[32] J. A. Rice, *Empress Marie Therese and Music at the Viennese Court, 1792–1807* (Cambridge, 2003), pp. 132–40; S. C. Wimmer, 'Die Hofmusikkapelle in Wien unter der Leitung von Antonio Salieri von 1778–1824' (MPhil diss., University of Vienna, 1998), pp. 132–40.

Queen Maria Carolina of Naples she grew up in an environment that gave primacy to vocal music. She played the harp, the piano, and was evidently a good sight singer, though commentators were rather circumspect about the actual quality of her voice. She became acquainted with the leading performers and composers of the day and took great pleasure in organizing and participating in private concerts at the imperial apartments in Vienna and the summer palaces of Schönbrunn, Laxenburg and Hetzendorf. A surviving musical diary of private concerts arranged between 1801 and 1803 lists the items performed, overwhelmingly vocal music, from solo arias (typically sung by professionals), through ensembles (in which the empress liked to participate), to concert performances of masses. Symphonies featured infrequently. Of the seventy-six concerts that are documented only nine included a symphony, mainly works by Paul Wranitzky.[33]

THE SYMPHONY IN ECCLESIASTICAL INSTITUTIONS: THE OLD TRADITION

Had Schönfeld been writing in the 1780s rather than the 1790s he would no doubt have commented on the impact of Joseph II's reforms on musical practices in monasteries and churches in the Austrian territories. One of the distinguishing and glorious features of Catholic worship for much of the eighteenth century was the prominent role given to music, an uplifting mix of plainsong, organ music, orchestrally accompanied masses, trumpet fanfares and instrumental music. More than one commentator remarked that attending a church service was akin to going to a concert. Symphonies played a part in these services, with individual movements often played as so-called Gradual music between the Gloria and the Credo.[34] A distinct sub-genre, the 'pastoral symphony' ('Sinfonia pastorella' and variants) existed, works that were specifically composed for use in church or were deemed suited by a local cataloguer to be performed there; the extensive collection of symphonies in the abbey of Göttweig, for instance, has pastoral symphonies by Hofmann, Pichl, Umstatt and Zechner.[35]

Joseph II's reforms were designed to make the religious community serve the population at large, and any expenditure that was not associated with the religious, educational and medical well-being of the people was viewed as extravagant. Accordingly, from 1782 onwards the emperor systematically

---

[33] An annotated transcription of the diary is given in Rice, *Empress Marie Therese*, pp. 279–309.

[34] N. Zaslaw, 'Mozart, Haydn and the *Sinfonia da Chiesa*', *Journal of Musicology*, 1 (1982), pp. 95–124.

[35] F. W. Riedel (ed.), *Der Göttweiger Thematische Katalog von 1830* (Munich, 1979), vol. 1, p. 441, p. 452, p. 456, p. 464.

reduced the role of instruments in church services.[36] By curtailing the tradition of orchestrally accompanied masses Joseph II's reforms also removed a common venue for the performance of symphonies, a practice, therefore, that gradually disappeared without ever being explicitly forbidden. In the process the fertile association of the symphony with religious sentiments was lost for ever. By 1800 it was already a distant memory.

Music, including the performing of symphonies, had also played an important recreational role in many monasteries in the Austrian territories. The *Tafelmusik* tradition was strong, music was played on name-days, birthdays and other special occasions and, as at the secular courts, performances were often dependent on the participation of members of the local community. Where the local ruler was an ecclesiastical one, as in the case of Grosswardein and Johannisberg where Dittersdorf served, the intertwining of secular and sacred musical traditions was particularly strong, as Bishop Patachich found to his cost. Many religious foundations, such as the abbeys of Göttweig, Kremsmünster, Lambach, Osegg (Osek) and St Florian, held significant quantities of symphonies, either ordered directly from Vienna or acquired as part of a local network.

On a visit to Melk in 1782 Joseph II was offered the customary *Tafelmusik* during the evening meal. He declined, commenting coldly 'Perhaps there will be a desire to converse at table and too little attention paid to the music.'[37] In fact the emperor had already set in motion a whole series of reforms that were to change not only the role of music in Catholic worship but, more fundamentally, the influence of monasteries in all aspects of Austrian society. Over the next few years some 400 sacred institutions were dissolved while those that survived were compelled to reduce the number of monks; in the case of Melk only fifteen remained in 1790 compared with the fifty or more before the reforms were enacted.[38] Many of the associated schools and theological seminaries were also closed. Thus, within eight years the recreational role of music in individual abbeys had either totally disappeared or had been severely reduced. A catalogue of the extensive music library of Göttweig abbey was completed in 1830. Together with a musical incipit each item was given a short description and, usually, the date when it had been acquired.[39] Over 350 symphonies are entered, the vast majority with dates of acquisition from the 1760s, 1770s and early

[36] For a summary see R. G. Pauly, 'The Reforms of Church Music under Joseph II', *Musical Quarterly*, 43 (1957), pp. 372–82.

[37] R. N. Freeman, *The Practice of Music at Melk Abbey Based upon the Documents, 1681–1826* (Vienna, 1989), p. 228, p. 464.

[38] Ibid., p. 25.   [39] Riedel (ed.), *Der Göttweiger Thematische Katalog*, vol. 1, pp. 415–66.

1780s; only twenty or so have dates later than 1785, a forcible indication of the transformation of musical life that occurred as a result of Joseph's reforms.

THE SYMPHONY IN PUBLIC CONCERTS: A HESITANT TRADITION

In comparison with other major cities such as Leipzig, London and Paris, and many smaller ones such as Dublin, Edinburgh, Frankfurt, Munich and Stockholm, Vienna had not developed a vigorous, continuing tradition of public concerts in the eighteenth century. Vienna did not have the equivalent to the Gewandhaus Concerts in Leipzig, the Concert Spirituel in Paris and the Salomon Concerts in London, that is a series of concerts presented in the same venue by a more or less consistent body of performers and to which admission was, at least nominally, available to all. In these concerts the symphony was a regular presence, the beginning of an association between genre, performers, venue and audience that was to inform its long-term development. In Vienna, the flourishing patronage of the symphony by private courts and ecclesiastical institutions, together with the conservative structures of social and economic society in general, meant that for much of the eighteenth century there was no pressing reason to copy trends elsewhere in Europe.

In the 1790s performances of symphonies in public in Vienna were numerically very few and often incidental in nature. Table 3.1 presents a summary of known performances of symphonies in Vienna between 1790 and 1800.

The precarious nature of these statistics should be stressed. Unlike Leipzig, London and Paris, Vienna did not have a commercially active press that regularly advertized musical and theatrical events; the *Wiener Zeitung* which appeared twice a week was a court newspaper and, although it did carry advertisements for all manner of goods (including music manuscripts and publications), it only infrequently carried advertisements for performances of operas and concerts, and reviews of such occasions were even less common. Such statistics as those presented overleaf have to be compiled from a variety of sources – documents, memoirs, extant posters, as well as the occasional report in the press – and the nature of the evidence ranges from the detailed to the cursory. There were probably further public concerts for which no sources have survived. On the other hand some of the individual tallies given in Table 3.1 may exaggerate the number of symphonies known to have been performed in a particular year, since the sources do not always distinguish between overtures and symphonies

Table 3.1. *Public performances of symphonies in Vienna, 1790–1800*

Year	No. of performances	Composers
1790	0	–
1791	15	Anon, Dittersdorf, Gassmann, Hasse, Haydn (5), Kozeluch, Mozart (2), Pleyel, Schenk (2)
1792	3	Haydn (2), Mozart
1793	10	Haydn (9), Ossowsky
1794	6	Haydn (4), Ulbrich (2)
1795	12	Cartellieri (2), Gyrowetz (2), Haydn (5), Paul Wranitzky (3)
1796	15	Anon (3), Haydn (9), Witt, Paul Wranitzky (2)
1797	6	Anon, Mozart (3), Paul Wranitzky (2)
1798	15	Eybler (4), Haydn (5), Seyfried (2), Anton Wranitzky, Paul Wranitzky (3)
1799	6	Anon, Gluck (2), Haydn (3)
1800	14+	Beethoven, Haydn (7+), Krommer, Mozart (3)

The information is drawn from the following sources: the calendar of public concerts in M. S. Morrow, *Concert Life in Haydn's Vienna: Aspects of a Developing Musical and Social Institution* (Stuyvesant, NY, 1989), pp. 275–307; and D. Edge, review of ibid., *Haydn Yearbook*, 17 (1992), pp. 157–66.

(the Gluck items in 1799 are certainly overtures, probably other items were too) and sometimes imply that several symphonies were played in a concert when, in fact, it may have been the constituent movements of one symphony spread across the programme. Nevertheless, the statistics are a helpful indication of the status of the symphony in public concert life in the period.

In 1790, no symphony is known to have been performed, largely because all public musical life was suspended for two months during the serious illness, death of and mourning for Joseph II. Excluding that year the average number of public performance of symphonies was about ten, one symphony every five weeks or, if one restricts the period to the social season of November through to May, one every fortnight, hardly a prominent feature of musical life in a city that was otherwise so active.

Most concerts were held in the theatres, principally the two court theatres, the Burgtheater and the Kärntnertortheater, plus Schikaneder's Theater auf der Wieden, on evenings when theatrical performances did not take place, so-called 'spielfreie Tage'. Earlier in the century 'spielfreie Tage' included all church holidays, that is the period 17–24 December and the whole of Lent, plus the anniversary of the eve and day of the death of the most recent emperor.[40] Gradually, managers whittled away at these days but it was always to their financial advantage to offer further performances of opera (or plays) rather than hire the theatre out for a concert. When Baron Peter Braun was in charge of the management of the theatres between 1794 and 1806 it was thought difficult for someone to hire the theatre, even more so if that person was a stranger to the city.[41] Those concerts that did take place were invariably single concerts rather than a series and were in the nature of benefit concerts, either for a charity or for an individual.

The most venerable charitable organization was the Tonkünstler-Societät.[42] Founded in 1771 its members were performing musicians in Vienna who raised funds to support the widows and orphans of past members. The principal means of raising funds were two bi-annual concerts, one during Advent and one at the end of Lent, each given twice, usually on consecutive evenings. All performers gave their services for nothing and since the object was to raise money their number was unusually large, typically in excess of 100. During the 1790s many of the programmes for the Tonkünstler-Societät consisted of a miscellany of items, such as the one in April 1792 that contained a symphony by Haydn, concertos for the oboe and for the cello, arias by Pleyel and Bianchi, a duet by Sacchini, a quintet by Albrechtsberger and choruses by Handel, Haydn and Albrechtsberger.[43]

While these four annual concerts were firm fixtures in the Viennese musical calendar, displaying a corporate sense of musical and social purpose, the many benefit concerts for individuals were more vainglorious. For instance, Joseph Seuche was the music director at the Theater auf der Wieden[44] and was entitled to an annual benefit concert. In 1792 the programme included a Mozart symphony alongside vocal items by Cimarosa and Sacchini, a violin concerto by Giornovichi and two items for mandolin; four years later his concert was more ambitious, Süssmayr's oratorio *Moses* preceded by a symphony by Haydn.[45] The pianist Josepha Auernhammer negotiated five concerts at the Burgtheater during the decade. As a former pupil of Mozart she often promoted the composer's music in the years after his death, her concert in 1797, for instance, including two symphonies and

[40] O. Biba, 'Concert Life in Beethoven's Vienna', *Beethoven, Performers, and Critics*, ed. R. Winter and B. Carr (Detroit, 1980), p. 77.

[41] *AmZ*, 6 (1803–4), cols. 470–71.

[42] The following remains the standard history: C. F. Pohl, *Denkschrift aus Anlass des hundertjährigen Bestehens der Tonkünstler-Societät, im Jahre 1862 reorganisirt als "Haydn", Witwen- und Waisen-Versorgungs-Verein der Tonkünstler in Wien* (Vienna, 1871).

[43] Morrow, *Concert Life*, p. 280.   [44] Schönfeld, *Jahrbuch*, p. 96.

[45] Morrow, *Concert Life*, p. 279, p. 290.

a piano concerto by him alongside a violin concerto and two arias by an unknown composer, and a set of variations by Auernhammer herself.[46]

Benefit concerts for composers were very rare. Following his first visit to London Haydn arranged a benefit concert in March 1793 at which he presented three of his latest symphonies; he repeated the exercise in December 1795, shortly after his second visit.[47] Thereafter, no further benefit concerts were organized by the composer. Although Beethoven had played at benefit concerts for other musicians on four occasions in the 1790s and twice for the Tonkünstler-Societät he did not present his own benefit until April 1800, at the Burgtheater; it accorded with standard practice in that it presented him as a performer (a piano concerto and an improvisation), unusual and ambitious in that it featured three substantial compositions by him, the First Piano Concerto, the Septet and the First Symphony.

A new kind of charity concert became evident in the 1790s, concerts to support the campaign against the threatening armies of France. For families who had recently lost men serving in the Austrian army, a couple of concerts were held in January 1794, each including a Haydn symphony.[48] Two years later, in the summer of 1796 Austria received a series of humiliating defeats in northern Italy at the hands of Napoleon's troops and, for the first time since the Seven Years' War, there was a real fear of invasion; Haydn's Symphony No. 94 ('Surprise') was performed in a number of concerts held in Vienna in the autumn to raise money for the volunteer corps that was to defend the city in the event of an attack.[49] Charity concerts such as these, with and without symphonies, were to be a regular feature of musical life in Vienna through to the end of the Napoleonic wars in 1814.

The only public concerts that were held in Vienna for musical reasons rather than to aid a declared cause were the summer concerts in the Augarten.[50] Although the concerts can be traced back to the early 1780s very little precise information is available and their repertoire is certainly under-represented in Table 3.1; in the 1780s and early 1790s many of the performing parts used in the concerts came from the library of Franz Bernhard Kees.[51] From 1798 the young Ignaz Schuppanzigh assumed the role of director; the concerts began at the startlingly early time of 7.00 a.m. and featured an orchestra in which the wind and double bass players were professionals and the violins, violas and cellos were amateurs.

---

[46] Ibid., pp. 293–4.

[47] Landon, *Haydn in England*, pp. 215–16; *Haydn: The Years of 'The Creation'*, pp. 59–60.

[48] Morrow, *Concert Life*, p. 284.   [49] Ibid., pp. 292–3.

[50] R. Klein, 'Musik im Augarten', *Österreichische Musikzeitschrift*, 26 (1973), pp. 239–48.

[51] Schönfeld, *Jahrbuch*, p. 74.

In addition to these formal occasions symphonies could also be heard informally, as part of the local serenading practice. As the following quotation from an almanac published in 1794 makes clear serenades in Vienna embraced all kinds of music.[52]

Every day during the summer months, if the weather is fine, one encounters serenading on the streets, and at all hours, sometimes at one o'clock, more often later. To a certain extent one is forced to hold the serenade very late in the day since the clatter of wagons, constantly trundling up and down the distant streets, comes to an end only very late. These serenades, unlike those in Italy and Spain, do not consist of a simple accompaniment to a voice, on a guitar, mandora or similar instrument – for one serenades here not to a send a sigh into the air, or to declare love, for which a thousand more suitable opportunities are found – rather these nocturnes [*Nachtmusiken*] consist of trios, quartets, mainly from operas, in several vocal parts, on wind instruments, often an entire orchestra; also the largest symphonies are played.

Equally difficult to document are performances of symphonies, or movements from symphonies, as interval music in a theatrical performance or even music to follow the main performance. Intermittent evidence from the 1770s onwards suggest that in Vienna as elsewhere in German-speaking Europe symphonies, as well as concertos and sonatas, could be performed in the theatre alongside the main stage presentation.[53] On three successive evenings in Schikaneder's Theater auf der Wieden in February 1798, three symphonies were performed, by Winter, Haydn and Henneberg, as interval music but, in general, such evidence as exists suggests that instrumental works with soloists were more common.[54]

Even though the repertoire in Table 3.1 is by no means a complete one, its narrowness is telling, eighteen composers only and as such a poor reflection of the content of the Traeg catalogue. Yet the symphonies are, for the most part, ones that were relatively new in the 1790s. The list is dominated by the symphonies of Haydn, over forty-nine performances, approximately half the total. As well as the two benefit concerts that the composer arranged in order to present some of the London symphonies, the two concerts of the Tonkünstler-Societät given in December 1793 were devoted almost entirely to the recent music of Haydn, three symphonies alongside two choruses; further, many performers in the 1790s sought to ensure good

---

[52] *Wiener Theater Almanach für das Jahr 1794*, quoted in Biba, 'Beobachtungen zur Österreichischen Musikszene', p. 225.

[53] E. Sisman, 'Haydn's Theater Symphonies', *Journal of the American Musicological Society*, 43 (1990), pp. 297–303.

[54] See the tables of performances given in P. Tomek, 'Die Musik an den Wiener Vorstadttheatern 1776–1825' (PhD diss., University of Vienna, 1989).

attendance at their benefit by including a symphony by the composer. Through the composition and many performances in Vienna from 1797 onwards of *The Creation* and the huge popular appeal of 'Gott erhalte Franz den Kaiser' Haydn acquired the status of an admired national figure. As with the affection that had been shown to Haydn in private in Kees's concerts, public perception of the man was now beginning to be associated with a reverence for his symphonies, a reverence that mingled musical superiority with national pride.

Although the number of known performances of symphonies by Mozart is much lower, nine, the perceived distinction of the works was part of a growing transcendence that marked the composer's image in the years immediately after his death. In his own lifetime in Vienna Mozart had always given priority to the piano concerto over the symphony (seventeen new concertos between 1781 and 1791 as opposed to six new symphonies); in the 1790s the situation was slowly being reversed with his symphonies profiting from the esteem that was accorded to those of Haydn. Alongside this emergent veneration of two individuals, Haydn and Mozart, there is the noticeable presence of Paul Wranitzky (1756–1808), with eight performances; on this evidence he is a more significant figure in the 1790s than his near contemporaries, Eybler (1765–1846), Gyrowetz (1763–1850) and Pleyel (1757–1831).

At the end of the eighteenth century in Austria the symphony was particularly vulnerable, even uniquely so, to the changes that were occurring in musical patronage. Having already lost the locus of performance in ecclesiastical surroundings, the symphony was now feeling the effect of the irreversible decline of orchestral music in the aristocratic courts, the mainstay of its support for much of the century. At the same time public concert life in Vienna, with its focus on single concerts for the benefit of an individual or a charity, was poorly equipped to take on the responsibility of promoting the symphony. For the next few years composers of symphonies were forced to combine dependency on the remains of the old forms of patronage with a willingness to grapple with the inadequacies of the new.

CHAPTER 4

A tale of two brothers: Anton and Paul Wranitzky

One of the defining characteristics of musical life in Vienna in the second half of the eighteenth century is the subtle relationship of the city with its hinterland, Upper and Lower Austria, Bohemia, Hungary and Moravia. It was not the nineteenth-century process of urbanization, with its attendant depopulation of the countryside and accelerating division between civic and peasant culture, but a more mutually supportive one that provided a measure of social cohesion. The aristocracy spent much of its time in the country estates, some like Prince Nicolaus Esterházy most of their time, and musical activity, as already discussed, was as dependent on musicians or musician-servants raised locally as those brought up in Vienna itself. The education system of the time, often rather basic until the reforms of Maria Theresia and Joseph II took hold, laid emphasis on musical accomplishment, one that was further nurtured outside school by the Catholic church. This was an aspect of musical life that caught the attention of Charles Burney in 1772 on his second tour in Europe to gather information for his General History of Music. The tour was organized around short periods of residence in major cities. After two weeks in Vienna in August-September he travelled north-westwards towards Prague noting with delight that all the local schools en route taught music. In Czaslau (Čáslav), a small town forty miles south-east of Prague, he wrote: 'I went in the school, which was full of little children of both sexes, from six to ten to eleven years old, who were reading, writing, playing on violins, hautbois, bassoons, and other instruments. The organist had in a small room of his house four clavichords, with little boys practising on them all: his son of nine years old, was a very good performer.'[1] Most of these children were destined to live their entire lives in the same locality, some might join the retinue of a local aristocrat as a servant and only the very gifted (such as the organist's

---

[1] P. A. Scholes (ed.), *An Eighteenth-Century Musical Tour in Central Europe and the Netherlands. Dr. Burney's Musical Tours in Europe vol. 2* (London, 1959), p. 132

son) would pursue a musical wider career in the Austrian territories and beyond. Gyrowetz, Joseph and Michael Haydn, Johann Antonin and Leopold Kozeluch, Krommer, Reicha and Vanhal are only a few products of this pervasive musical culture, one that is rather obscured by the term Viennese Classical School.[2]

Two brothers raised in Neureisch (Nova Říše), Paul Wranitzky (1756–1808) and Anton Wranitzky (1761–1820) are especially interesting figures in the history of the symphony at the turn of the century. Between them they composed sixty symphonies, the last composers in the Viennese tradition to contribute so prolifically. Although the brothers lived in Vienna and often participated in the same musical events, their careers were fundamentally different, reflecting the changing nature of musical life and the role the symphony played in it. The younger brother, Anton, spent most of his working life as Kapellmeister to Prince Lobkowitz; Paul, on the other hand, had a more varied career, one that skilfully capitalized on circumstances.

THE SYMPHONIES OF ANTON WRANITZKY (1761–1820)

As a boy in Neureisch Anton Wranitzky learnt the violin and nurtured a distinctive treble voice. After attending the school associated with the local Premonstratensian monastery he studied law and philosophy at the Jesuit seminary in Brno. By December 1783 he had become choirmaster at the Theresianisch-Savoyische Akademie in Vienna, an institution dedicated to the training of sons of the aristocracy. The role of music in the liturgical services of the school was curtailed by Joseph II's reforms which led Anton Wranitzky in his mid-twenties to embark on a freelance career as a violinist, although little of detail is known. It was probably at this time that he turned to composition as well as playing and directing, and he is said to have studied with Albrechtsberger, Haydn and Mozart. His earliest dateable works are six quartets, published by Hoffmeister in 1790 (perhaps 1791), where he is described as a pupil of Haydn ('Eleve de Mr. J. Hayden'); more significantly the quartets are dedicated to Prince Lobkowitz, then only eighteen years old, with whom he was to be associated for the rest of his working life.[3]

He taught the prince the violin and soon became his advisor and confidant in all musical matters, arranging concerts and, especially notable, composing a large symphony in C major on the occasion of his marriage in

[2] For an account of Bohemians in the musical life of Vienna see T. Antonicek, 'Musiker aus den böhmischen Ländern in Wien zu Beethovens Zeit', *Beethoven und Böhmen*, pp. 43–61.
[3] Copy of print in Lobkowitz library, Nelahozeves: X. I. a. 52 and 53.

1792. It was also during this period that he consolidated his reputation as a teacher of the violin, counting amongst his pupils the young Ignaz Schuppanzigh. Later, in 1804, he published a treatise on violin playing, *Violin Fondament nebst einer vorhergehenden Anzeige über die Haltung sowohl der Violin, als auch des Bogens*.

Shortly before Prince Lobkowitz reached the age of majority Anton Wranitzky was charged with establishing a permanent body of musicians at the Lobkowitz court, initially five in number, later stabilizing at seven, and Wranitzky was himself formally appointed Kapellmeister in 1797. He soon became the central figure of authority in the musical life of the Lobkowitz family, playing, directing, composing and dealing with all the associated administrative work of supervising the acquisition of new music and the engagement of additional performers.[4] His own compositions reflected his expertise as a string player, including quintets, quartets, trios, sonatas and fifteen violin concertos as well as symphonies, but he also composed a few sacred works.

Since Anton Wranitzky's musical life was linked firmly with the unending enthusiasm of his patron, Prince Lobkowitz, his name figures infrequently elsewhere in the musical life of Vienna. He led the second violins in the first public performances of *The Creation* in 1799 and was subsequently entrusted by Haydn with arranging the work for string quintet (published by Artaria in 1799). Haydn wanted him do the same for *The Seasons* commenting favourably on his musicianship and integrity;[5] he had to decline and the work was undertaken by the Leipzig musician August Eberhard Müller. When Prince Lobkowitz along with eight other aristocrats formed a consortium to run the Burgtheater, Kärntnertortheater and the Theater an der Wien in 1807 he appointed his Kapellmeister as orchestra director, though it is difficult to imagine that he actually participated in many performances given the other demands that the prince was making on his time and, in particular, the five months or so the musical retinue was resident in the various Bohemian palaces. Prince Lobkowitz relied heavily on Wranitzky's advice when he took over the Hoftheater-Musik-Verlag from Thadé Weigl in 1811 and guided its troublesome activities until 1816.[6] While Prince Lobkowitz's distressing financial circumstances led him to end the employment of most of his full-time musicians, Wranitzky remained in

---

[4] His signature can be seen on documents in the following volumes: *Beethoven und Böhmen* and *Ludwig van Beethoven im Herzen Europas*.
[5] Landon, *Haydn: the Late Years* (London, 1977), p. 79.
[6] A. Weinmann, *Verzeichnis der Musikalien aus dem K. K. Hoftheater-Musik-Verlag*. Beiträge zur Geschichte des Alt-Wiener Musikverlages, Reihe 2, Folge 6 (Vienna, 1982), pp. 6–8, pp. 15–27.

post until the prince's death in 1816 and was retained in what was now a virtual sinecure by his successor, Prince Ferdinand Lobkowitz. Aged fifty-five Wranitzky seems to have already retired from composition, to judge from known dates of publication, and the remaining four years of his life were probably spent fulfilling his playing duties in the theatres in Vienna and noting the burgeoning careers of his two sons, Anton (violin) and Friedrich (cello), and a daughter, Katharina (a singer).

There are fifteen extant symphonies by Anton Wranitzky all found in the Lobkowitz library in the family palace in Nelahozeves (Mühlhausen), located on the banks of the Moldau to the north of Prague. With one exception, the *Aphrodite* symphony in C major (C1), the Lobkowitz sources are the only ones.[7] Taken with the fact that there are no symphonies by Anton Wranitzky in the Traeg catalogues of 1799 and 1804 this might suggest that the works were considered the intellectual property of the court and were not allowed to be disseminated. This is unlikely for several reasons. Other instrumental works by Wranitzky, especially his quintets, quartets and trios were advertized by Traeg, and published by Hoffmeister in Vienna and André in Offenbach.[8] While Wranitzky's contract with the prince has not been located, that for his fellow Kapellmeister Joseph Rössler has survived and it does not stipulate that his works should remain the exclusive property of the court.[9] In any case such an obligation would have been decidedly old-fashioned c.1800. Best known from the first contract that Haydn signed with the Esterházy family in 1761, it was omitted from the second contract, signed in 1779, and that composer, like Dittersdorf and others, was able to distribute his music outside the confines of his employment. If, as is likely, Wranitzky worked under the same liberal conditions this begs the question why there are no further sources for his symphonies, manuscript or published, from outside the court. From 1807 there is evidence in correspondence between the composer and André in Offenbach that Wranitzky had explored the possibility of publishing some symphonies; André was reluctant because of changing musical taste and the idea was quietly forgotten.[10] Only one public performance of a symphony in Vienna is known: at a benefit concert for Josepha Dussek on 29 March 1798 at the Jahnscher Saal, given alongside the singer's party piece, 'Non, più di fiori' from Mozart's *La clemenza di Tito*.[11]

[7] Brook (ed. in chief), *The Symphony 1720–1840. Reference Volume*, pp. 558–9.
[8] See Weinmann, *Johann Traeg. Die Musikalienverzeichnisse*; Weinmann, *Hoffmeister*; Matthäus, *André*; Constapel, *André*.
[9] Transcription of contract in *Ludwig van Beethoven im Herzen Europas*, p. 491.
[10] Constapel, *André*, p. 116.   [11] Morrow, *Concert Life*, p. 296.

Table 4.1. *The symphonies of Anton Wranitzky*

Work[a]	No. on ms source in Lobkowitz library	Instruments added later
C1 (1792)	8	
C2	10	
C3	3	
C4	6	
D1 (1796)	14	
D2	7	
D3	9	clarinets
D4	2	
D5	16	
E♭1	1	
E♭2	5	trumpets and timpani
F1	15	
G1	11	trumpets and timpani
A1	13	clarinets, trumpets and timpani
B♭1	4	trumpets and timpani

[a] The catalogue numbers are those given in B. S. Brook (ed. in chief), *The Symphony 1720–1840. Reference Volume: Contents of the Set and Collected Thematic Indexes* (New York, 1986), pp. 558–9. Lobkowitz shelfmarks are given in this catalogue.

The picture that emerges of Kapellmeister Wranitzky is that he was content in his old-fashioned working environment; a generation earlier he might have been more successful selling his symphonies outside the court in a casual manner but he seems to have accepted the changes that were taking place in the status of the symphony at the end of the century and to have retreated into the comfort of the Lobkowitz court. Table 4.1 summarizes his symphonic output.

Only two of the fifteen symphonies carry a date: 1792 for the *Aphrodite* symphony (C1) and 1796 for another programme symphony (without an overall title), a symphony in D major (D1). The manuscript parts, prepared by Viennese copyists with a few examples of additional or replacement parts by more local scribes, are contained within folders that postdate the original acquisition and carry a sequence of numbers from '1' to '16', offering the possibility that one symphony ('12') has disappeared. Lurking in this sequence there may, too, be a semblance of chronology, since works with low numbers (E♭1, D4 and B♭1) tend to be for smaller orchestra and stylistically cautious, whereas the last two symphonies in the sequence (F1 and D4) are for fuller orchestra and have a more modern idiom.

Another aspect of the chronology is that several of the symphonies show elements of revision. A symphony in B♭ (B♭1) that was originally scored for strings, flute, two oboes, two bassoons and two horns in B♭ alto has later, additional parts for trumpet and timpani in the first movement, minuet and finale. Trumpets and timpani in this key, as opposed to the traditional ones of C and D, were still a comparatively novel sound in the 1790s; Wranitzky's first version reflected older sonorities, the revision newer ones. Trumpets and timpani were added also to three other symphonies, E♭2, G1 and A1, again reflecting the more prevalent use of trumpets and timpani and the consequent disassociation of sonority and key that occurs c.1800. A further two works, D3 and A1, have clarinet parts that were added later. A final form of revision consists of the addition of a slow introduction to two works, E♭2 and G1 (works that also had trumpets and timpani added); compared with those slow introductions that were contemporaneous with the original work these additional ones are rather short and perfunctory, perhaps done quickly with an imminent performance in mind.

As a former pupil of Haydn, Wranitzky clearly reveals his influence. With the exception of the two programme symphonies (C1 and D1), where the subject matter encourages an expansion of the genre in particular ways, all the symphonies are in four movements, usually with a slow introduction. Within the four-movement scheme Haydn's spectre is especially noticeable in slow movements, many of which are sets of variations, an approach never found in Mozart's symphonies. The theme of the Adagio of E♭1 is a regularly phrased tune, similar to that in the slow movement of Haydn's Symphony No. 85, which is then subjected to three variations, the first in sextuplet rhythms, the second a *minore*, and the third back in the major and marked *legato*. Wranitzky also explores the mixing of variations and rondo in slow movements, but without the bold contrast of mood and the engrossing cross-references that characterize such movements in the symphonies of Haydn.[12] Thus the slow movement of D4, an Adagio molto, presents a theme in G, a contrasting theme in G minor and then two variations of the G-major theme. The slow movement of D3 is a rudimentary set of variations on two alternating themes of the kind Haydn begins to explore towards the end of the 1770s: main theme, contrasting section, repetition of main theme, variation of contrasting section, and variation of main theme.

Although none of the slow movements has that sense of overt drama that is found in many symphonies by Haydn from the 1780s and 1790s,

---

[12] E. R. Sisman, *Haydn and the Classical Variation* (Cambridge, Mass., 1993), pp. 150–63.

where the prevailing tunefulness is disturbed by a noisy outburst, several movements (variations and otherwise) include trumpets and timpani as part of the orchestral colouring. The slow movement of G1, a five-part rondo (ABACA) on a 2/4 theme in E minor, has the unusual distinction of featuring a cor anglais as the solo instrument in the second episode, though the writing is uncomfortably high rather than being placed in the lower, plangent register.

Sonata form in the first movements of Wranitzky's symphonies is invariably formulaic, with attractive thematic material never prompting musical thought processes that are distinctive to a given movement; contrasting second subjects are the norm. The first movement of D4 is typical in this respect, but then captures the attention through an unorthodox repetition of music from the end of the slow introduction to conclude the movement.

This blend of the Haydnesque, the formulaic and the unexpected is evident in a Symphony in C minor (C4), one of two symphonies in a minor key by Wranitzky (D5 is the other).[13] Unusually for a work in the minor key it has a slow introduction in the major, part of an attractive management of keys in the work as a whole. The first movement concludes in C minor; the slow movement is in Eb major but encloses a stormy middle section in C minor; the minuet is in C minor, but the trio in C major evokes the pastoral with its regularly phrased theme in the wind over held pedal points; the finale returns to C minor but the recapitulation in C major of the slow-moving homophonic second subject provides a moment of resolution that is well-calculated.

The symphony opens with a descending opening unison that incorporates the headmotif of the first subject of the ensuing Allegro vivace in C minor. An arresting thematic idea that demands attention throughout the movement, it is reminiscent of similar openings in two C-minor symphonies by Haydn, Nos. 78 and 95, but unlike both of those movements the motif never provokes any symphonic consequences. Wranitzky's tutti sound in C minor is stirring enough with agitated rhythms and full use of horns (in Eb) and trumpets (in C) in the middle of the texture. The slow movement is headed *Romance* and offers echoes of the similarly titled movement in Haydn's Symphony No. 85, including the doubling of the theme at the higher octave by the flute. The authority of the minuet theme in C minor played by full orchestra is sapped by some nondescript triplet passages after the double bar, though the real deficiency is the complete absence of any

---

[13] Modern edition by E. Hennigová-Dubová, *The Symphony 1720–1840*, ed. in chief, B. S. Brook, B/XII (New York, 1984), pp. 235–329.

disruption to the regular flow of four-bar phrases, whether by accentuation, syncopation or manipulation of phrase lengths. The finale provides a strong contrast between an energetic first subject in C minor (with an insistent anacrustic figure of three quavers) and a lyrical slow-moving theme in the major. Not only is the recapitulation of the theme in C major a well-judged moment of resolution, its subsequent transformation into an energetic, climactic C major, complete with three-quaver motifs and assertive cadential figures is fully convincing. Here it is Beethoven not Haydn who is brought to mind.

If claiming Wranitzky as a chronologically appropriate link between Haydn and Beethoven is suspiciously neat, such an idea is difficult to avoid in another symphony, F1, probably one of his last. The slow introduction, with its wide contrasts of register, double-dotted figuration and move to the flattened submediant, represents an amalgam of features from the slow introductions to Haydn's symphonies No. 104 and No. 100, while the trio, in a *pianissimo* dynamic and with a persistent thematic nudge on the third rather than first beat, recalls the trio of the 'Oxford' symphony (No. 92). What happens after the *da capo* of the minuet is, however, more akin to Beethoven, as the composer seeks to expand the dimensions of the dance movement: a coda makes as if to repeat the trio but then leads into a final repetition of the main theme of the minuet.

Wranitzky's two programme symphonies are strikingly ambitious works that stand apart from the rest of his output. Prompted by notable events in the life of Prince Lobkowitz they are closely related to them and are written on a scale unusual in the symphony of the time. They are court symphonies of the most exclusive and rarefied kind, and presentation scores as well as parts survive for them. The earlier work is the *Aphrodite* symphony of 1792, written to celebrate the wedding in August of that year at the Lobkowitz palace in Raudnitz (Roudnice) of the prince, then nineteen, to Maria Carolina Schwarzenberg, aged seventeen. Unlike many eighteenth-century operas or serenatas performed on such occasions this is not a musical celebration through extended allegory, but a nuptial gift by the prince, a portrait of the Greek goddess of love, Aphrodite, a gift that is placed on display for all to admire. Programme symphonies based on classical stories had recently acquired particular esteem through Dittersdorf's twelve Ovid symphonies (1781–6) and there is little doubt that Wranitzky and Lobkowitz saw these works as a stimulus. Both composers were writing for an audience that were familiar with classical stories and Dittersdorf, certainly, had thought long and hard about how best to link narrative and

Table 4.2. *Anton Wranitzky, Aphrodite symphony*

Music	Summary of programme
Part 1	
Adagio, C major, ℂ–	Peaceful, gentle sea
Allegro con fuoco, C min., ℂ–	Storm
Poco Adagio, C major, 3/4 –	Aphrodite emerges 'bathed in the splendour of heavenly beauty'
Poco Allegro, C major, ℂ	Celebration
Part 2	
Andante, F, 3/4 –	A zephyr beckons towards Cyprus, the traditional home of Aphrodite
Tanz: Allegro, A min. – A major, 2/4	Dance of the joyful Graces
Part 3	
Adagio, C major, 3/4 –	Aphrodite in the company of the gods
Triumphlied: Allegro vivace, C major, ℂ	Song of triumph

Orchestra: strings, two flutes, two oboes, two bassoons, two horns, two trumpets, timpani and strings.

evocation with symphonic traditions.[14] Wranitzky's challenge was a less demanding one in that narrative events are kept to a minimum. Instead, the symphony offers an idealized image of Aphrodite, one that avoids the treachery, jealousies and mixed loyalties of the myth in favour of an extended evocation of her sensuous beauty, a beauty that is then openly celebrated in the concluding *Triumphlied*. A detailed programme is written into all the parts for the benefit of the players; perhaps the listeners were given the same information in the form of a specially printed book akin to presentation librettos associated with opera.[15] The symphony is presented in three parts, each subdivided (Table 4.2).

Several musical traditions are evoked and combined here. The two sections that promote celebration and triumph, at the end of Part 1 and Part 3 respectively, predetermined the choice of C major as the home tonic, a key long associated with symphonies with trumpets and timpani and, more generally, with settings of the Te Deum and the mass. The raucous splendour at the end of Part 1 and even more in the 157-bar-long *Triumphlied* draws powerfully on these overlapping associations of power and might,

---

[14] R. Will, *The Characteristic Symphony in the Age of Haydn and Beethoven* (Cambridge, 2002), pp. 29–82.

[15] The programme is given in Will, *Characteristic Symphony*, pp. 291–2.

Table 4.3. *Anton Wranitzky, Symphony in D (D1)*

1. Allegro maestoso, D major, ₵: Ausbruch einer lebhaften Freude (Outbreak of spirited joy)
2. Andante, G major, 3/4: Sanftes Dankgefühl (Feeling of tender gratitude)
3. Minuet with two trios, D major, 3/4: Munterer Ausbruch der Gegenliebe (Cheerful outbreak of mutual love)
4. Adagio sostenuto, A major, 3/4: Zärtliche Rührung (Fond compassion)
5. *Finale*: Allegro, D major 2/4: Segenswünsche (Good wishes)

the divine and the secular. Opera and ballet are evoked too, particularly of the Gluckian variety: in Part 1 a storm is followed by a lyrical section of pristine beauty, while the *Tanz* in Part 2 provides momentary unease, an exotic number in A minor that moves comfortingly to A major.

Wranitzky's second programme symphony dates from four years later and again survives as a dedicatory score and a set of parts. The title page of the score states clearly the occasion for which it was written: 'Symphony/To his noble highness/Joseph/Prince von Lobkowitz of the Holy Roman Empire/on his twenty-fourth birthday 1796/ dedicated/by Anton Wranitzky/Kapellmeister to his noble highness'. Lobkowitz's birthday was on 7 December and clearly this symphony was an expression of gratitude for the recent formation of a small permanent retinue of musicians at the court, Wranitzky's imminent assumption of the title of Kapellmeister as well as Lobkowitz's forthcoming year of majority that had made all this possible. The work has an extravagance of gesture and resource that is unmatched in the eighteenth-century symphony (Table 4.3).

The orchestra is a large one: two flutes, two oboes, two clarinets (mainly in A, also in G), two bassoons, two horns, four trumpets (two 'clarino', two 'principale'), timpani and strings. The work is set out in five movements, a more focused plan than found in *Aphrodite*, each with a title.

Each of the movements has a verse by an unknown person – poet would be too dignified a word – that expands on the sentiments of the title. That for the first movement reads as follows:

> Er kömmt, Er kömmt! Dem unser Herz schon lange huldigte:
> Mit Ihm wird unsern Fluren Saat und Segen!
> Dank Ihm, Sie sind erfüllt, der Wünsche sehnlichste:
> Eilt! Brüder, eilt und wallet jachzend Ihm entgegen.

He comes, He comes! He to whom our heart has long given homage/With him our fields are sown and blessed/Thank him. You are replete with ardent best wishes/ Hurry brothers, hurry and rejoice in him.

Example 4.1 Anton Wranitzky, Symphony in D (D1), first mvt., bb. 1–36

The opening of the symphony gives full rein to these excitable emotions, with flamboyant use of the four trumpets and timpani. Ex. 4.1. Underneath the bottom line of the presentation score the constituent phrases of the verse are underlaid in such a way that they are clearly associated with the rhythms of the music, here in single lines (b. 22, bb. 33–6), later in multiple lines,

Example 4.1 (*cont.*)

a practice apparent throughout the five movements. For this most musical of princes it was a wonderful conceit, a subliminal declamation of repeated homage in a symphony that was, to all apparent purposes, musically self-sufficient.

There was a precedent for this approach, one almost certainly known to Wranitzky. In 1787 when Haydn was overseeing the publication by Artaria

Example 4.1   (*cont.*)

of the original orchestral version of *The Seven Last Words* as well as the quartet arrangement, he went to great lengths to ensure that the text was presented in the first violin part under the opening thematic line of each movement.[16] More broadly both Haydn and Wranitzky exploit what must

[16] Letters of 14 February and 23 June 1787; H. C. Robbins Landon, *Haydn: Chronicle and Works. Haydn at Eszterháza 1766–1790* (London, 1978), pp. 688–9, p. 695.

Example 4.1   *(cont.)*

have been a common sensation for orchestral musicians of the time in performances of the Ordinary of the mass and other well-known liturgical texts, the subconscious association of text and music.

Wranitzky, Lobkowitz and the assembled orchestral players, in particular the four trumpeters and timpanist, would all have been aware of the rich symbolism of the prime sonority of this symphony. Ceremonial life,

Example 4.1 (cont.)

church services, theatre performances were punctuated by fanfares, often excessively noisy ones, and symphonies, operas and church music drew repeatedly on these associations, particularly in C major but, increasingly towards the end of the century in D major.[17] The opening of Wranitzky's symphony places this tradition in the foreground of the composition and

---

[17] A. Peter Brown, 'The trumpet overture and sinfonia in Vienna (1715–1822): rise, decline and reformulation', *Music in eighteenth-century Austria*, ed. D. W. Jones (Cambridge, 1996), pp. 13–69.

Example 4.1 (*cont.*)

includes one astonishing detail, a rapid rising scale to a notated c" for clarino 1 (bb.32–3), florid writing that had died out in the Austrian tradition in the middle of the century; in the remainder of the symphony the trumpet writing is entirely conventional. Less spectacular, but no less unusual, are the several notated leading notes (b') in the second horn part.

Example 4.1 (*cont.*)

Given that Lobkowitz's patronage of music was untypical of its time, it is appropriate that the sentiments of the symphony are also steadfastly old-fashioned, more suited to 1756 than 1796. In a year in which Austria feared imminent invasion from French forces from the west and from the south, and during which Haydn's symphonies were performed to raise money for the Vienna Volunteer Corps, Lobkowitz's birthday symphony is

Example 4.1 (*cont.*)

magnificently indifferent, as 'Brüder' are urged to praise their master rather than help their countrymen, never mind forcibly embrace everyone in a declaration of classless humanity.

THE SYMPHONIES OF PAUL WRANITZKY (1756–1808)

Born on 30 December 1756 Paul Wranitzky was nearly five years older than Anton. He had attended the same monastery school in Neureisch

Dem   un - ser Herz   schon   lan-ge hul- dig-te

Example 4.1 (*cont.*)

but then continued his education in Iglau (Jihlava) and at Olmütz where
he studied theology, which suggests that he was contemplating a career in
the church. He continued to follow this path in Vienna but his capabili-
ties as a violinist, also an organist, led to his appointment as choirmaster
at the theological seminary he was attending. The lexicographer Gerber
claimed that he studied with Haydn, a claim that is given credence by the

title-page to the Imbault print of a symphony in C (P8) where he is described as 'Elève du Célèbre Haydn'.[18] More doubtful is the statement that he studied with his exact contemporary Joseph Martin Kraus (1756–92), the German composer who was employed at the court of Gustav III in Stockholm and who was in Vienna for seven months in 1783; the claim was first made in the middle of the nineteenth century.[19]

In 1784 Paul Wranitzky became music director at the court of Count Johann Baptist Esterházy (1748–1800), a distant cousin of Haydn's patron who had a palace on the Krugerstrasse in the south-eastern corner of the inner city and several more in Hungary. A competent oboe player and an enthusiastic music lover who, for instance, attended Mozart's subscription concerts in 1784, he maintained a small orchestra for which Wranitzky wrote his first symphonies. The count was also a Freemason and it was through his influence that Wranitzky joined the craft; from 1784 he is listed as a member of the lodge 'Zur gekrönten Hoffnung' (Crowned Hope)[20] and in December of the following year two specially composed symphonies by him were performed in the lodge.[21] Wranitzky remained in the employ of the count until 1791. His first published music, a set of oboe quintets (op. 1), was issued by André in 1789 and was, appropriately, dedicated to the count.

Unlike his brother, Paul was evidently encouraged to develop his career as a violinist and composer outside the aristocratic court. Already in November 1785 a symphony of his was played at the Kärntnertortheater between the acts of the singspiel *Die eingebildeten Philosophen* (a translation of Paisiello's *I filosofi immaginari*) and he is listed as a member of the orchestra for that season, moving to the Burgtheater in 1787.[22] 1790 was a significant year in Wranitzky's career. He wrote a symphony in C (P8) to commemorate the resolution of tension between the Habsburg court and the Hungarian nobility, a work that brought him to the attention of the imperial court. His first opera, the singspiel *Oberon, König der Elfen*, was performed no fewer than twenty-four times in Frankfurt during the festivities surrounding the crowning of Leopold II as Holy Roman Emperor. Finally, it was here that he met the publisher André with whom he struck up a lasting friendship;

[18] E. L. Gerber, *Historisch-biographisches Lexikon der Tonkünstler* (Leipzig, 1790–92), vol. 2, col. 830. Title page transcribed in M. Poštolka, 'Thematisches Verzeichnis der Sinfonien Pavel Vranickýs', *Miscellanea musicologica*, 20 (1967), p. 110.
[19] See I. Leux-Henschen, *Joseph Martin Kraus in Seinen Briefen* (Stockholm, 1978), p. 112.
[20] H. C. Robbins Landon, *Mozart. The Golden Years 1781–1791* (London, 1989), pp. 116–17.
[21] D. Edge, Review of Morrow, *Concert Life* in *Haydn Yearbook*, 16 (1992), pp. 149–50.
[22] D. Link, *The National Court Theatre in Mozart's Vienna: sources and documents* (Oxford, 1998), p. 71, p. 418, p. 423, p. 427, p. 431, p. 438.

the firm was to publish the vast bulk of his instrumental music (including symphonies), reaching the opus number 53.[23] Wranitzky became his eyes and ears in Vienna, facilitating the contact between Traeg and André and, later, between Constanze Mozart and André. The closeness of the relationship is suggested by the fact that André's son, Johann Anton, dedicated his second symphony (op. 5) to the Viennese composer when it was published in 1795.[24] Less successfully Wranitzky attempted to promote his music in London. He had met the publisher John Bland in the winter of 1789–90 and in a subsequent letter, dated 12 December 1790, sought to press his case, citing Haydn and Salomon as two people who could vouch for his music.[25]

From these various activities in 1790 a vivid picture of Wranitzky's personality emerges. He had the support of the Viennese aristocracy, was known at the imperial court, he was well regarded as a violinist and he had an eager business sense. He never became a victim of changing musical practices; on the contrary, he was someone who was able to exploit them. Within a few years he was a key figure in the musical life of Vienna.

As his contact with the imperial court developed, he wrote a symphony (P5) to celebrate the crowning of Leopold's successor, Franz, as Holy Roman Emperor, and a further one (P18) for the wedding of Archduke Joseph in 1800. By this time he had become a favourite of Empress Marie Therese, regularly directing her private concerts and indulging her fondness for music with toy instruments by writing symphonies and, incongruously, even adding them to a score of Mozart's mass in C (K220).[26] He became director of the orchestra at the Burgtheater, later transferring to the Kärntnertortheater, making him well placed to pursue his career as a composer of German opera and to present his own symphonies at benefit concerts and, possibly, as interval music too. Three symphonies, op. 33 (André, 1798), were dedicated to Baron Peter Braun, the director of the court theatres between 1794 and 1806. Having joined the Tonkünstler-Societät in 1793 he became its secretary the following year and began to re-energize its outlook.[27] A long-standing grievance between Haydn and the society was ameliorated[28] and Beethoven, too, was made an honorary member.[29] Wranitzky even busied himself with improving the acoustics for the concerts

[23] Constapel, *André*, p. 169.   [24] Matthäus, *André*, p. 288.

[25] Landon, *Haydn in England*, pp. 27–8.

[26] Rice, *Empress Marie Therese*, pp. 101–106, pp. 139–41.   [27] Pohl, *Tonkünstler-Societät*, p. 9, p. 107.

[28] H. C. Robbins Landon, *Haydn: Chronicle and Works. Haydn: the Years of 'The Creation' 1796–1800* (London, 1977), p. 246.

[29] T. Albrecht (ed.), *Letters to Beethoven and other Correspondence* (Lincoln, Nebraska, 1996), vol. I, pp. 46–7.

given by the society at the Burgtheater, spending a substantial amount of money on a reflecting dome that, in the event, proved unsuccessful.[30]

He was much in demand as a leader and director of performances; he led the orchestra in the first public performance of *The Creation* in 1799 at the Burgtheater and at Beethoven's first benefit concert in the same theatre the following year. With his hectic lifestyle as a composer, player and general *animateur* it is not surprising that Wranitzky was accused of neglecting his day-to-day duties at the theatre; one report in the *Allgemeine musikalische Zeitung* remarked that because he absented himself from some rehearsals, subsequent performances directed by him were deficient.[31] His last known public appearance was in April 1808 when he led the orchestra in a charity performance of *The Creation* at the Burgtheater.[32] He died the following September.

In 1967 the Czech scholar Milan Poštolka published a detailed thematic catalogue of Paul Wranitzky's symphonies.[33] It lists 51 symphonies ordered according to key. Six of these works are clearly sextets, the *Sei Sestetti a Flauto, Oboe, Violino, Due Viole è Violoncello*, published by Hoffmeister in 1788. Of the remaining 45 works, 23 were published and 22 are known in manuscript only. Apart from the first few years of service at the court of Count Johann Esterházy the published symphonies, issued singly or in groups of three, cover the whole of Wranitzky's working life and form a convenient backbone for any chronology. They are presented first in Table 4.4; later published editions of the same works are given in Poštolka's catalogue. They are followed by symphonies that exist only in manuscript; only one of the latter, P33, can be dated. While some of these symphonies represent Wranitzky's earliest efforts in the genre, the style of others, together with some circumstantial evidence, suggests that a wide span of the composer's creative life is represented here too.

Of the manuscript works, P9 in C, P26 in D and P43 in G minor are representative of Wranitzky's symphonies in the 1780s, comparatively short in duration and cautious in their content. Like its companions the opening sonata form of the second of these, P26 in D, is very regular in its paragraphing: first subject, transition (beginning with first subject), second subject in a contrasting texture, and a reference back to the first subject. The reference is to the rhythmic pattern, ♪♪♪ | ♪, which in the hands of Haydn (as in the first movements of No. 28 and No. 73) and

[30] Pohl, *Tonkünstler-Societät*, pp. 36–7.

[31] *AmZ*, 3 (1800–01), cols. 624–5.   [32] Morrow, *Concert Life*, p. 350.

[33] Poštolka, 'Verzeichnis', pp. 101–128. Paul Wranitzky is a major composer of symphonies who is not represented in the sixty volumes of B. S. Brook (ed. in chief), *The Symphony 1720–1840*.

Table 4.4. *The symphonies of Paul Wranitzky*

Published symphonies			
Date	Opus	Publisher	Work
1790	2	André	P8
1791	11	André	P11, P37, P46
1792	16	André	P14, P47, P24
1791	17	Bossler	P2
1791	18	Bossler	P49
Aug. 1792	19	André	P5
July 1793	25	André	P25
1797	31	Gombart	P12
Oct.–Dec. 1798	33	André	P48, P7, P34
[1800]	35	André	P1, P40, P32
Feb. 1800	36	André	P18
Nov. 1799	37	André	P23
1804	50	André	P39
1804	51	André	P44
1804	52	André	P21

Manuscript works
P3, P6, P9, P10, P15, P16, P17, P19, P20, P22, P26, P27, P28, P30, P31, P33 (1786), P35, P38, P42, P43, P45, P50.
Note: Poštolka's dates of publication have been amended to take account of information in W. Matthäus, *Johann André Musikverlag zu Offenbach am Main: Verlagsgeschichte und Bibliographie 1772–1800* (Tutzing, 1973) and B. Constapel, *Der Musikverlag Johann André in Offenbach am Main. Studien zur Verlagstätigkeit von Johann Anton André und Verzeichnis der Musikalien von 1800 bis 1840* (Tutzing, 1998).

Mozart (first movement of K201) would have led to a stronger integration of the thematic and the harmonic, but Wranitzky allows it to stand as a point of contact only. In the development section, however, the motif does encourage the music to the distant harmonic territory of F major and F minor. The following recapitulation is entirely regular.

Like his brother Anton, Paul Wranitzky had an unfailing ear for orchestral balance, displayed in the slow movement of this symphony, an Adagio in A major. It is a set of five variations in which the violins are marked *con sordini* (favoured in many slow movements by Paul Wranitzky) and each variation is strongly coloured, as in Haydn's symphonies of the 1760s: semiquaver decoration; a homophonic *minore*; cello solo over a pizzicato accompaniment; a second *minore*; and a double variation led by solo flute. The minuet is fully scored and with an enterprising tonal excursion after the double bar (to F, E♭, and B♭), while the trio is led by the oboe. The finale (Allegro, 2/4) is a simple rondo (ABACA).

P43 in G minor is almost certainly the earliest of Wranitzky's symphonies in a minor key, eventually to total six in number.[34] Again the music looks back to the 1760s and 1770s and can be placed alongside a number of symphonies in G minor by Haydn (No. 39), Mozart (K183), Vanhal (Bryan g1 and g2) and Kozeluch (Poštolka I: 5); like those examples it concludes in the tonic minor rather than turning to G major at some point. Symphony P9 in C reflects an even more common symphonic type, energetic C major works with plenty of rhythmic posturing, particularly at ends of movements, a facet of compositional technique that was to serve Wranitzky well throughout his career. Even though the only extant source for this symphony (in the Österreichische Nationalbibliothek) has parts for two oboes, two horns, one bassoon and strings it is possible, even likely, that two trumpets and timpani were present in the original.

The first symphony by Wranitzky to be published by André was also a work in C major (P8), composed in 1790. Equally notable are the explicit reasons for the composition of the work, ones that reflected a moment of acute crisis in Austrian politics. Most of the original title page of André's publication is not written in the usual French or German, but in Hungarian. Plate 4.1. It gives the general title for the work, followed by the headings for each of the three movements.[35]

Joy of the Hungarian Nation at the Restoration of its Laws and Freedoms. Effected by the Emperor and King Joseph II on the 28th Day of the post-Christmas Month (Januarius) of the Year 1790. A Grand Symphony Comprising Three Parts. I. First Joy of the Nation, and its Diffusion. II. Pleasant Sentiments of the Estates of the Realm and the Restored Unity Among Them. III. Joy of the Community at the Return of the Holy Crown. Dedicated to the Hungarian Nation by Pál Wraniszky, Music Director to János Esterházy, Count of Galantha.

Within the Austrian Monarchy, Hungary had long enjoyed greater independence, particularly in comparison with Bohemia. New Habsburg rulers were traditionally crowned as the King of Hungary in a ceremony held in Pressburg and any proposals for changes in taxation and other administrative arrangements had to be approved by a national diet. Joseph's campaign to create a unified and homogenous Austrian state had run roughshod over many of these traditional distinct privileges. He had signalled his

---

[34] The others are P10, P11, P12, P30, P42. P14 is excluded from this total; it has a slow introduction in C minor but thereafter the home tonic is C major.

[35] Translation from preface to modern edition of score by Ferenc Bonis (Budapest, 1978).

Plate 4.1 Original title page of Paul Wranitzky, Symphony in C, op. 2 (André, 1790).

intention immediately in 1780, on accession to the throne, by refusing to attend a coronation ceremony in Hungary; he later compounded the insult by ordering the transfer of the Hungarian crown to Vienna. He refused to summon the diet and attempted to impose changes unilaterally. Lack of diplomacy was compounded by the far-reaching nature of the actual reforms that were imposed, including the enforced use of German as the official language rather than the traditional Latin and Hungarian, and the systematic dismantling of the land tax system that had allowed most of the money raised in Hungary to stay there rather than being forwarded to Vienna. By the end of the 1780s national disenchantment threatened to turn into open insurrection as the Hungarian nobility sought the support of Austria's traditional enemy, Prussia. For Joseph II this was only one of three simultaneous crises that openly challenged Habsburg authority; with Russia he was involved in a costly and unpopular war against the Turks, and late in 1789 Belgian patriots in the Austrian Netherlands removed their Habsburg rulers to form the United States of Belgium.

Grudgingly Joseph began to make conciliatory noises towards Hungary. On 28 January 1790, the date referred to in the title of Wranitzky's symphony, he issued a letter revoking virtually all his reforms. Specifically he agreed to summon the Hungarian diet (the sentiments of the second movement), ordered the return of the crown to Hungary (the subject matter of the third movement) and indicated that he would attend a coronation in Pressburg. Joseph, however, was in poor health and died in February 1790. His successor, Leopold II, was by temperament more diplomatic and by persuasion more democratic and over the first few months of his reign he managed not only to defuse the tension in Hungary, but secure a ceasefire in the war with Turkey, placate Prussia and regain the Austrian Netherlands. It was with a renewed sense of dynastic authority, therefore, that Leopold was crowned King of Hungary in Pressburg on 15 November.[36] Possibly prompted by Wranitzky, André prepared a new title page, a bilingual one in Latin and Hungarian, that allowed the same work to commemorate Leopold's achievements: 'Joy of the Hungarian Nation for the Celebration of the Coronation of Leopold II. A Grand Symphony Composed and Dedicated to his Majesty by Pál Wranitzky.'[37] Plate 4.2.

Wranitzky was a Moravian, not a Hungarian and this symphony should not be regarded as a *Kossuth* symphony over a hundred years before it was written; in any case the triumph of Habsburg diplomacy is as much the subject of the symphony as the patriotism of the Hungarians. The impetus for its composition and the unusual linguistic character of its subsequent publication reflected the political responsibilities of Count Johann Esterházy, Wranitzky's employer. Hungary was divided into fifty-four counties, each with a sheriff who ensured that his county was administered according

---

[36] C. Ingrao, *The Habsburg Monarchy 1618–1815* (Cambridge, 1994), pp. 203–204, pp. 206–211. C. A. Macartney, *The House of Austria. The Later Phase 1790–1918* (Edinburgh, 1978), pp. 13–15, pp. 17–24.
[37] Translation from preface to modern edition of score by Ferenc Bonis (Budapest, 1978).

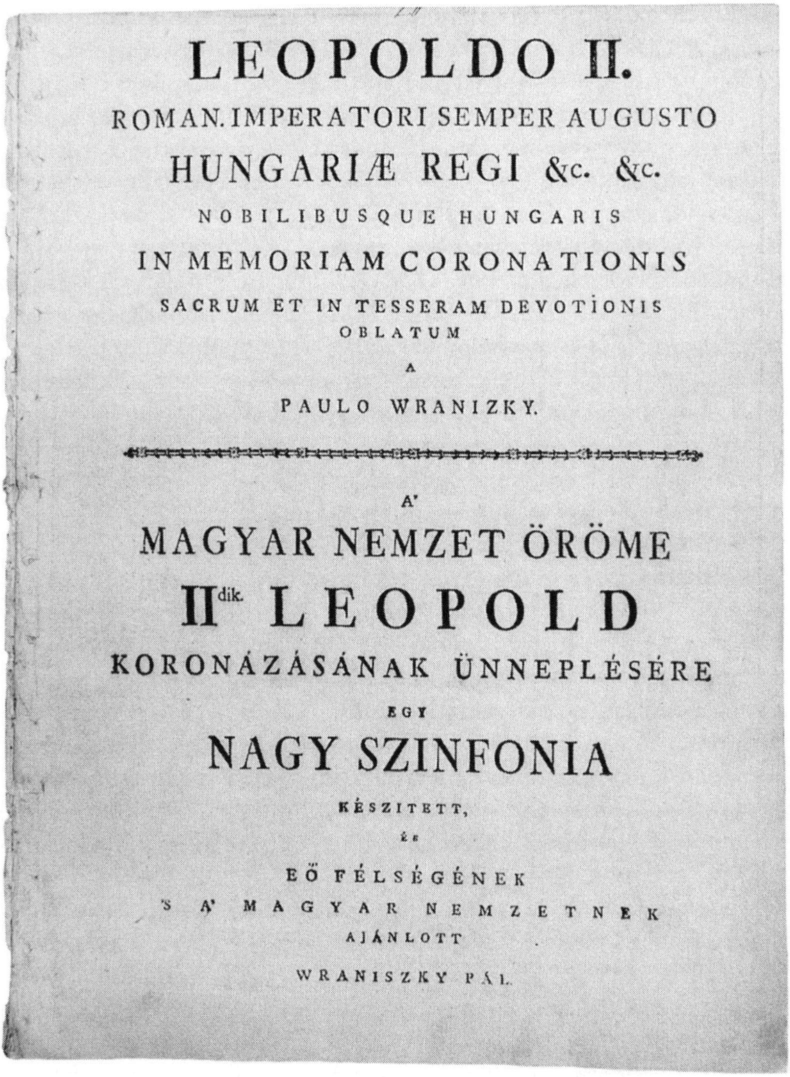

LEOPOLDO II.

ROMAN. IMPERATORI SEMPER AUGUSTO

HUNGARIÆ REGI &c. &c.

NOBILIBUSQUE HUNGARIS

IN MEMORIAM CORONATIONIS

SACRUM ET IN TESSERAM DEVOTIONIS
OBLATUM

A

PAULO WRANIZKY.

A'

MAGYAR NEMZET ÖRÖME

II^dik LEOPOLD

KORONÁZÁSÁNAK ÜNNEPLÉSÉRE

EGY

NAGY SZINFONIA

KÉSZITETT,

és

EÖ FÉLSÉGÉNEK

'S A' MAGYAR NEMZETNEK

AJÁNLOTT

WRANISZKY PÁL.

Plate 4.2 Revised title page of Paul Wranitzky, Symphony in C, op. 2 (André, 1790).

to the needs of the diet. Count Esterházy was the sheriff for the counties of Pressburg and Bereg, someone who had experienced the impact of Joseph's reforms, the accelerating crisis at the end of the decade and the hurried climbdown in 1790. At first Joseph had wanted to do away with the county system, later he tried to enlist its support; with the accession of

Leopold the county system was once more recognized and Count Johann Esterházy regained his influence as sheriff.[38] It was in this environment that the count must have instructed his Kapellmeister to compose a celebratory symphony, one that reflected a new spirit of co-operation between the King of Hungary and his subjects. In the absence of direct evidence it is likely that the symphony was first performed at his court and, later, at the time of Leopold's coronation in Pressburg.

In the history of the symphony this is a significant moment. Single works had often evoked national characteristics, Turkish, French, German, Italian, English, and all five in Dittersdorf's *Sinfonia nazionale nel gusto di cinque nazioni*, but as entertainment rather than as political propaganda.[39] When a peace treaty with Turkey was signed in August 1791 Hoffmeister, in his rather opportunistic way, wrote a symphony to which he gave the title *La festa della pace 1791*, one of the new works offered in his ambitious plans to publish all his symphonies, but only the finale, a *Turchesco*, alludes to the circumstances that had ostensibly stimulated it.[40]

Wranitzky's symphony is a resplendent, on occasions exhilarating work lasting twenty-five minutes. Scored for two flutes, two oboes, two bassoons, two horns, two trumpets, timpani and strings it draws on the long association of C major with pomp and ceremony and, although the last movement contains some allusions to Hungarian thematic material, contrast of mood rather than narrative is the concern of the symphony as a whole. As a concession to the subject matter there is no minuet, yielding one of only four symphonies by Wranitzky in three movements. The opening slow introduction (Adagio maestoso) is only nine bars long but it is the composer's control of orchestral sonority and colour that immediately holds the attention, both of them distinctive features of Wranitzky's symphonies in general. A clearly articulated sonata form (Vivace assai) begins with a unison theme that is then stated up a tone (Ex. 4.2). Thereafter the movement follows Wranitzky's usual very clear sonata form, compensated by a coda section that cleverly works the music into a frenzy of fanfare figuration.

Instead of a variations movement in a gently ambling tempo, the slow movement of P8 is an eloquently lyrical Larghetto con moto in F major in which the main theme is presented by strings, with muted violins and divided violas. Wranitzky also reveals his fondness for thematic lines

[38] R. Gates-Coon, *The Landed Estates of the Esterházy Princes. Hungary during the Reforms of Maria Theresia and Joseph II* (Baltimore, 1994), pp. 78–84.
[39] A list of such symphonies is given in Will, *Characteristic Symphony*, pp. 300–301.
[40] Modern edition by R. Hickman, *The Symphony 1720–1840*, B/5 (New York, 1984), pp. 51–71.

Example 4.2 Paul Wranitzky, Symphony in C (P8), first movement, bb. 1–29.

Example 4.2   *(cont.)*

Example 4.2 *(cont.)*

Example 4.2 (*cont.*)

Example 4.2 (*cont.*)

doubled at the lower octave by bassoon and/or at the upper octave by flute. A ternary movement, the return of the main theme is decorated and the movement culminates in a passage for wind ensemble. The finale is a five-part rondo (ABACA) in 2/4 in which the swaggering main theme shows why Wranitzky was to become a successful composer of theatre music; the contrasting sections in C minor and F are more introspective with the occasional harmonic and thematic inflection *al ungarese*. In the first movement the horns had been marked C basso; in the finale they are instructed to play in C alto to provide, in effect, an additional pair of trumpets.

Wranitzky's symphonic output continued to follow the course of Austrian politics for a while. Having restored some degree of composure in the Habsburg territories and embarked on governmental reforms that sought to engage his subjects rather than offend them, Leopold II, quite unexpectedly, died on 1 March 1792 after a short illness. He was succeeded by his son, Franz, who, in a comparatively trouble-free succession, was crowned King of Hungary in June, elected Holy Roman Emperor in July and crowned King of Bohemia in August. By now Wranitzky had assumed the position of orchestral director at the court theatres. He composed another C major symphony with trumpets and timpani, P5, this time in four movements and without movement headings. It was published by André just a month after the celebrations in Frankfurt and it is likely that it was first performed in that city rather than Vienna. With an awareness of the wider impact of his actions Wranitzky, probably in conjunction with his close friend André, this time ensured that the title page was in German, the language of the Empire: 'Grosse Sinfonie bei Gelegenheit der Erhebung Franzens zum Deutschen Kaiser verfertiget und Ihre Kaiserlich-Königlichen Apostolischen Majestät allerunterthänigst gewidmet von Paul Wranitzky' (Grand symphony composed for the occasion of the election of Franz as German Emperor and most humbly dedicated to His Imperial-Royal Apostolic Majesty by Paul Wranitzky).

For five years, from 1792 to 1797, Austria and France were at war. The population at large felt, at least initially, that it was an unnecessary war, sentiments that were confirmed as Austria lost one ally after another; nevertheless the new sense of Austrian identity that was whipped up by the government in 1796–7 was real enough and when the treaty of Campo Formio was signed in October 1797 it seemed to have managed to convert resentment into national pride. By now Wranitzky was at the centre of musical life in Vienna. At the previous two Christmas concerts of the Tonkünstler-Societät he had been able to present a symphony as part of a mixed

Table 4.5. *Paul Wranitzky, Grand Characteristic Symphony for the Peace with the French Republic*

---

1. The Revolution
   Andante maestoso (C minor, C) – Allegro molto (C minor, C) with two interpolations, March of the English (C major, ₵) and March of the Austrians and Prussians (E♭, ₵).
2. The Destiny and Death of Louis XVI
   Adagio affettuoso (E♭, ₵) with one interpolation, Funeral March (C minor, C)
3. March of the English (from 1) (C major, ₵), March of the Austrians and Prussians (from 1) (C major, ₵), Tumult of the Battle (Allegro, C major, C)
4. Peace Negotiations – Jubilation at the Restoration of the Peace
   Andante grazioso (G major, 6/8) – Allegro vivace (C major, 2/4)

---

programme.[41] For the pair of concerts in December 1797 he wrote a new programmatic work that sought to give public expression to the national joy, a *Grand Characteristic Symphony for the Peace with the French Republic* (P12) (Table 4.5). Since the work carried movement titles, permission had to be sought from the censors. Two days before the planned performance permission was declined,[42] even though the work had already been advertized for sale by Traeg in the *Wiener Zeitung* on 29 November.[43] Evidently the Habsburg authorities could not overcome five years of nervous, occasionally ruthless, repression of anything that might be misconstrued as disaffection or disloyalty and though Wranitzky's broad aim in this symphony had been to chart the history of the war that had now culminated in peace, they obviously felt it was better not to remind the public of what had happened.

Movement titles alone cannot convey the real sense of contrast, drama and narrative that is in the work, as it moves from a sombre C minor to a jubilant C major in Wranitzky's most triumphant manner. When the work was published by Gombart (Augsburg, 1798) it was with French titles but it is likely that Wranitzky's first wrote them in German, as is suggested by the title 'Friedensymphonie' that appears in Traeg's advertisement and the manuscript source for the work in the Lobkowitz library.[44]

This symphony is clearly fashioned around a standard four-movement pattern, adjusted to accommodate the programme. Conveniently, the two interpolated marches in the first movement, which represent the attempts of

---

[41] Morrow, *Concert Life*, p. 290, p. 293.
[42] Pohl, *Tonkünstler-Societät*, p. 50.   [43] Weinmann, *Die Anzeigen*, p. 63.
[44] Lobkowitz Library: X. G. e. 11. Modern edition, based on the Gombart print, by Joseph Wagner (Vienna, 1997).

the allies to halt the French Revolution, allow Wranitzky not to develop his existing material. The funeral march contained within the slow movement revisits the C minor of the first movement. The third movement rather than having the controlled sense of statement – contrast – return that always characterizes minuets has a strong forward momentum prompted by the programme, the two marches in C for the countries of the coalition, followed by the battle. After this unremitting tension and tumult the opening of the finale associates the prospect of peace with the conventional pastoral imagery of lilting melodies in thirds over a drone bass. The ensuing allegro vivace is a full sonata form in 2/4.[45]

By allowing the programmatic to modify and extend the standard structures of the symphony Wranitzky produced a work of imagination and impact, immeasurably helped by a new sense of rhetorical power and the composer's customary ear for orchestral colour. The symphony is scored for pairs of woodwind including clarinets; they lead the windband in the funeral march but, very strikingly, this windband is doubled at the lower octave by divided violas, cellos and double basses. For the battle a piccolo is added to the top of the texture, and bass drum and military drum provide the cannon and musket shots. Here and elsewhere there is a full range of stylistic gestures that can only be called Beethovenian, except that Beethoven was not yet deploying them, insistent rhythms, tremolo, accents on and off the beat, *fortissimo* pauses on dominant sevenths and stark apposition of chords between strings and wind.

Political events soon led to a third commemorative symphony by Wranitzky, a work in D major, op. 36 (P18). Following the treaty of Campo Formio the Austrian Foreign Minister, Franz Thugut, and Count Colloredo, the emperor's principal minister, sought to strengthen the relationship with Russia. Carefully nurtured by the Austrian ambassador in St Petersburg, Count Johann Ludwig Cobenzl, it was cemented by that old-fashioned instrument of Habsburg diplomacy, a dynastic marriage. Archduke Joseph, one of the emperor's brothers, was married to the favourite daughter of Tsar Paul, Alexandra Pawlowna.[46] The wedding took place in October 1799 in the summer palace of Gatchina, not far from St Petersburg. The *Wiener Zeitung* gave regular formal reports of the marriage, the journey back to Vienna and the various celebrations (church service, presentation at court, formal attendance at the Burgtheater and at the Kärntnertortheater, and several balls) that took place in January 1800. Since 1795 Archduke

---

[45] For further discussion see Will, *Characteristic Symphony*, pp. 205–209.
[46] Macartney, *House of Austria*, pp. 29–31.

Joseph had been the Hungarian palatine, representing his brother in the kingdom and acting as a link between the Hungarian authorities and the Habsburg court, a role that he carried out with considerable diplomatic skill and success. The formal celebrations were continued, therefore, in Ofen, where a special performance of Haydn's *Creation* was given on the archduke's birthday on 19 March.

In all these reports there is no mention of a performance of a symphony by Wranitzky. The D major symphony was published by André in February with the title page clearly indicating that it was written specifically for the wedding celebrations: 'Symphony on the occasion of the high wedding of his Imperial-Royal highness, Archduke Joseph, Palatine of Hungary, with her Imperial Highness the Archduchess Alexandra Paulowna, composed and humbly dedicated to the high bride and groom by Paul Wranitzky, first orchestra director of the two Imperial-Royal court theatres in Vienna.' The fact that it was published in February suggests that it was performed in January. Two possibilities offer themselves. On 8 January the couple attended a performance of the play *Der Tod der Kleopatra* at the Kärntnertortheater; perhaps the symphony was performed between the acts, as a contrast to the inappropriate subject matter of the play. Alternatively it could have been performed at a reception at court.

Scored for double wind (including clarinets), timpani and strings Wranitzky's four-movement symphony in D major is appropriately celebratory but a number of unexpected features prompted by the occasion for which it was written give it an individuality of expression too. At twenty-nine bars the slow introduction is the lengthiest in Wranitzky's output and one of the lengthiest between Mozart's 'Prague' symphony (thirty-six bars) and Beethoven's Second Symphony (thirty-three bars). The opening, with its dotted-note figuration, scales and targeted harmonic dissonance suggests the influence of Mozart's Symphony in E♭ (published by André two years previously) but the introduction then moves on towards a secondary idea before returning to the opening material. The following Allegro molto begins *piano* with a theme that seems lightweight after the introduction; a strategic ploy in Haydn, Wranitzky lacks the ability to convert the flimsy into the significant and, consequently, the movement relies even more than usual on the composer's mastery of orchestral colour and the occasional arresting gesture. Typical of the latter is the *fortissimo* plunge at the beginning of the development into F major, following the A major of the exposition. Several sonata forms by Wranitzky use this harmonic relationship at this juncture and it was one that caught the attention of Carl Zelter, the Berlin composer and writer, who thought it too redolent of Haydn (as in the first movements of Symphonies Nos. 80, 97 and 100): 'we have heard it all so many countless times, and are still hearing it, to the point of nausea; the gentlemen should really find another way out especially since they creep home in the exactly the same way with the chord of the augmented seventh [*recte* augmented sixth].'[47]

The second movement provides the first of Wranitzky's diplomatic surprises. Instead of an expansive slow movement or a set of variations on a simple theme he presents a *Russe*, a measured dance in honour of the new archduchess. Ex. 4.3 An earlier *russe* by Wranitzky, from his ballet *Das Waldmädchen* (1796) was already very popular in Vienna, prompting Beethoven to use it as a theme for a set of variations (WoO 71). In the symphony Wranitzky uses the dance as the first section of a ternary design in which the middle section then turns to the tonic minor and the return of the dance is resourcefully expanded. In the middle section trumpets come to dominate the sonority, momentarily upsetting the overall mood. The use of trumpets and timpani in slow movements is a characteristic of Wranitzky's symphonies (e.g. P1, P5, P34, P40 as well as the present work) and was another feature that irritated Zelter. Once again he may well have had the composer in mind when he wrote the following: 'Haydn, in some stately passages in his G or F major adagios, had the trumpets and timpani in D or C enter with great surprise and noble effect; he did this discreetly and with care; but now the tail comes – and nowadays there is hardly a symphony, the andante of which does not have trumpets and timpani . . .'[48]

Instead of a minuet and trio Wranitzky provides a delicately scored *Polones* and *Trio*. The polonaise was a favoured social dance of the day, particularly popular at the Russian court where it invariably began the evening. Wranitzky's diplomatic gesture could not have been more gracious: the expected Viennese minuet gives way to the Russian polonaise. The final surprise is the fifteen-bar largo introduction to the finale, scored for Harmonie alone, and evoking the very Viennese practice of serenading. A trumpet fanfare moves the atmosphere from the private to the public; into a 6/8 rondo that, yet again in a Wranitzky symphony, culminates in a blaze of trumpet calls.

An unusual corner of Wranitzky's output are the three symphonies that include toy instruments. None was published and all owed their origin to Empress Marie Therese who had a fondness for such works; they occupy a territory somewhere between the charming and the silly. The smallest

[47] *AmZ*, 1 (1798–9), cols.152–3; English translation from Landon, *Haydn: the Years of 'The Creation'*, p. 339.
[48] *AmZ*, 1 (1798–9), col. 153; English translation from Landon, *Haydn: the Years of 'The Creation'*, p. 339.

Example 4.3   Paul Wranitzky, Symphony in D (P18), second mvt., bb. 1–16.

in scale and forces is in G major (P38), in two movements and scored for strings, four panpipes and glockenspiel. Much larger is a D major work (P20) which has an orchestra of piccolo, pairs of flutes, oboes, clarinets, bassoons, horns, four trumpets, timpani and strings to which is added a large percussion section of one Turkish drum, a pair of cymbals, two bass drums, tambourine and a large rattle. There is no indication of a programme to the work but the description of the two bass drums as 'Grosse Trommel zum Cannoniren' (large drum for the cannon fire, their function too in the *Grand Characteristic Symphony*) and the fact that they, together with the Turkish drum, appear only in the third movement suggest a broad narrative of imminent battle, battle itself, victory and rejoicing. The third work, P27 in D major, is scored for a large orchestra, including three trombones but no percussion instruments. Written for performance at one of the private concerts of Empress Marie Therese it is akin to one of those paintings that reproduces the painting within itself, in that it depicts the course of a private concert in the imperial quarters of Marie Therese; the musicians enter in turn and tune up, play a symphonic movement and then embark on a medley (quodlibet) of material from contemporary operas and ballet, plus a folksong; a concluding Andante sees the musicians departing one by one, an obvious influence of Haydn's 'Farewell' symphony.[49]

The most substantial work in the quodlibet prepared by Wranitzky is the overture to Mozart's *Zauberflöte* (this is the item that required trombones), a particular indication of the extraordinary popularity of this work in Vienna in the 1790s, a popularity further indicated by the use of the panpipes and glockenspiel in the G major work (P38). Yet another symphony by Wranitzky, P23 in D published by André in November 1799 as op. 37, reflects Mozart's opera, this time within the appropriate context of a work written to accompany the wedding celebrations of two aristocrats, identified on the title page as Count Nicolaus Esterházy and 'Fräulein Françoise de Roisin'. The count was the son of Wranitzky's first employer, Johann Esterházy, and the wedding took place on 1 June 1799 in Vienna.[50] Scored for Wranitzky's standard full orchestra of double wind, timpani and strings, the symphony uses the expected four-movement pattern with slow introduction, but in a less exultant manner than in the later wedding symphony for Archduke Joseph. Unusually trumpets and timpani are silent in the slow movement and do not dominate the concluding moments of the first and last movements. The absence of the instruments in the Andante (G major, 6/8) allows a ternary movement to present a simple melody over a pizzicato accompaniment, the ends of phrases charmingly marked by five-note scales on an instrument described as 'floetino in D alla Papageno', that is the panpipes with which Papageno seeks to capture his prey. It is likely that

---

[49] Rice, *Empress Marie Therese*, pp. 103–106; Jan LaRue, 'A "Hail and Farewell" Symphony', *Music and Letters*, 37 (1956), pp. 250–59.
[50] Landon, *The Golden Years*, p. 255.

the success of this wedding symphony led to the more ambitious one a few months later for the archduke and his Russian bride.

In Vienna there is no doubt that in the 1790s and early 1800s Paul Wranitzky was the one contemporary composer who was consistently associated with the composition of symphonies. His style had evolved from a careful and studied modelling of Haydn's symphonies up to c.1780 and gathered individuality by responding imaginatively to extra-musical influences. Apart from his earliest works Wranitzky's symphonies were always contemporary even when they were not topical, and offered something that was clearly different from Haydn, Mozart and other composers. It was this fashionability that André was able to promote from his publishing offices in Offenbach. Within Vienna the composition and performance of the composer's symphonies were always entirely dependent on Wranitzky's links, carefully cultivated, with the imperial court, the aristocracy, the theatres and the Tonkünstler-Societät. It is a measure of this dependence that within a few years of the composer's death his symphonies were forgotten.

CHAPTER 5

Loose ends and faltering beginnings

With sixty symphonies between them Anton Wranitzky and Paul Wranitzky were the most prolific composers of symphonies in Vienna at the turn of the century. Others who wrote symphonies included Krommer (1759–1831), Antoine Reicha (1770–1836) and Anton Eberl (1765–1807) but their combined output during these years was only thirteen works. The decline in private patronage – with the notable exception of Prince Lobkowitz – and the unsupportive nature of public concert life combined to ensure that they contributed interestingly but not extensively to the genre. Consideration of the circumstances in which the symphonies were composed reveals much about the diminishing presence of the genre in Viennese musical life.

Coupled with this decline in quantity was an increased sense of individuality as the vestiges of the old practice of a group of works with shared characteristics still evident in the symphonies of the Wranitzky brothers disappeared and gave way to single works that sought to be different. Rarity and individuality came also to embrace an element of emulation, a developing sense of tradition that evaluated the new alongside the achievement of the past, in particular the symphonies of Haydn and Mozart. Intermittent in nature and inchoate in conception, it characterized the private concerts sponsored by Joseph Würth between 1803 and 1805 and the Liebhaber Concerte of 1807–8.

KROMMER'S SYMPHONIC OUTPUT TO 1807

Like the Wranitzky brothers, Franz Vinzenz Krommer was born in Moravia, in November 1759 in Kamenitz (Kamenice) near Iglau (Jihlava) where his parents ran the local inn.[1] At the age of thirteen or fourteen and having already shown a talent as a musician Krommer went to live with an uncle,

---

[1] A detailed account of Krommer's life is given in K. Padrta, *Franz Krommer (1759–1831). Thematischer Katalog seiner musikalischen Werke* (Prague, 1997), pp. 15–38. Supplementary information on Krommer's relationship with André is to be found in Constapel, *André*, passim.

Anton Krommer, in Turas (Tuřany), not far from Brünn (Brno). Anton was a respected figure, the head teacher of the local school, music director at the church and composer of sacred music. Under his guidance Franz became an accomplished violinist and organist, and began to compose.

Krommer left Turas at the age of nineteen or twenty to seek employment further afield. He went to Vienna where he met Count Carl Styrum whose principal residence was in Simontornya in Hungary; Krommer entered his service, probably in the typical dual role of servant and instrumentalist. Early in 1782 Krommer moved to Fünfkirchen (Pécs), the largest town in southwest Hungary, where he was employed as cathedral organist and also composed a number of sacred works. In 1787, still at Fünfkirchen, he became Kapellmeister to Count Antal Károlyi, who had responsibility for the local regiment; Krommer remained Kapellmeister until the death of the count in August 1791 and wrote a number of windband pieces for the regiment.

At the age of nearly thirty-two Krommer had hitherto led a rather humdrum existence in the Hungarian provinces. With his next employment his career became centred on Vienna, where he was to live for the rest of his life. Around 1790–1 the Kapelle of Prince Anton Grassalkovicz, whose principal residence was in Pressburg, saw a number of changes. Haydn was offered the post of Kapellmeister in the autumn of 1790 but turned it down in favour of the chance to visit London; Anton Kraft, one of the cellists at the Esterházy court, joined the orchestra; and in August 1791 Krommer became director of the violins, probably the senior figure in the retinue but without the formal title of Kapellmeister that Haydn would have received had he joined the court. In the next few years Krommer's career as a composer of string quartets and string trios began to blossom. Probably through Paul Wranitzky, Krommer established a secure business relationship with André in Offenbach that led to regular publication of his music: three quartets op. 1 (1793), three duos op. 2 (1793), three quartets op. 3 (1794), three quartets op. 4 (1795), three quartets op. 5 (1796), three violin duets op. 6 (1796), three quartets op. 7 (1797), three quintets op. 8 (1797), variations for violin and basso op. 9 (1797), three quartets op. 10 (1798), three quintets op. 11 (1798) and, eventually, his first symphony op. 12 (1797).

In 1795 Prince Grassalkovicz dismissed his orchestra, replacing it with the fashionable Harmonie. Since Krommer's position was primarily as a violinist rather than a composer he too left; rather ironically, later in his life Krommer was to become a popular composer of Harmoniemusik. Without a full-time position but well known in musical circles in Vienna,

Krommer set about a varied freelance career as a violinist, composer and teacher, though very little of detail is known. As early as December 1797 he unsuccessfully applied for a position in the Hofkapelle; he may have worked for Count Fuchs for a while in 1798; the number of items of Harmoniemusik dedicated to Archduke Joseph (the Hungarian Palatine) suggest that they were first commissioned by him; and from at least 1800 he participated in the weekly concerts of Count Harrach who later gave him a small yearly honorarium to write chamber works involving the flute, the count's instrument.[2] In 1806 he applied for a second time for a position in the Hofkapelle, again without success. Krommer did not gain a salaried post until he was appointed leader for ballet performances at the court theatres in 1810, a secondary role to Anton Wranitzky who led performances of opera.

By 1810 Krommer had written over 160 instrumental works, most of which were published by André. Many of these publications contain a dedication, revealing the network of patronage that Krommer cultivated: Archduke Joseph (several items of Harmoniemusik, op. 57, op. 67, op. 69, op. 71, op. 73 and op. 76); Count Moritz von Fries (three quartets op. 16, three quartets op. 18, three quartets op. 48, six violin duets op. 33, six violin duets op. 51); Count Karl Leonhard Harrach (concertino op. 18, flute quintet op. 49); Prince Lobkowitz (three quartets op. 34) and Count Razumovsky (three quartets op. 68). It is against this background that Krommer's symphonies need to be considered. They were not a priority for the composer and only three were composed between 1797 and 1807.

The publication of the first symphony in F major was announced by André on 1 December 1797; Johann Traeg announced its availability in Vienna on 20 December.[3] The publication by André represented a natural extension of the composer's output issued over the previous four years. The original circumstances of its composition are unknown and the work does not carry a dedication. It may have been composed a few years earlier when Krommer worked for Prince Grassalkovicz; more likely is that it was written with publication rather than a planned performance in mind and, indeed, it may have been instigated by André rather than the composer.

The symphony is scored for a smaller orchestra than was customary in Paul Wranitzky's works by this time, one flute, two oboes, two bassoons, two horns and strings, all used rather cautiously with no conspicuous solo instruments. As with the earlier symphonies of Paul Wranitzky the shadow

---

[2] O. Biba, 'Nachrichten zur Musikpflege in der gräflichen Familie Harrach', *Haydn Yearbook*, 10 (1978), pp. 40–41.

[3] Matthäus, *André*, p. 342. Weinmann, *Die Anzeigen*, p. 64.

Example 5.1 Krommer, Symphony in F, op. 12, first movement, bb. 1–4.

of Haydn hangs over the four movements of the work. The slow introduction (Adagio) heard over repeated quavers, and with a harmonic occlusion in
the second bar (offering the possibility of D minor as a tonic rather than F)
before the formal move to a cadence at the fourth bar reflects Haydn's
Symphony No. 97. Ex. 5.1. The slow movement (Andante) is a sectional
Romanze, featuring a short-breathed theme in 2/4 that is later contrasted
with a noisy interlude with trumpets and timpani. The main theme of the
minuet is a distant cousin of the minuet of Haydn's Symphony No. 89; it is
even more Haydnesque than Haydn in that it is propelled by the three-note
crushed figure that occurs throughout that composer's output but not, as
it happens, in the minuet of No. 89. Krommer's finale is a 2/4 movement
marked Allegro assai; even though it is in sonata form it is headed rondo,
an indication of thematic character rather than structure.

The only known public performance in Vienna in this period of a symphony by Krommer occurred in a benefit concert for two wind players,

Sebastian Grohmann (oboe) and his 13-year-old pupil, one Formaezko, that took place in the Jahnscher Saal on 4 April 1800, two days after Beethoven's first benefit concert in the Burgtheater.[4] Three works by Krommer were included, a flute concerto, an oboe concerto and a symphony; the programme also included the piano and wind quintet by Mozart (K452), an unidentifiable symphony by Haydn and an arrangement for Harmonie of arias from Paer's opera, *Camilla*. Krommer's symphony was described as being given for the first time which suggests that it may have been the composer's second symphony, eventually published by André in 1803. But given that presenting symphonies in public concerts was an unusual and difficult enterprise and that Krommer was assiduously cultivating a career as a composer and performer of chamber music, the 1800 concert may have been the first opportunity he had of presenting the F major symphony.

Krommer's second symphony, in D major, was published by André in 1803 as his op. 40. It is an assured work and the best of his early symphonies. The orchestration is varied, imposing in its tutti sonorities (now including two clarinets) and with some attractive solo writing, especially for flute and bassoon. The structure of the slow movement is ABACA plus coda, in which A is varied each time and the nominally contrasting sections also allude to the main theme. Throughout there is a new adventurousness in harmonic colour. The slow introduction is entirely in D minor but instead of changing to D major at the beginning of the ensuing Allegro, D minor is retained for twelve bars before switching to the major key. Such harmonic idiosyncrasies were an occasional feature of Krommer's style but they always appear as local harmonic quirks with no long-term consequence on symphonic thought.

Krommer's fruitful relationship with André led the publisher to encourage the composer to write further symphonies. In a letter of 9 December 1806 he wrote: 'But I wish that you now wanted to compose three or six symphonies . . . your first two have pleased very much and although *in general* symphonies do not sell I would like to have *ones composed by you.*'[5] By the following May Krommer had completed his next symphony. When it was eventually published in 1808 as op. 62 it was dedicated to Baron Alexander Wetzlar, a notable Viennese patron of chamber music but not of large-scale orchestral music which suggests, once more, that the main impetus for composition was publication by André rather than performance

---

[4] Morrow, *Concert Life*, p. 304.   [5] Constapel, *André*, p. 96.

in Vienna; in the event there is no record of either a private or a public performance in the city.

Very oddly, Krommer decided to place this third symphony in the same key as his second one, D major. As well as the key, Krommer's third symphony is scored for the same orchestra and has the same four-movement pattern of fast, slow, minuet and fast with a slow introduction and a sonata-form finale in duple time (₵ in op. 40, 2/4 in op. 62). As well as a shrewd businessman André was a practised composer who often rejected submitted compositions on musical as well as commercial grounds, and he duly expressed his concern to Krommer: the public might think that the new work was merely the second symphony newly engraved and that genuinely new works could not be expected from him.[6] Evidently Krommer managed to counter André's reservations and the work was published a few months later as op. 62, but the damage had been done and the publisher's earlier wish for 'three or six symphonies' was never fulfilled. Krommer, who had never exerted much energy towards having his symphonies performed in Vienna, lost the only incentive he had to compose in the genre and was not to return to it until 1820 when the musical environment in the city became more conducive.

Krommer's wider reputation as a symphonist was damaged by the negative review of the third symphony that appeared in the *Allgemeine musikalische Zeitung* in June 1808.[7] The unknown writer remarked that the form of the first and last movements was too similar and objected to the 'coarse transitions to distant keys', quoting a passage from the minuet that moves from D major to B♭ major in four bars. In his view the most original movement was the Andante Allegretto in D minor, with its striking opening of a *pizzicato* walking bass in quavers, over which a melodic line later appears. This movement is, indeed, the highlight of the work, initially arresting and making colourful use of full orchestra, but with a structure that is repetitive rather than organic.

ANTOINE REICHA'S STAY IN VIENNA, 1802–8

The composer and musical theorist Reicha is very much associated with Paris where he lived for a quarter of a century until his death in 1836, but he spent six years in Vienna before moving permanently to the French capital. He wrote a large number of works in Vienna – Reicha's own estimate was

[6] Ibid., p. 116.   [7] *AmZ*, 10 (1807–8), cols. 566–70.

more than fifty – yet failed to secure a niche in the musical life of the city. His expectations, as well as his disappointment, are evident in the following paragraphs from his autobiography.[8]

Everyone knows that real and fine instrumental music was created by Haydn and Mozart. But it had been played so much that already in 1800 its popularity, among the blasé public of Vienna, was on the wane; a new music, more or less baroque in style, was replacing it. French operas translated into German, and Italian operas were performed at the theatre. German translations had been made of my two operas *Obaldi* and *L'Ouragan*, but they were turned down here as they were in Paris. Prince Lobkowitz, great patron of music, had the whole orchestra play at his house the music of *L'Ouragan*, a kindness which did me little good as he did not have the right to insist on a public performance of my work. I might have had an opera presented had I been willing to set a nonsensical German libretto.

For Empress Marie Therese, Reicha wrote a two-act Italian opera, *Argene regina di Granata*, from which only extracts were performed at court.[9] Even more frustrating was the fate of a cantata entitled *Lenore*, a setting of a ballad by Gottfried Bürger for soloists, chorus and orchestra that failed to get past the imperial censors and remained unperformed. Reicha did, however, make an impact with the publication in 1805 by the Chemische Druckerei of an unusual work for the piano: *Trente-six Fugues pour le Piano:Forté composées d'après un nouveau système* (Thirty-six fugues for the pianoforte, composed in a new way). Dedicated to Haydn, this compendium of fugal technique aimed to combine reverence for the past with an up-dating of musical technique fit for the new century. Alongside fugues with subjects that wilfully distort the old standard intervallic and rhythmic patterns there are others that use first subjects from sonata forms by Haydn (the quartet op. 20 no. 5) and Mozart ('Haffner' symphony), and, even more radical, complete fugues are composed in 5/4, 7/4 and 8/8. Equally subversive, Reicha challenges the long-standing principle of fugal construction that emphasized harmonic relationships of a fifth or a fourth between successive entries in favour of mediant relationships. Extended relationships of this kind lead to most of the fugues ending in a different key from which they had begun.[10]

Reicha's autobiography suggests that instrumental music in the tradition of Haydn and Mozart was on the decline, a misleading comment that is

---

[8] J.-G. Prod'homme, 'From the unpublished Autobiography of Antoine Reicha', *Musical Quarterly*, 22 (1936), p. 348.

[9] Rice, *Empress Marie Therese*, p. 234.

[10] O. Šotolová, *Antonín Rejcha. A Biography and Thematic Catalogue* (Prague, 1990), pp. 22–25; pp. 242–51.

undermined by the large quantities of chamber music that Reicha himself composed in Vienna, nine string quintets and nine quartets. If the focus is narrowed to the symphony, however, then Reicha's comments do fairly reflect a rather frustrating period for the composer.

In 1803, shortly after Reicha arrived in Vienna, Breitkopf and Härtel published two symphonies by him, originally written in Paris in 1799, op. 41 and op. 42, both in E♭; the latter was advertized by Johann Traeg in February 1804.[11] Neither of these symphonies was performed in public in Vienna and though performances at the Lobkowitz court are more likely than not, there is no evidence of any.[12] A further two symphonies, in G and F, were composed in the summer of 1808. It is not clear whether Reicha was contemplating performances in Vienna or whether he had already decided to leave for France; in the event neither work was ever published and only the F major is known to have been performed, at the Paris Conservatoire on 7 May 1809.[13]

The untidy, sometimes unclear autograph score of the symphony in G major in the Bibliothèque Nationale, Paris has a number of revised passages and approximately sixty bars are missing from the beginning of the sonata-form finale. Given that Reicha was already an experienced composer of symphonies with at least four, perhaps as many as seven to his credit, the work is a very deferential one, with the thematic material of the first movement and the minuet revealing kinship with two G major symphonies by Haydn, No. 92 ('Oxford') and No. 94 ('Surprise'). Only in the development section of the first movement does Reicha show any evidence of that harmonic adventurousness that characterized his music in general; it moves through C minor, F major and B♭ major before returning to the home tonic via G minor.

The symphony in F major is a more individual work, one that embraces some of the composer's eccentricity.[14] Again the autograph in the Bibliothèque Nationale shows evidence of reworking, and the slow introduction was almost certainly composed in Paris rather than in Vienna. The recurring motif of a descending diminished fourth in the introduction is certainly ear-catching but nothing comes of it. On the other hand the chromaticism of the bass line of the following first subject encourages

---

[11] Weinmann, *Die Anzeigen*, p. 99.

[12] In 1807 Reicha was paid the substantial sum of 419 gulden by the Lobkowitz court for something that is not specified; Macek, 'Franz Joseph Maximilian Lobkowitz', p. 164.

[13] Šotolová, *Rejcha*, pp. 156–7. Šotolová implies that two other symphonies, in C minor and F minor, were composed in Vienna, but both autographs are written on French paper; ibid., pp. 154–6.

[14] Modern edition by S. C. Fisher, *The Symphony 1720–1840*, ed. in chief, B. S. Brook, B/IX (New York, 1983), pp. 179–241.

a tortuously adventurous development section that moves from C major to E minor and then D minor, C minor and, through the dominants of D minor and G minor, back to the tonic. In the finale Reicha's questing imagination as a contrapuntist are evident, an aspect of compositional technique entirely absent from the symphonies of the Wranitzky brothers and Krommer. The generating motif is a three-note figure that rises through the arpeggio, punctuating the texture in a way familiar from any number of works by Haydn and Mozart. At the beginning of the development the motif is extended by a descending chromatic figure in crotchets that leads into a series of fugal entries entirely in a *piano* dynamic; with two exceptions the relationship between the entries is not the standard fourth or fifth but a third or a second: C, A, G minor, C minor, E♭, F minor, G minor and D minor. Homophony, full scoring and a *forte* dynamic return at the point of the recapitulation.

ANTON EBERL (1765–1807): 'CULTURED TASTE AGREEABLY GRATIFIED'

On 11 March 1807, after eight days of suffering from scarlet fever, the composer and pianist Anton Eberl died in Vienna at the age of forty-one. His career had taken him to some of the principal German cities, Hamburg, Leipzig and Mannheim, and to St Petersburg, and this wide esteem was reflected in a generous obituary, eight columns long, in the *Allgemeine musikalische Zeitung*;[15] 'the early death of an artist has seldom been so universally regretted' it opined. During the previous four years Eberl had composed two major symphonies, in E♭ (op. 33) and D minor (op. 34), which following their first performance in Vienna were published in Leipzig and played several times in Germany. From the pan-German perspective of the *Allgemeine musikalische Zeitung* the author of the obituary lamented the early death of not merely a Viennese composer of interest but a German composer of burgeoning stature. This dual outlook had been skilfully developed by Eberl for much of his career.

Unusually for a Viennese composer he was actually born in the city, on 13 June 1765. His father was a servant at the imperial court and this connection probably facilitated lessons with three court composers, Wagenseil (1715–77), Steffan (1726–97) and Kozeluch (1747–1818). He wanted his son

---

[15] *AmZ*, 9 (1806–7), cols. 423–30; the following biographical account is largely taken from this source. See also the useful chronicle in J.-A. Kim, *Anton Eberls Sinfonien in ihrer Zeit. Hermeneutisch-analytische Aspekte der Sinfonik 1770–1830*, Schriften zur Musikwissenschaft aus Münster, vol. 17 (Eisenach, 2002), pp. 13–42.

to study law but by the age of eighteen Eberl had committed himself to a musical career. He composed several German operas, established himself as a pianist and between 1784 and 1785 wrote three symphonies, in D, G and C. The opening movement of the last one is blatantly modelled on the first movement of Mozart's 'Haffner' symphony.[16] Although all three works were advertised by Traeg in his 1799 catalogue there is no other indication that they were part of the repertoire in Vienna in the 1780s and 1790s; certainly Eberl himself composed no further symphonies in this period. He was on friendly terms with the Mozart family and may have studied formally with the composer, though there is no direct evidence. Within a week of Mozart's death in December 1791 Eberl composed a laudatory cantata for soloist, chorus and orchestra, *Bey Mozarts Grabe*; in December 1794 he was the soloist in a Mozart piano concerto that was played between the acts of the concert performance of *La clemenza di Tito* at the Kärntnertortheater organized by Constanze Mozart; and in the autumn of 1795 he accompanied Mozart's widow and her sister, Aloysia Lange, on the first part of her concert tour in Germany, performing a piano concerto and a piano quartet by Mozart at a concert in Leipzig in November, and appearing in four concerts in Hamburg. While the two sisters continued their journey to Berlin and Dresden, Eberl returned to Vienna, where in March 1796 he married Anna Maria Scheffler.

The following three years were spent in St Petersburg as a pianist and teacher in the imperial court and the houses of the nobility. For the marriage of the Grand Duchess Alexandra Pawlowna and Archduke Joseph – the occasion for which Paul Wranitzky had written his D major symphony, op. 36 – Eberl provided a major celebratory cantata, *La gloria d'Imeneo*. At the end of 1799 Eberl and his wife returned to Vienna, perhaps with the intention of settling in the city; it was then that he probably began to enjoy the occasional patronage of Count Moriz von Dietrichstein to whom he dedicated a number of piano works. Baron Braun, the director of the court theatres, commissioned a fashionable magic opera from him, *Die Königin der schwarzen Inseln*, a modestly successful work that received eight performances. This limited success may have inhibited any plans the composer may have had to seek a benefit concert at one of the court theatres, which would have provided an opportunity for a new symphony; certainly, it seems to have encouraged him to return to St Petersburg.

[16] This led to the work being published as a newly discovered symphony by Mozart: *Sinfonia in do maggiore*, ed. N. Negrotti (Milan, 1944). H. C. Robbins Landon, 'Two Orchestral Works Wrongly Attributed to Mozart', *Music Review*, 17 (1956), pp. 29–34. S. C. Fisher, 'Die C-dur-Symphonie KV Anh. C. II.14: ein Jugendwerk Anton Eberls', *Mitteilungen der Internationalen Stiftung Mozarteum*, 31 (1983), pp. 21–6.

There he dedicated three new quartets to Tsar Alexander and directed three performances of Haydn's *Creation*, sung in French.

Despite the niche that Eberl had carved for himself in the musical life of St Petersburg, the composer was restless and in 1802 returned once more to Vienna, where he remained until his death in 1807. As a composer he concentrated more and more on piano music, including a large-scale sonata (op. 12) dedicated to Haydn. Josepha Auernhammer played his C major concerto (op. 32) at her benefit concert in the Burgtheater on 25 March 1803 and his most gifted pupil, Fräulein Hohenadel, performed the same work in the summer concerts at the Augarten that year. The fact that Eberl's E♭ symphony was dedicated to Prince Lobkowitz suggests that his music must have featured in Lobkowitz's concerts from at least 1803 onwards. On 6 January 1804 Eberl presented his own benefit concert in the Jahnscher Saal. Like Beethoven's benefit concerts, it featured Eberl both as a performer and a composer and was similarly ambitious in scope. There were five items on the programme: the overture to the cantata *Imeneo*, the premiere of a new piano concerto in E♭ (op. 40), a cello duet by Pleyel, the first public performance of the Symphony in E♭ (op. 33) and the premiere of a double piano concerto in B♭ (op. 45) played by the composer and his pupil Fräulein Hohenadel.

A review of the concert in the *Allgemeine musikalische Zeitung* in the following April[17] noted that the room was pressingly full, the applause unanimous and noisy, but that the standard of performance was at best middling; 'the flutes, oboes and trumpets were accident prone; only the first clarinet was well played.' The symphony, however, was singled out for special praise.

A large new symphony by Eberl, dedicated to Prince Lobkowitz, was rather more interesting for the lovers of music, since so few great masters have worked successfully in this taxing genre of music. This symphony is extraordinarily successful, full of bold and new ideas, and, in particular, Eberl has demonstrated a profound and extensive knowledge of instruments. Each one is used in the most appropriate and fitting way . . . After the first beautifully worked-out, but very long, Allegro in E♭ follows a splendid Andante in C minor, in which the wind instruments are beautifully deployed; the passage where the cellos, clarinets and bassoons present the theme makes an extraordinary effect. Of true originality and artistic merit is the finale in E♭, full of new and exciting modulations and transitions, in which the attention is excited and captivated, and cultured taste agreeably gratified. The most pleasing passage was where Eberl modulates from A♭ to C major by means of an enharmonic change through G♯. May this symphony be made generally available in print, and Herr Eberl further employ his talent in this genre!

[17] *AmZ*, 6 (1803–4), cols. 468–70.

The remainder of the report uses this notably successful concert as a pretext for a critical assessment of concert life in Vienna in a way the author hopes will benefit any musician contemplating visiting the city. He draws attention to the unfavourable facilities in the city for concert giving. With no adequate concert hall that is favourable to the music or has sufficient room for the listeners the artist is compelled to turn to the court theatres, the Redoutensaal and the Jahnscher Saal. Only with the highest recommendation ('besonders hohe Empfehlung') can the co-operation of Baron Braun, the director of the court theatres, be ensured and he would rather leave them empty. As regards the Jahnscher Saal the headroom and the width are not favourable and it holds only 400 people, making it very difficult to recoup costs.[18]

Nevertherless Eberl himself must have been pleased with his first benefit concert for almost exactly a year later, on 25 January 1805, he presented a second one, again at the Jahnscher Saal. The overture to *Imeneo* was given again as was the double piano concerto with Eberl and Hohenadel as soloists; this was followed by the first performance of the Symphony in D minor (op. 34), a set of variations for two pianos on a theme from Grétry's *Raoul Barbe-bleue*, a set of variations for violin, and, rather peculiarly, an arrangement for orchestra of an unidentified chorus (possibly from *Imeneo*). In the subsequent report on the concert in the *Allgemeine musikalische Zeitung* Eberl's symphony was again given special attention.[19]

An entirely new symphony in D by Eberl also belongs to his most successful compositions. It begins with a short Largo, in D minor, which is then interrupted by a bold, beautifully executed march in D major. There follows a very beautifully worked-out Allegro, then a beautiful, expressive Andante, and finally the whole concludes with a majestic double fugue.

While the first performance of two major symphonies in two benefit concerts in two years was a significant achievement in the history of the symphony in Vienna in the early nineteenth century, it should be remembered that Eberl's success as a composer in Vienna was, like that of Beethoven, bound up with his appearances as a soloist in his own piano concerto and, particularly novel, as a performer alongside his favoured pupil in a double concerto. Performing and directing concertos alongside presenting new symphonies was clearly a viable if difficult way for Eberl to maintain a public career. Publishing the symphonies in Vienna was out of the question and Eberl, like Krommer, Paul Wranitzky and others, turned to publishers

---

[18] Ibid., cols. 470–71.   [19] *AmZ*, 7 (1804–5), col. 322.

in Germany. The E♭ symphony was issued by the firm of Kühnel in Leipzig in 1806 and dedicated to Prince Lobkowitz; the D minor symphony was published by Breitkopf and Härtel in 1805–6 and dedicated to his former patron in Russia, Tsar Alexander I. Plate 5.1.

To promote his complementary career as a pianist and composer Eberl undertook a six-month tour of Germany in 1806, performing and directing his music in Dresden, Berlin, Leipzig, Weimar, Frankfurt and Mannheim. Performances of the two symphonies are known to have taken place in Leipzig and Mannheim and were favourably reviewed in later reports in the *Allgemeine musikalische Zeitung*.[20] From the 1790s onwards, principally through the firm of André, symphonies by composers resident in Vienna such as Gyrowetz, Krommer and Paul Wranitzky had made some impact in the major cities of Germany. Unlike those three composers Eberl was willing to travel and to perform as a soloist, so that a difficult career in Vienna could be supported by one of widening popularity in Germany.

Eberl returned to Vienna in July 1806 and set to work on a new piano concerto and on a new double concerto, this time for violin and piano; it is reasonable to assume that these concertos would have been joined in due course by a further symphony, all designed for performance in Vienna before being published in Leipzig and performed on a concert tour of Germany. At the height of his ambition Eberl contracted scarlet fever in March 1807 and died after eight days of illness. It was with this sense of a potential only partly realized that the warm obituary in the *Allgemeine musikalische Zeitung* was written. In a further indication of the veneration in which Eberl was held, the obituary garnishes its account with two images of abstracted genius identical to those found in representations of Mozart and Beethoven: he was said to compose works in his head before putting them down on paper, and to work through compositional problems on lonely walks when, totally preoccupied, he would fail to acknowledge anybody.

Eberl's symphony in E♭ is scored for an orchestra of two flutes, two oboes, two clarinets, two bassoons, two horns, two trumpets, timpani and strings and its four impressively contrasting movements produce a work that lasts over twenty-five minutes in performance.[21] There are a number of features in the construction of the work that show Eberl's imagination

[20] *AmZ*, 8 (1805–6), col. 462 (Leipzig); *AmZ*, 9 (1806–7), col. 215 (Leipzig), col. 754 (Mannheim); *AmZ*, 13 (1811), col. 830 (Leipzig).
[21] Modern edition by S. C. Fisher, *The Symphony 1720–1840*, ed. in chief, B. S. Brook, B/IX (New York, 1983), pp. 245–317.

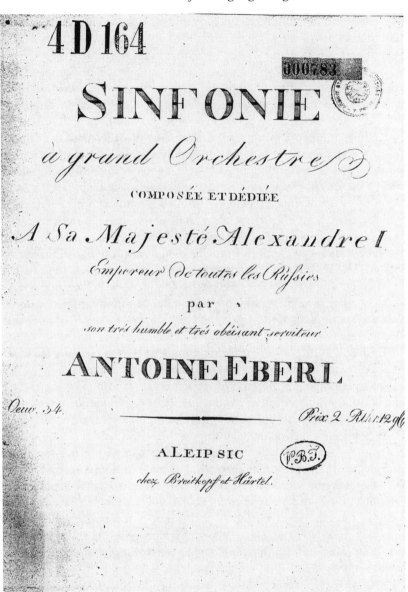

Plate 5.1 Title page of Anton Eberl, Symphony in D minor, op. 34 (Breitkopf and Härtel, 1805–6).

as a composer but throughout the symphony it is his grasp of harmonic tension and use of varied phrase rhythms that mark him as a consistently superior composer to the Wranitzky brothers and Krommer.

The first movement opens with a slow introduction of eighteen bars, Andante sostenuto, that avoids the traditional rhetoric of dotted rhythms and strong contrasts of dynamic in favour of a measured unfolding of a lyrical idea alternating between strings (*con sordini*) and full wind (including trumpets and timpani). Initially the first subject of the Allegro fuoco e vivace seems to lack the fire and energy promised by the tempo heading, lamely presenting a syncopated figure in the strings linked by wind into its repetition up a tone, considerably less striking than Paul Wranitzky's use of similar techniques at the beginning of his C major symphony (see Ex. 4.2). Eberl's superior mastery of musical continuity becomes evident at the beginning of the tutti that launches the transition, where the syncopated idea is placed in the bass underneath repeated quavers in violins. The second subject area presents two melodic ideas, the first led by clarinets and bassoon, the second by first clarinet, but on both occasions Eberl returns the music to the material of the first subject to provide a sense of focus rare outside the symphonies of Haydn, Mozart and Beethoven.

Although, at fifty-one bars, the development section occupies less than one-sixth of the movement as a whole, its single paragraph in a *forte* dynamic has plenty of bold juxtaposition of register together with rhythmic energy and harmonic incident; it reaches the dominant of G minor before moving to an extended dominant preparation, with a number of minor ninth inflections (a favourite harmonic colouring in this work), and, via a signalling timpani roll, into the recapitulation. The 136 bars of the recapitulation provide an almost perfect mathematical balance to the 135 of the exposition, but it is rewritten to avoid the excessive symmetry that characterizes the sonata forms of Krommer in particular and to provide a new carefully judged climax in the coda; from b.295 the music is underpinned by a chromatically rising bass from D♯ to B♭, with harmonic surprise and astringency (including augmented fifth chords) supported by the melodic highpoint in the movement (g''').

A strong contrast is offered by the following movement, a contrast which is itself then transformed. Set in C minor and in 2/4 time the movement is headed Andante con moto, but it is clearly a march. For modern listeners following a lengthy sonata form movement in E♭ with a march in C minor is unavoidably redolent of the *Eroica* Symphony, composed in 1803. But Eberl's symphony was completed before the *Eroica* and certainly lacks the emotional turbulence of Beethoven's *Marca funebre.*[22] The distant models for Eberl's march are rather different, those inscrutable 2/4 movements in a minor key by Haydn, such as the slow movements of the piano trios in C minor (Hob.XV:13, 1789), G minor (Hob.XV:19, 1794) and D minor (Hob.XV:23, 1795). As an active pianist Eberl would have had such movements under his fingers and the slow movement of his symphony shares the same thematic emphasis on a syncopated second quaver, dotted figuration, *sforzando* accents in a predominant *piano* dynamic and expressive melodic emphasis on the submediant degree; in addition Eberl has the Haydnesque idea of punctuating the ends of phrases with a tutti *forte* chord.

The standard ternary structure can be sensed in the overall shape of the movement but, as in the opening Allegro, it is coupled with a real sense of organic development that works in conjunction with, and modifies, structural procedures. After the sixteen-bar opening theme the music moves towards E♭ and a contrasting lyrical idea, initially for strings, later for clarinet and strings; fragments of the march theme then feature in a well-paced bridge passage to the return of the main section. This reprise (b. 57 onwards) was one of the moments in the symphony that caught the particular attention of the reviewer in the *Allgemeine musikalische Zeitung*: it is entirely rescored for full orchestra but in a *piano* dynamic and with the theme played by violas, cellos and bassoons against a new countermelody in octaves in the violins; the trumpets and timpani colour the sonority with repeated martial figuration. The movement seems to be moving to a close in C minor, with echoes of the first theme over repeated sextuplet figuration, when the sextuplets force an extended crescendo that culminates in a dominant seventh. A new section in C major, a coda of thirty-three bars, follows, one that simultaneously transforms C minor into C major, prevents an overly neat ternary structure to the movement as a whole and effects a true moment of emotional release. The material itself is a major-key version of the march, this time led by an Harmonie of flute, two oboes, two clarinets, two horns and two bassoons, with the strings providing *pizzicato* underpinning. Again the dynamic is *piano* rather than a triumphant *forte*. The movement ends with dotted figuration, *perdendosi* until the final *pianissimo*.

The third movement is headed *Menuetto* but the tempo marking of Allegro vivace and the rhythmic energy of the music invites performance at one-in-a-bar. To answer the increasingly pressing problem of how to make a minuet equal in substance to the surrounding movements while still retaining its distinctive character Eberl provides two trios and a coda

[22] For discussion of the relationship between Beethoven and Eberl see Chapter 6, pp. 170–74.

to make an overall structure of minuet, trio 1, minuet, trio 2, minuet, coda. Only one symphony by Haydn (No. 51 from c.1772) has two trios, the composer preferring to expand from within, and there are no examples by Mozart though a number of minuets in the leisurely orchestral serenades have two trios (e.g. K250 and K320). What is more surprising and resourceful in Eberl's symphony than the mere presence of two trios is the contrasting attitude to their content. Trio 1 in C minor arises naturally from the minuet, taking a repeated crotchet figure first heard in bar five and using it as a generating motif for a new *fortissimo* theme. While Trio 1 acts as an intensification of the minuet, Trio 2 instead offers a contrast, an appoggiatura-laden melody for oboe over a *pizzicato* accompaniment.

The finale, Allegro assai, is a sonata form in which the four even minims of the opening of the first subject with the thematic profile 1↘3↗5↘7 occur throughout the movement, standing out against an active background, mainly of quavers. Stephen C. Fisher views the movement as a distinct response to the finale of Mozart's 'Jupiter' symphony ('the model for the movement'), a view taken up by Jin-Ah Kim who uses it as a basis for an investigation of sonata and fugue in finales in symphonies.[23] While such an association is easily made, and perhaps was easily made in the first decade of the nineteenth century when Mozart's 'Jupiter' symphony was becoming one of the most frequently performed of the composer's symphonies, further investigation of the movement shows that the comparison cannot be sustained; in fact there is nothing in the movement that can be properly labelled fugal. There are no fugal expositions, not even pairs of entries, no countersubjects, no stretto (though the 'subject' does lend itself to a number of possibilities) and certainly no peroration in the coda. In technique it does not have the contrapuntal ambition of the 'Jupiter' symphony, the finale of Haydn's Symphony No. 95 or even the finale of Reicha's contemporary symphony in F.

A more sympathetic and productive reading of the movement is to link the appearances of this four-note motif with the creative outlook on sonata form that Eberl had shown in the first movement, in particular the principle of returning to a main idea after a contrasting one to provide cohesion. As in the exposition of the opening movement Eberl has two thematic ideas in the second subject area. The first (b.86 onwards), heard after a teasingly extended dominant preparation, is a repetition of the four-note motif but with a new quaver accompaniment. This, in turn, reaches a more forceful dominant preparation via the flattened sixth, prompting a new thematic

[23] Fisher, *The Symphony*, B/IX, p. xxxix; Kim, *Anton Eberls Sinfonien*, pp. 260–94.

idea. Once more this leads to a return of the opening motif, *fortissimo* in violas, cellos, basses and bassoons, later at the top of the texture. Stark contrasts of *piano* and *fortissimo*, the latter with bold chromatic harmonies, signal the end of the exposition.

With 114 bars to the 181 of the exposition the development is proportionately slightly longer than that of the first movement. It contains one major surprise. The first paragraph is guided by the four-note motif, the paragraph concluding on the dominant of Bb (b.233). From this chord the music slides chromatically into Db major and to what is ostensibly a new theme, the most overtly lyrical in the movement and one that resourcefully avoids lame four-bar units in favour of a phrasing pattern of 3+3+7+6. Its first three notes are those that dominate the movement as a whole. It is here that Eberl's compositional strategy differs once more from that of Mozart: whereas Mozart's four-note tag becomes ever more assertive in the movement, Eberl's motif is transformed into lyricism, a natural outcome of the initial downwards movement of his motif, compared with the upwards move of the 'Jupiter' motif.

The recapitulation is 152 bars long, slightly shorter than the exposition but, as in the first movement, featuring compression so that expansion can take place towards the end. The moment of the recapitulation in Eb features the opening motif not in its first subject guise but in its second subject format, thus effectively lopping off over eighty bars. Thereafter, the progress of the recapitulation follows that of the exposition. The music seems to be moving to a resolute conclusion in Eb when it is deflected, at the equivalent point to the first movement, into a series of chromatic chords, once more on a bass that rises by semitones, from Bⁿ up to F. This was the second passage that elicited particular comment from the critic in the *Allgemeine musikalische Zeitung*, though he misreads the harmonic destination as C major rather than Eb major. The movement is then able to justify its lengthy, excitable emphasis on the tonic.

Eberl's imaginative handling of symphonic form continued in his next, final symphony, in D minor. Rather than the four movements that were now the accepted norm for a symphony the composer uses a novel three-movement structure.

1. Andante maestoso e sostenuto (D minor, 3/4) – Tempo di Marcia (D major, C) – Allegro agitato (D minor – D major, 3/4)
2. Andante con moto (A major, 3/4)
3. *Finale*: Vivace assai (D major, 2/4)

A minuet movement is omitted, as in Mozart's 'Prague' symphony, Wranitzky's Symphony in C (P8) and Symphony in D (P24), and many

Plate 5.2 Anton Eberl, Symphony in D minor, op. 34 (Breitkopf and Härtel, 1805–6), first page of violin 1 part.

other examples in the eighteenth century, but alongside this standard process of omission there is a very individual expansion of the format of the first movement. Instead of the slow introduction leading into a sonata form a substantial march (in full ternary form with internal repeats) is interpolated between the introduction and the Allegro. Plate 5.2. There are a number of intertwining thought processes at work here which certainly show a musical imagination that is fertile and bold, but there is, too, an equally impressive desire that the result should be convincing and not merely idiosyncratic.

The starting point is the unusual choice of key, D minor. Two of Haydn's London symphonies in D major have slow introductions in D minor, Nos. 101 ('Clock') and 104 ('London'), and it is to the first of these that Eberl turns, very deliberately, at the beginning of his work. Haydn's 'Clock' symphony begins very atmospherically with a six-note ascent up the minor scale, *piano* to *forte*; Eberl has the same pattern, but staccato and *fortissimo*, and immediately repeated up a tone to a set up an harmonic excursus that is very different from Haydn's beginning. Also different from Haydn is the intention to have the subsequent sonata form in D minor rather than D major, and it is in order to maximise the impact of that sonata form (the Allegro agitato) that Eberl inserts a march in D major. With this interpolation Eberl sets up an alternation of minor and major that anticipates that of the ensuing sonata form. Delightfully insouciant in itself, even dangerously so, the march is integrated into the movement as a whole in other ways. Its melodic climax is the same forceful ascent up the scale that had opened the symphony, now in dotted rhythms (into the fifth stave of Plate 5.2, also later), two characteristics that recur in the second subject area of the Allegro agitato.

As in the symphony in E♭, Eberl favours a sonata form with two well-separated themes in the second subject area. In addition to this contrast and Eberl's usual deft manipulation of phrase patterns, the momentum of the movement owes a good deal to phrases that are left harmonically open. Eberl has one further structural surprise: the recapitulation reverses expectations, beginning in D major with second subject material before concluding with the first subject material, now also in the major. At no point in this substantial movement does the compositional energy flag.

The Andante con moto provides an immediate contrast of mood, a lyrical theme in A major announced by the clarinet. The middle section of the ternary form plunges into F major followed by a second switch to the flattened sixth, D♭ major; this is then enharmonically changed to C sharp from where the music makes its way to the dominant of A. The return of the main theme is colourfully rescored with an extended decorated line for solo violin.

The exposition of the sonata-form finale has many characteristics already encountered in Eberl's two mature symphonies, three clear themes, harmonic surprise (A minor and F major both appear during the course of the second subject area) and well-timed references to the main theme, in this case its opening three-note motif. Startlingly the subsequent development section is entirely fugal, 116 bars in the prevailing tempo of Vivace assai and entirely *forte* or *fortissimo*. The initial subject (in bass instruments) is a mixture of two conventional types, a descending chromatic line followed by rising fourths with no apparent relationship to the material in the first part of the movement. Ex 5.2. The apparently complete fugal texture then cleverly incorporates the three-note motif from the first subject that had featured extensively in the exposition (b. 203 onwards) to produce the double fugue mentioned by the critic of the *Allgemeine musikalische Zeitung*. A lengthy section of dominant preparation leads to the recapitulation. As in the first movement the second subject area is presented first which allows for a suitable peroration of the first subject and attendant emphasis on the main motif. In spirit, this movement too reveals the influence of Haydn's 'Clock' symphony, finding contrapuntal ingenuity in material that is apparently contentedly homophonic.

THE PATRONAGE OF JOSEPH WÜRTH: NEW CONCERTS IN A NEW PALACE

In April 1804, in one of his regular reports on musical events in Vienna, the correspondent of the *Allgemeine musikalische Zeitung* noted that the previous winter had witnessed a significant new venture, private concerts on Sunday mornings sponsored by 'Herr von Würth'. Since Würth was a banker the patronage was inevitably compared with that of the late Franz Bernhard Kees, both affording a welcome opportunity to hear major works during the winter season.[24]

Joseph Würth was not an aristocrat by birth.[25] Like his father he was a merchant who in 1800, in his mid-twenties, married Theresia Fellner, the nineteen-year-old daughter of Baron Andreas Fellner. Fellner was a successful purveyor of military equipment and a banker who lived and worked in a credit bank on the Hoher Markt, an elegant square between the Graben and the Danube canal. Joseph joined him in the business, lived in the same house and assumed the name of 'von Würth'. In 1801 Fellner purchased six small adjacent properties and converted them into a spacious new palace that included an elegant music salon measuring 48 feet (14.7 metres) by 25 feet (7.6 metres) and about 13 ft 6 ins high (4.1 metres), only slightly

---

[24] *AmZ*, 6 (1803–4), col. 467.
[25] W. Brauneis, "'. . . composta per festeggiare il sovvenire di un grand Uomo." Beethovens "Eroica" als Hommage des Fürsten Franz Joseph Maximilian von Lobkowitz für Prinz Louis Ferdinand von Preußen', *Jahrbuch des Vereins für Geschichte der Stadt Wien*, 52–3 (1996–7), pp. 74–8.

Example 5.2 Eberl, Symphony in D minor, op. 34, third movement, bb. 197–212.

Example 5.2 (*cont.*)

smaller than the music salon in the Lobkowitz palace. Joseph Würth was himself a capable violinist[26] and soon after the building was completed began using it as the venue for weekly concerts on Sunday mornings, probably beginning in early December and continuing into the following Lent. Professional players were joined by gifted amateurs under the direction of Franz Clement (the leader of the orchestra at the Theater an der Wien) and the concerts were noteworthy for avoiding vocal music and the vapid display pieces of most benefit concerts in favour of overtures, concertos and symphonies.[27] The first season, 1803–4, included several overtures by Mozart and Cherubini, and Eberl's overture *La gloria d'Imeneo*, but the critic of the *Allgemeine musikalische Zeitung* was particularly enthusiastic about the performances of two symphonies by Mozart, the 'Jupiter' (K551) and the G minor (K550).[28]

In the second season, during the winter of 1804–5, the concerts consisted mainly of overtures, concertos and symphonies, as before; the last concert was given over to a rare performance of the original, orchestral version of Haydn's *Seven Last Words*. In January 1805 the correspondent of the *Allgemeine musikalische Zeitung* commented on the early part of the season, noting the 'humane, accommodating demeanour of the host' and the presence of a 'very select company'. Mozart's 'Jupiter' symphony had once more been a highlight and the writer was looking forward to forthcoming performances of the latest symphonies of Beethoven and Eberl, works which had already made such an impact on connoisseurs in Vienna.[29] The concert on 13 January included Beethoven's First Symphony, the following week the *Eroica* was given; the performing parts for the latter were supplied by Prince Lobkowitz, who also paid some incidental expenses. Eberl's Symphony in E♭ was given the following week, on 27 January, and since that work too was dedicated to the prince, it is likely that he supported the performance in a similar manner. When the *Allgemeine musikalische Zeitung* next reported on the concerts it focused on these three symphonies.[30] Beethoven's Symphony in C was described as 'a splendid artistic creation', characterized by 'coherence, order and light'. The *Eroica* symphony perplexed him deeply, 'a very far extended, audacious and wild fantasy. It is not lacking in striking and beautiful passages, in which one must acknowledge, the energetic,

---

[26] O. Biba, 'Beethoven und die "Liebhaber Concerte" in Wien im Winter 1807/08', *Beiträge '76–78: Beethoven Kolloquium 1977: Dokumentation und Aufführungspraxis*, ed. R. Klein (Kassel, 1978), p. 90.

[27] The programmes of the concerts, as far as they can be established, are given in Morrow, *Concert Life*, pp. 401–03.

[28] *AmZ*, 6 (1803–4), col. 467.   [29] *AmZ*, 7 (1804–5), cols. 242–4.

[30] *AmZ*, 7 (1804–5), cols. 321–2.

talented spirit of its creator; but very often it seems to lose itself in the irregular.' Eberl's symphony in E♭ was much more warmly received.

The Eberl work in E♭ really pleased once more, and really has so much beauty and strength, is handled with so much genius and art, that its effect is hardly anywhere lost . . . Quite admirable is the last movement, where a lovely idea governs the whole and is beautifully and artistically turned throughout.

While the actual number of concerts in each of the two series hosted by Joseph Würth in the new palace is a matter of conjecture – twelve to fifteen concerts in 1803–4, perhaps a few more in 1804–5 – some interesting trends are safely inferred. First the names of the composers whose works were represented in the second season demonstrate an emerging sense of hierarchy that was a natural consequence of the wish to concentrate on substantial works. Mozart is the most featured composer with nine works (three overtures, two piano concertos, three symphonies and a piano quartet); at least three performances of Haydn's music took place (including two symphonies and *The Seven Last Words*) and Beethoven was represented by three works (the First Symphony, the *Eroica* and the C minor piano concerto). Another discernible trend is the frequent performance of opera overtures as concert works, a different practice from the eighteenth-century one of presenting overtures shorn of their titles as symphonies, since they are now to be readily associated with the subject matter of the operatic work that they precede; several overtures by Cherubini, Méhul and Mozart appear on the programmes. Finally, over nine symphonies were performed in the season, with those of Haydn and Mozart forming the standard against which the newest works of Beethoven and Eberl could be compared. The absence of contemporary symphonies by the Wranitzky brothers and Krommer may be significant in this regard. Certainly the private views of one commentator, Georg August Griesinger, on a symphony by Friedrich August Kanne (1778–1833) that was played suggests that the genre was gaining an aura of discrimination and value.

Griesinger (1769–1845) was a diplomat who worked in the Saxon legation in Vienna. A keen music lover, he acted as an agent for Breitkopf and Härtel in the city, ensuring that the music of Haydn and Beethoven, in particular, was published by the firm. He reported regularly to Breitkopf and Härtel on musical life in Vienna, especially developments in instrumental music. Writing on 13 February 1805, he offered his views on recently performed symphonies.[31] Other commitments had prevented him

---

[31] O. Biba (ed.), *"Eben komme ich von Haydn . . ." Georg August Griesingers Korrespondenz mit Joseph Haydns Verleger Breitkopf & Härtel 1799–1819* (Zurich, 1987), pp. 235–7.

from hearing Beethoven's *Eroica* symphony but he reported favourably on its reception and in a way that could not be more different from the views articulated by the critic of the *Allgemeine musikalische Zeitung*: 'here is more than Haydn and Mozart, the symphony-poem ['Simphonie-Dichtung'] taken to a higher standpoint.' He mentions the performance of Eberl's symphony on 27 January but offers no critical comment. As regards the symphony of the young Kanne he regarded it as worthless.

> The creator, so-called, must study for a few more years before he can entertain us; his work stands far below the symphonies of Vanhal, Gyrowetz and other good masters, and one does not like to hear these after Haydn and Mozart. I tell you this in confidence for I do not want to shame the young man. Kanne himself was present at the burial of his symphony . . .

THE LIEBHABER CONCERTE OF 1807–8

It is safe to assume that the success of Würth's concerts over two seasons would naturally have led to a third season, in the winter of 1805–6. Any hopeful plans were, however, dashed by the course of the Napoleonic Wars. In October 1805 France declared war on Austria and following a military campaign of ruthless efficiency, French troops entered Vienna the next month where they stayed until January 1806. Many aristocratic palaces as well as the imperial summer palace at Schönbrunn were requisitioned by the French troops, and although the public theatres remained open, private musical entertainment was scarce. The success of Würth's concerts had encouraged the planning of a second, new subscription series for that winter. Baron August Neuwirth (1754–1826) planned sixteen subscription concerts to be held on Sundays between noon and 2 pm in the hall of the university. Gyrowetz and Paul Wranitzky were entrusted with artistic responsibility and the baron secured the provisional support of many members of the aristocracy.[32] These concerts too fell victim to the French occupation of Vienna.

In 1807 similar aspirations emerged once more when a new private subscription series was established, variously called the Liebhaber Concerte, Musikalisches Institut, Freunde der Tonkunst and Gesellschaft von Musikfreunden, which in the event ran for one season only.[33] In December the

---

[32] R. Perger and R. Hirschfeld, *Geschichte der K. K. Gesellschaft der Musikfreunde in Wien. 1. Abteilung: 1812–1870* (Vienna, 1912), p. 4.

[33] Biba, 'Liebhaber Concerte', pp. 82–93.

Pressburger Zeitung, which often reported on musical events in Vienna for the benefit of its readers, contained the following announcement.[34]

Music-lovers in the capital have long desired to see the creation of a musical institution which would perform the works of great masters to perfection and give virtuosos opportunity to show their art. Two years ago the von Würth concerts let us experience the great worth of music properly played. This winter a group of seven persons has come together for the sole purpose of creating and operating such an institution . . .

Leading members of the organizing consortium included Count Moriz von Dietrichstein, Prince Lobkowitz, Prince Ferdinand Trauttmansdorff and, for a few weeks until an undocumented squabble intervened, the banker and businessman Johann Baptist Häring. The organization represented a pooling of patronage by several figures, rather like van Swieten's Gesellschaft der Associierten that had promoted performances of choral music in the 1780s and 1790s. But, unlike Swieten's group who underwrote the costs themselves, the Liebhaber Concerte depended on subscriptions from the wider aristocratic community. Seventy individuals were sought who could buy any number of tickets, tickets that could then be distributed as gifts to friends and acquaintances; unused tickets had to be returned. Members and guests willingly bought into the lofty objective of the series: 'Every concert must be distinguished by the performance of significant and decidedly excellent musical works, since the institute wishes to affirm the dignity of such art and to attain still higher perfection.'

As well as concerts of ambition and status the organization offered an opportunity for gifted amateur performers to play alongside professional performers in an established orchestra of fifty-five players. The very capable Häring was the first leader but he was soon succeeded by Franz Clement. The first violins included Joseph Würth who played alongside Conradin Kreutzer, best known as a composer. Gifted amateurs formed the bulk of the violins, violas and cellos, plus two flutes and one clarinet; double basses, oboes, a second clarinet, bassoons, horns, trumpets and timpani were paid professionals, recruited mainly from Clement's orchestra at the Theater an der Wien. The customary one rehearsal for a concert was held no more than two days before the event; for particularly large and difficult works two rehearsals were held.

The first concert on 12 November 1807 was given in the Mehlgrube but proved too small for the 1309 people who were expected to attend, and from

---

[34] M. Pandi and F. Schmidt, 'Musik zur Zeit Haydns und Beethovens in der Preßburger Zeitung', *Haydn Yearbook*, 8 (1971), p. 225, p. 285.

the second concert onwards the series was held in the hall on the first floor of the university; even here it is likely that some audience members had to stand. Twenty concerts were given, on varying days of the week, between 17 November and 27 March 1808. With the exception of the very last concert, a performance of Haydn's *Creation* given in honour of the composer, all the programmes consisted of orchestral music with, as in Würth's concerts, a preponderance of overtures, concertos and symphonies. Table 5.1 presents a complete list of the content of these programmes.[35]

Apart from the final concert, given in honour of the aged Joseph Haydn, each concert consisted of four of five items built round a typical plan of two overtures, a concerto and a symphony, plus a vocal item from an opera. While the concertos and vocal items provided the familiar focus on the performer – singers from the opera houses, leading performers such as Clement, Hohenadl and Nicolaus Kraft, and gifted noblemen such as Franz von Cerrini de Monte Varechi and Count Hrzan – priority was given to substantial works by Beethoven, Cramer, Krommer, Mozart and Steibelt rather than to vapid display pieces. Alongside several concertos for the piano and for the violin the series contained a notable performance of Mozart's Clarinet Concerto, in which the soloist was a player from the Theater an der Wien, Joseph Friedlowsky; this was one of the first performances in Vienna not given by the original player, Anton Stadler.[36]

Following on the practice evident in Würth's concerts, operatic overtures were the most frequently performed works, with thirty-one different works in nineteen concerts. Gluck is represented by the overtures to *Alceste* and *Iphigénie en Aulide*, Mozart by the overtures to *Die Entführung, Le nozze di Figaro, Don Giovanni* and *Così fan tutte*, plus the march from the first act of *La clemenza di Tito*. However, most of the overtures were from recent operas by composers such as Carl August Cannabich (son of Christian Cannabich), Cherubini, Dalayrac, Méhul and Winter; in the case of Romberg's overture *Ulysses und Circe* the opera had only just received its first performance, in Berlin.

The music of over thirty composers figured in the series and though the repertoire of overtures might suggest a desire to be thoroughly contemporary, there is too a distinct feeling of an emergent Viennese tradition. Mozart

---

[35] In his article on the concert series Otto Biba ('Liebhaber Concert') was able to present summary details only of the works of Haydn, Mozart and Beethoven that were performed. I am extremely grateful to the author for presenting me with a copy of his research notes on the series, based on material in the family archive of Count Dietrichstein.

[36] This performance should be added to those documented in C. Lawson, *Mozart. Clarinet Concerto* (Cambridge, 1996), pp. 36–9.

Table 5.1. *Programmes of the Liebhaber Concerte, 1807–8*

12 November 1807 (Mehlgrube)
Mozart: Overture, *Le nozze di Figaro*
Gluck: Overture, *Iphigénie en Aulide*
Cramer: Piano Concerto, played by Fräulein Spielmann
Beethoven: Symphony No. 2 in D

22 November 1807 (University)
Mozart: Overture, *Die Entführung aus dem Serail*
Himmel: Overture, *Die Sylphen*
Rode: Violin Concerto, played by Herr von Cerrini
Haydn: Symphony No. 100 ('Military')

29 November 1807 (University)
Beethoven: Overture, *Die Geschöpfe des Prometheus*
Müller: Flute concerto, played by Herr Kessler
Mozart: Symphony in C [K551]
Paer: Aria from *Sargino*, sung by Fräulein Biró
Cherubini: Overture, *Epicure*

6 December (University)
Bernhard Romberg: Overture, *Ulysses und Circe*
Andreozzi: Aria, sung by Herr Rathmayer
Beethoven: Symphony No. 3 ['Heroische Symphonie in Es']
Cherubini: Storm and chorus from *Anacreon*

13 December (University)
Haydn: Symphony in D
Rode: Violin Concerto, played by Count von Yermoloff
Beethoven: Overture, *Coriolan*
Righini: Aria from *Tigrane*, sung by Mademoiselle Buchwieser
Mozart: Overture, *Così fan tutte*

20 December (University)
Mozart: Symphony in G minor [K550]
Devienne: Flute Concerto, played by Count Hrzan
Cherubini: Overture, *Médée*
Paer: Duet from *Sargino*, sung by Fräulein von Baroni and Kapellmeister Liverati
Méhul: Overture, *Adrien*

27 December (University)
Winter: Overture, *Tamerlan*
Mozart: Piano Concerto, played by Herr Llora
Beethoven: Symphony No. 4 in B♭
Variations for oboe, played by Herr Flad
Cherubini: Overture, *La prisonnière*

3 January (University)
Mozart: Symphony in C [probably K551]
Krommer: Violin Concerto, played by Herr Sieber
Cherubini: Overture, *Anacréon*
Paer: Duet from *Sargino*, sung by Mademoiselles Elise Teyber and Thérèse Kaiser
Righini: Overture, *Tigrane*

(*cont.*)

Table 5.1. (*cont.*)

17 January (University)
Beethoven: Symphony No. 1 in C
Vogel: Overture, *Demophon*
Mozart: Aria, sung by Herr Möglie
Cherubini: Storm from *Médée*
Weber: Overture, *Wilhelm Tell*

24 January (University)
Haydn: Symphony in E♭ [probably No. 99]
Clement: Violin concerto, performed by the composer
Cherubini: Overture, *Elise*
Boieldieu: Overture, *Ma tante Aurore*

31 January (University)
Mozart: Symphony in D [probably K504]
Beethoven: Piano Concerto No. 1 in C, played by Herr von Felsenberg
Kreutzer: Overture, *Konradin von Schwaben*
Guglielmi: Aria from *Cleopatra*, sung by Mademoiselle Campi
Cherubini: Overture, *Der portugiesische Gasthof* [*L'hôtellerie portugaise*]

2 February (University)
Beethoven: Symphony No. 3 ['Heroische Symphonie']
Eybler: Aria, sung by Herr Weinmüller
Beethoven: Overture, *Coriolan*
Devienne: Variations for flute, played by Count Hrzan
Cherubini: Overture, *Médée*

7 February (University)
Haydn: Symphony in E♭ [probably No. 99]
Kraft: Cello concerto, played by Nicolaus Kraft
Gluck: Overture, *Alceste*
Righini: Recitative and aria, sung by Mademoiselle Fischer
Méhul: Overture, *Joanna*

14 February (University)
Mozart: Symphony in C ['Nro. 2' = K425]
Kreutzer: Piano concerto, performed by the composer
Mayer: Duet, sung by Mademoiselle Laucher and Herr Radicchi
Dalayrac: Overture, *Das Schloss von Montenero* [*Léon, ou Le château de Monténéro*]

22 February (University)
Beethoven: Symphony No. 2 in D
Rode: Violin concerto, played by Herr Schmieding
Vogler: Overture, *Samori*
Liverati: Aria, sung by Mademoiselle Müller
Mozart: March from *La clemenza di Tito*

28 February (University)
Haydn: Symphony in B♭
Kreutzer: Overture, *Die zwei Worte*
Mozart: Clarinet concerto, played by Herr Friedlowsky
Cherubini: Overture, *Lodoïska*

(*cont.*)

Table 5.1. (*cont.*)

6 March (University)
   Mozart: Symphony in C [probably K551]
   Steibelt: Piano concerto, played by Herr von Moyer
   Mayseder: Overture
   Asioli: Aria, sung by Mademoiselle Buchwieser
   Cherubini: Overture, *Faniska*

13 March (University)
   Haydn: Symphony in C minor [probably No. 95]
   Krommer: Flute concerto, played by Count Hrzan
   Cherubini: Overture, *Anacréon*
   Weigl: Recitative and aria, sung by Herr Holbein
   Mozart: Overture, *Don Giovanni*

20 March (University)
   Beethoven: Symphony No. 1 in C
   Eberl: Piano concerto, played by Fräulein Hohenadel
   Kreutzer: Overture, *Konradin von Schwaben*
   Nasolini: Aria, sung by Mademoiselle Campi
   [Carl August] Cannabich, Overture, *Orfeo*

27 March (University)
   Haydn: *The Creation*

is the best represented composer with fourteen performances; the popularity of Cherubini's overtures resulted in twelve performances, one more than the total numbers of performances of works by Beethoven. The fourth most frequently performed composer was Haydn: six performances, with the last concert devoted entirely to the esteemed grand old man of Viennese music. As well as honouring Haydn, the series was clearly a landmark in the posthumous reception of Mozart, the first series of concerts to feature his music since the heyday of the composer's own benefit concerts in the mid-1780s. Alongside these composers there is the new veneration accorded to Beethoven. The statutes of the organization mention that 'decidedly significant and excellent music' was to be performed, a viewpoint that produced a second, unwritten principle that every concert should include at least one work by these composers, and very often two.

Linked to the elevation of Haydn, Mozart and Beethoven is the presence of the symphony. While the concertos and vocal items are by a wide cross-section of composers, the symphonies focus exclusively on Haydn, Mozart and Beethoven. The symphonies of Eberl, Krommer, Anton and Paul Wranitzky, as well as those of earlier composers, are noticeably absent.

'Decidedly significant and excellent music' has become presciently linked with decidedly significant and excellent composers, a moment of crystallization in the history of music in Vienna. To promote this excellence as well as to aid appreciation of the works in question the series included repeat performances of several symphonies: Haydn's Nos. 99 and 104 (if that is the D-major work in question), Mozart's 'Jupiter', and Beethoven's Nos. 1, 2 and 3. In another very conscious narrowing of the potential repertoire Beethoven's newest symphonies are placed alongside the last symphonies of Mozart and Haydn, rather than ones from earlier in their careers.

The Viennese correspondent of the *Allgemeine musikalische Zeitung* provided enthusiastic accounts of the success of these concerts; although he never deals at length with a particular concert or a particular work, some of the casual comments reflect the sense of discrimination that the programmes no doubt stimulated. The performance of the 'Jupiter' symphony on 29 November prompted the coining of the description 'Giant Symphony' ('Riesensinfonie', a play on the common 'Grosse Sinfonie', 'Grand Symphony') for the work, in addition to the adulatory comment 'this triumph of instrumental music, hitherto unsurpassed'.[37] In his next report the critic was able to compare Haydn's Symphony in D (possibly No. 104) with Mozart's G minor symphony, suggesting that the former was only politely received whereas the latter seized the imagination: 'all the strings of the soul are so vigorously and powerfully struck that they resound still.'[38] Here are the beginnings of that outlook that enabled Mozart to be enthusiastically captured by the nineteenth century while Haydn was politely but firmly kept in the eighteenth, an outlook that even in 1807–8 was yielding, however incipiently, the faulty chronology of Haydn, to Mozart, to Beethoven.

[37] *AmZ*, 10 (1807–8), col. 184.   [38] *AmZ*, 10 (1807–8), col. 238.

CHAPTER 6

A rare and rarefied genre

The Liebhaber Concerte of 1807–8 were potentially one of the most sig-nificant developments in the entire history of music in Vienna: a well-planned, ambitious series of concerts, presented to a high standard by a regular orchestra, and with the symphony playing a defining role in the programmes. Although the series relied on the enthusiasm of a few key figures from the aristocracy, the concerts were well-attended, proving that there was a genuine desire for music-making of this kind. Sharing the costs and controlling the distribution of tickets enabled the organizers to present themselves as arbiters of taste, not within the confines of their palaces but in an increasingly public way. The move from the Mehlgrube to the university after the first concert suggests the concerts were less exclusive than originally conceived and for the planned second series the rules of the distribution of the tickets were to be relaxed.[1] Had the concert series established itself as a continuing feature of musical life in the city it is likely that it would have evolved quite naturally into a fully public one and that the symphony would have completed its journey from private entertainment to public statement. This change would not have been the reluctant adjustment of hide-bound traditionalists anxious to maintain their role as patrons, since it was the kind of support that governed the opera houses in Vienna. From January 1807 the Burgtheater, the Kärntnertortheater and the The-ater an der Wien were financially underwritten and directed by a group of aristocrats, including Prince Nicolaus Esterházy, Prince Lobkowitz, Count Ferdinand Palffy and Prince Joseph Schwarzenberg.[2] Their investment of time and money to provide theatrical entertainment for a wide audience mirrored the emerging practice of the Liebhaber Concerte.

Although the consortium that ran the theatres soon encountered prob-lems that dented their early ambition and enthusiasm there was never any

---

[1] Biba, 'Beethoven und die "Liebhaber Concerte"', p. 84.
[2] F. Hadamowsky, *Wien Theater Geschichte von den Anfängen bis zum Ende des Ersten Weltkriegs* (Vienna, 1994), pp. 308–10.

doubt that the theatres themselves would continue with full and active programmes. The Liebhaber Concerte, on the other hand, was a new organization that had not yet secured a permanent place in the musical life of the city and was vulnerable to the first awkward threat. Plans for a second season, from December 1808 to March 1809, were put in hand but had to be abandoned because the whole of Austrian society was being prepared for a major assault on Napoleon's conquered territories in Germany and the former Habsburg dominions. Emperor Franz and his advisors acted partly out of a sense that Napoleon was vulnerable, militarily overstretched and facing criticism at home. Austria tried to secure the support of other nations but failed; by the spring of 1809 it stood alone. With pent-up patriotism, but little real hope, Austria declared war on France in April 1809. Within a few weeks Napoleon's troops had occupied Vienna, where they remained until the autumn. During this period of national fervour followed by national humiliation there was no room for a second series of Liebhaber Concerte.

Austria's financial situation was becoming increasingly unstable. The costs of the failed campaign were exacerbated by the rapid decline of the purchasing power of the currency. When Napoleon's troops left the economy was in a state of hyperinflation, leading ineluctably to state bankruptcy in 1811 and an 80 per cent devaluation of the currency. This proved only a temporary solution as the renewed campaign against Napoleon in 1813 once more took its toll on the state finances. Between 1809, when Napoleon invaded Vienna, and 1814, when he was finally defeated, the cost of living in the city increased by a staggering 542 per cent.[3]

In this political and economic climate, patronage of music in Vienna was affected along with every other aspect of life. It was in this period that the endless extravagance of Prince Lobkowitz's musical expenditure came to an ignominious end. There were no successful attempts to establish a subscription series following the Liebhaber Concerte and most concerts were benefit ones for charitable purposes, including the war effort itself. Here the instant appeal of the music in performance was more important than the challenging appeal of the music as music. Inevitably the symphony, with its comparatively new image of inherent greatness and inherited value, became less and less evident in musical life. While Beethoven completed two new symphonies, Nos. 7 and 8, Krommer composed none, and there was no new figure equivalent in presence to Paul Wranitzky (from the 1790s

[3] C. Ingrao, *The Habsburg Monarchy 1618–1815* (Cambridge, 1994), pp. 203–04, pp. 234–9; J. Moore, 'Beethoven and Inflation', *Beethoven Forum*, 1 (1992), pp. 198–204, p. 212.

and early 1800s) or Eberl (from the middle of the first decade). It was fast becoming a neglected genre that was in danger of disappearing completely.

One of the declared aims of the Liebhaber Concerte had been to lead artistic taste and expression. In the following season, 1808–9, there is evidence that benefit concerts in Vienna responded to this agenda, with Beethoven the symphonist gaining some prominence. He directed a symphony for a charity concert at the Burgtheater on 15 November 1808, the pianist Marie Bigot de Morogues included a Beethoven symphony in her benefit concert in the Kleiner Redoutensaal on 16 December, and Franz Clement included Beethoven's Fifth Symphony in his benefit at the Theater an der Wien on 23 December. The last-mentioned was a partial repeat of the concert of the previous evening, Beethoven's own benefit concert which had featured the first public performance of the Sixth as well as the Fifth Symphony. Haydn's 'Military' symphony (No. 100) enjoyed renewed popularity in the bellicose atmosphere of spring 1809 with four performances at benefit and charity concerts, usually opening lengthy miscellaneous programmes that contained other stirring items such as Weigl's chorus, 'Der Kriegs Eid' (The Battle Oath), Süssmayr's song 'Der Genius Oesterreichs' and Weigl's chorus 'Oesterreich über alles'. These few months also saw the performance of a symphony by the fifteen-year-old Moscheles (1794–1870), performed at the Kärntnertortheater on 12 March, and the first performance of a symphony by a former pupil of Haydn, Paul Struck (1776–1820), at the benefit concert of a Russian bassethorn player, Iwan Müller;[4] neither symphony has survived. But this promising presence of old, recent and new symphonies was not to be maintained as public concerts in Vienna became ever more populist in the final years of the Napoleonic period.

There was an indication of this malaise in the autumn of 1811 when Baron August von Neuwirth tried for a second time to organize a series of subscription concerts, having failed six years earlier. A double-column advertisement in the *Wiener Zeitung* in German and French – the bilingualism was an indication of the enforced alliance with France – sought support for sixteen concerts in the hall of the university, beginning on 1 December, and to be given by an orchestra of sixty players; replies were needed by 15 October. The response must have been inadequate since the

---

[4] Morrow, *Concert Life*, pp. 350–55.

concerts never took place. He tried a third time in Lent 1813 but again with no success.[5]

The Tonkünstler-Societät continued to offer the bi-annual pair of concerts at Easter and Christmas but, whereas during Wranitzky's period of office as secretary the programme often included a symphony alongside the main choral work, between 1809 and 1814 none was presented; performances of Haydn's two late oratorios, *The Creation* and *The Seasons*, were the most reliable means of raising money and the society presented one or other of these works on sixteen evenings out of twenty.[6] From 1804 onwards another organization, the 'Wohltätigkeits-Anstalten' (Charity Institute), held concerts twice a year, at Whitsuntide and in November, that were designed to raise money for charitable causes in general. Taking their cue from the Tonkünstler-Societät the organizers usually presented large-scale choral works; the appearance of an unspecified Haydn symphony in the concert held in November 1810 was a rare event.[7]

One of the most conspicuous features of concert life in Vienna in the last years of the Napoleonic Wars was the increase in the number of benefit concerts given by violinists, who now enjoyed the kind of attention previously accorded to pianists. Franz Clement, director of the orchestra at the Theater an der Wien, had already assumed a pivotal role in musical life. He was a competent composer, but he never wrote a symphony and the programme of his benefit concert on 22 March 1812 at the theatre is typical of many in avoiding the genre; it included Paer's overture to *Numa Pompilio*, a violin concerto in E by Clement, a cantata by Andreas Romberg that set a text by Schiller, *Das Lied von der Glocke*, an improvisation by Clement on the violin, and, to end, the march and chorus from Beethoven's incidental music to *The Ruins of Athens*. Earlier the same day, the leader of the orchestra at the Burgtheater, Joseph Mayseder (1789–1863), had given his benefit concert to a full house in the Kleiner Redoutensaal, dominated by his own compositions, an overture, a violin concerto and a set of variations for violin and orchestra.[8] The violin concerto was by far the most frequently encountered instrumental genre on concert programmes, possessing the easy appeal of the virtuoso performer standing in front of an orchestra and directing his own music, something that the symphony could not offer.

[5] T. Antonicek, *Musik im Festsaal der Österreichischen Akademie der Wissenschaften*, Veröffentlichungen der Komission für Musikforschung, ed. E. Schenk (Vienna, 1972), pp. 81–2, p. 85.
[6] Pohl, *Tonkünstler-Societät*, pp. 67–9.   [7] Morrow, *Concert Life*, p. 52, p. 178, p. 362.
[8] *AmZ*, 14 (1812), cols. 282–3.

The most celebrated violinist of the day was Louis Spohr (1789–1859) who spent just over two years in Vienna, from December 1812 to March 1815.[9] The nature of his success in the city is instructive. He was appointed leader of the Theater an der Wien in succession to Franz Clement and presented several benefit concerts in which he featured as soloist in his own music. His recent oratorio, *Das jüngste Gericht*, was successfully presented, he provided a cantata for the Congress of Vienna, *Das befreite Deutschland*, and for the active chamber music culture he composed three quartets, two quintets, an octet and a nonet. But he never composed a symphony in Vienna.

A year before he arrived in the city, Spohr had written a symphony in Eb for the music festival at Frankenhausen in central Germany, a substantial work in four movements that was subsequently published by Kühnel in Leipzig when it was diplomatically dedicated to the Gewandhaus orchestra. He brought the symphony with him to Vienna where it was played on two occasions but with little success. The first performance in the city was of the first movement only, on 14 January 1813 at the Kleiner Redoutensaal at a benefit concert for Spohr and his wife, the harpist Dorette Scheidler. The Vienna correspondent of the *Allgemeine musikalische Zeitung* wrote enthusiastically about Spohr's gifts as a violinist and as a composer for the instrument, wondrously displayed in a new violin concerto (A major), a pot-pourri based, improbably, on a Russian folksong and Mozart's 'Là ci darem la mano', and an Allegro for violin and harp; the movement of the symphony was not successful, mainly because of its 'unreasonable length'.[10] The second, complete performance took place the following year, at the Theater an der Wien on 25 March 1814, as part of a charity concert to raise money for a local army regiment. The first half of the concert consisted of Beethoven's *Coriolan* overture, a song by Weigl ('Der österreichische Grenadier'), an Adagio and variations for horn and orchestra by Joseph Blumenthal and a chorus, 'Von dir, o Ewiger', by Schulz; the second half opened with Spohr's symphony and was followed by two movements from a flute concerto by Krommer, a duet from Paer's opera *Griselda* and, to end, a patriotic chorus by Salieri, 'Der Vorsicht Gunst beschütze, beglücktes Oesterreich'. The symphony was indifferently received, with the first movement once again attracting criticism; this time the critic offered the considered view that the main theme was not capable of sustaining the length of the movement and was more suited to a minuet.[11] In the context of a patriotic concert

[9] See C. Brown, *Louis Spohr. A Critical Biography* (Cambridge, 1984), pp. 75–109.
[10] *AmZ*, 15 (1813), cols. 115–6.   [11] *AmZ*, 16 (1814), cols. 286–7.

which also had a good deal of music for soloist and orchestra, winning the enthusiasm of the audience for a substantial symphony was always going to be difficult.

From an early age Spohr had been an avid diarist, producing material that was later incorporated into a substantial and entertaining autobiography. The Vienna years are covered in some detail with full, enthusiastic accounts of his triumphs as a player, the performance of *Das jüngste Gericht*, and the ready market for his chamber music, plus his impressions, ambivalent but always honest, of the music of Beethoven. Nowhere in this account does Spohr mention his symphony.[12] When Spohr and his wife left Vienna in March 1815 they headed first for Brünn (Brno), then Breslau (Wroclaw), Würzburg, Nürnberg and finally Munich. In the Bavarian capital he wrote an enthusiastic account in his diary of the annual subscription concerts in the city and, although he does not specifically mention Vienna by name, his favourable comments on the status of the symphony in Munich clearly reflect the experience of the Viennese years.[13]

Our stay here afforded us much artistic enjoyment. Already on the day after our arrival we were present at an interesting concert, the first of twelve winter-concerts given every year by the royal orchestra upon their own account. These concerts are numerously attended, and merit it in high degree. The orchestra consists of the simple harmony [Harmonie], twelve first, twelve second violins, eight violas, ten violoncelli and six double-basses. The violins and basses are excellent, and the wind instruments, also, up to the horns. At every concert, a *whole* Symphony is performed; (which is the more praiseworthy, from its becoming unfortunately daily more rare, and that the public for that reason are losing more and more the taste for that noble kind of instrumental-music); then an overture, two vocal, and two concert pieces.

As well as violin concertos and other solo works for the instrument, concerts in Vienna in the period 1809–1814 saw the increasing presence of programmes that mixed music with public readings of poetry, typically advertized as a 'musikalische und declamatorische Abendunterhaltung' (musical and declamatory evening entertainment). Held in all the venues hitherto associated with public concerts in Vienna, they represented a transfer to the public domain of an entertainment popular in salon culture, a move that inevitably came to favour the rousing and the rhetorical over the subtle and the sentimental. On 8 April 1811, for instance, a benefit concert for the court actor and poet Friedrich Reil – now best known as the author of the text of Schubert's song 'Das Lied im Grünen' – was held in the

---

[12] *Louis Spohr's Autobiography. Translated from the German* (London, 1865), vol. 1, pp. 161–203.
[13] Ibid., vol. 1, p. 213.

Kärntnertortheater, the same evening as the Tonkünstler-Societät was presenting Haydn's *Creation*. The critic of the *Allgemeine musikalische Zeitung*
gave a full list of the items in Reil's concerts, sixteen in number, together
with some comments.[14]

Part 1. 1) Symphony (C major) by Mozart, but only the first movement. 2) Bürger's
'Song of the worthy Man', recited by Herr Reil. His voice has too little variety
and flexibility. 3) 'The Cow', by Bürger, recited by Mademoiselle Koberwein: she
exerted herself *too much*; less would have been more. 4) 'The Ruins of Antiquity',
by Overbeck declaimed by Herr Roose; the poem failed to please the audience.
5) 'The Townspeople' by Schiller, recited by Herr Krüger in a splendid, authentic
and always understandable manner. Of all the actors he won the laurels. 6) A
flute concerto (G minor), entirely new, composed and played by Herr Professor
Bayer. He received enthusiastic applause. 7) 'The eternal Jew', a lyrical rhapsody by
Schubart, recited by Herr Koch – whom we treasure in plays – but without exertion
and understanding. 8) 'Morning Celebration', ode by Klopstock, music by Zum-
steeg, was extremely tedious because of the uncertain presentation of Herr Reil.
9) Romance from the opera *Aschenbrödel*, sung by Mademoiselle Josefa Demmer,
which was agreeable to listen to. *Part 2.* 10) 'Emperor Max on the Martinswand'
by Collin, diligently presented by Mademoiselle Adamberger. 11) 'The Struggle
between the Lion and the Python', by Kind; good, but rather too quickly spoken by Herr Koberwein. 12) 'The Tobacco Pipe'; presented by Herrn Koch and
Koberwein. 13) A trio by Winter, sung by Mademoiselle Meier, and Herrn Ehlrer
and Meier: pleasing. 14) 'Rudolph von Habsburg', by Schiller, with a new musical
accompaniment by Herr Gyrowetz, played on the piano by Herr Neumann, singer
at the Imperial-Royal court theatres, and declaimed by Mademoiselle Krüger. Her
presentation revealed more practice than true feeling. Herr Neumann who is usually very accomplished – particularly in his compositions – was today not entirely
certain in his playing. 15) 'To Joy', by Schiller. The verses were presented in alternation by Herr Reil and the chorus. This poem would have made more effect
with music and singing. 16) To end: duet from the opera *Aschenbrödel*, sung by
Mademoiselle Demmer and Herr Ehlrer, again very pleasing. Because the house
was packed, Herr Reil had good takings.

The sixteen numbers were all short items, with the first movement of the
Mozart symphony, probably the 'Jupiter', providing the most significant
orchestral item. The penultimate item, the declamation of Schiller's 'An
die Freude', shared between Reil and a chorus of actors, is an eye-catching
anticipation of Beethoven's Ninth Symphony. It is difficult to imagine that
Beethoven would have attended a concert of this kind, but he was an avid
reader of the *Allgemeine musikalische Zeitung* and the remark that a musical
setting would have been more effective than a recited performance may have

---

[14] *AmZ*, 13 (1811), cols. 360–61.

caught his attention. Certainly a year later he began sketching an overture that was to include a setting of the text.[15] The Ninth Symphony has a long prehistory, encompassing a lost song from the 1790s based on Schiller's text, the principal melody of the Choral Fantasy (itself based on an earlier song) and the aborted overture from 1812; this concert warrants a mention in that prehistory, if only because of the character of the event, abstract musical works alongside the public declamation of ardent and uplifting poetry by Collin and Klopstock, as well as Schiller.

Two other mixed concerts that took place in 1814 are interesting for the light they shed on the continuing development of Mozart's posthumous image. On 5 April in the Theater an der Wien and for the benefit of impoverished theatre personnel (the Theater-Armenfond) a concert of thirteen items was given, nine musical, two poetic and two *tableaux vivants*.[16] The evening opened with a work described as a 'Grand Symphony in F minor by W. A. Mozart, arranged for full orchestra by Herr I. v. Seyfried, first Kapellmeister of this theatre.' Ignaz Seyfried (1776–1841) was one of Vienna's most successful composers of German opera and had been associated with the Theater an der Wien since its opening in 1801. His new symphony consisted of three carefully chosen movements by Mozart arranged for full orchestra (including four horns): the first movement of the Piano Quartet in G minor (K478) transposed down a tone; the Andante of the same work but in the original key, B♭; and the Fantasia in F minor (K608), originally written for a mechanical organ.[17] Undoubtedly Seyfried's principal motivation was to honour the memory of Mozart, but in a way that shaded it for contemporary ears. With a symphony in F minor, Seyfried was able to extend Mozart's symphonic output in the minor key to two ardent works (the early symphony in G minor, K183, was forgotten); the choice of the first movement of the G minor piano quartet was particularly shrewd, one of Mozart's most motivically arresting movements, while the fugal content of the Fantasia allowed the work to pose as a legitimate companion to the 'Jupiter' symphony.

Seyfried had already provided another 'new' symphony by Mozart, an orchestration of the C minor fantasia (K475) and associated sonata (K457),[18] which was performed a few days later, on 10 April, at yet another musical and declamatory concert, this time for the benefit of the general charity,

---

[15] B. Cooper, *Beethoven and the Creative Process* (Oxford, 1990), p. 112.

[16] *AmZ*, 16 (1814), cols. 353–4.

[17] B. van Seyfried, *Ignaz Ritter von Seyfried. Thematisch-Bibliographisches Verzeichnis. Aspekte der Biographie und des Werkes* (Frankfurt, 1990), pp. 390–92.

[18] Ibid., pp. 388–90.

the Wohltätigkeits-Anstalt.[19] This substantial four-movement work again allowed orchestral music in the minor key by Mozart to be heard in a concert of exaggerated public emotion; the evening ended with the singing of the national anthem, 'Gott erhalte Franz den Kaiser', prompted by the news that coalition troops had entered Paris.

As a composer who devoted himself to the theatre, Seyfried never wrote an original symphony and he may well have thought there was little point in trying since the heyday of the genre seemed to have passed. His devotion to the music of Mozart was part of an increasingly prevalent outlook in Vienna that saw him as a great national figure, an icon around whom a sense of Austrian, more specifically Viennese, musical identity could be created. In 1814, the symphony was not yet part of this consciousness; that was to come later.

Amongst the increasing number of charity concerts that were taking place in Vienna in the last years of the Napoleonic wars were ones promoted by a new society of female aristocrats, the Gesellschaft der adeligen Frauen. The first concert organized by the society was a musical and declamatory one, held in the Burgtheater on 27 February 1811; the proceeds were given to the blind institute. Fourteen months later, on 16 April 1812, the society organized a second concert, this time entirely of music, at the newly built concert room in the house of the pianist Andreas Streicher in the Landstrasse; on this occasion the proceeds were given to the deaf institute. Neither programme included a symphony, though Beethoven's overture to *Coriolan* was given in both concerts.[20] Following a devastating fire in Baden the society then proceeded to organize its most ambitious concert to date, a performance of Handel's *Alexander's Feast*. A preliminary notice reveals that the leading figures in the Gesellschaft were Baroness Fanny von Arnstein, Countess Dietrichstein and Princess Lobkowitz; the banker Count Moritz Fries looked after the finances.[21] The performance took place on 29 November 1812 at the winter riding school and was such a resounding success that it had to be repeated three days later.

From the success of these concerts grew the impetus to found a more broadly based society, the Gesellschaft der Musikfreunde which, like its precursor, sought to unite musical ambition with charity, except that the charitable purposes were now to be specifically musical ones. As a public organization it sought to ally the venerable charitable tradition associated with music making in Vienna with the ambitious musical standards of

---

[19] *AmZ*, 16 (1814), col. 355.
[20] *AmZ*, 13 (1811), cols. 226–7; 14 (1812), cols. 362–3.   [21] *AmZ*, 14 (1812), col. 772.

the short-lived Liebhaber-Concerte and the still-remembered enlightened patronage of individuals, and to apply them to a range of musical activity in Vienna in order to raise expectations and standards. By 1814 it had drawn up its statutes, ninety-six in number, mingling lofty ideals with a carefully worked out bureaucratic structure and a pragmatism that ensured that the society was more important than any individual.[22] The statutes gave priority to founding a conservatoire, bringing major works to performance, establishing a musical journal, setting up a music library and supporting excellent musical talent in general. Statute 47 dealt very crisply with the essential dual purpose of concerts: 'Partly to propagate true musical taste, partly through lucrative receipts to secure sound finances.' It was to take several years for the Gesellschaft to establish itself as a driving force in the musical life of the city as its initial aims were developed and modified. The earliest concerts of the Gesellschaft capitalized on the success of *Alexander's Feast*; the same work was given again in 1813, followed by another oratorio by Handel in the following year, *Samson*.[23] On 3 December 1815 in the Kleiner Redoutensaal a miscellaneous concert of six items was held, including an unspecified symphony in D by Mozart,[24] but axiomatic association of 'true musical taste' with the symphony was not to occur for several years.

PONDERING THE FUTURE

One of the most regular contributors to the *Allgemeine musikalische Zeitung* was Ernst Ludwig Gerber (1746–1819) who had lived his entire life in Sondershausen, Thuringia, where he held a mixture of musical and administrative posts at the court of Prince Schwarzburg-Sondershausen. He had spent most of his adult life compiling two notable music dictionaries, the *Historisch-biographisches Lexicon der Tonkünstler* (Leipzig, 1790–2) and the *Neues historisch-biographisches Lexikon der Tonkünstler* (Leipzig, 1812–14). As the latter was being completed he wrote a leading article in the *Allgemeine musikalische Zeitung* dealing with what he clearly sensed was a moment of crisis for the symphony, 'A friendly discourse on cultivated instrumental music, especially symphonies'.[25] Gerber had never visited Vienna and the perspective of his essay is a broadly German one. Haydn is his hero, and he sees the composer's mastery of phrasing, wit and instrumentation together with his projection of a single unifying idea as the founding principles of

[22] *Statuten der Gesellschaft der Musikfreunde des österreichischen Kaiserstaates Wien* (Vienna, 1814).
[23] Hanslick, *Geschichte des Concertwesens*, vol. 1, pp. 145–9.   [24] Ibid. p. 156.
[25] 'Eine freundliche Vorstellung über gearbeitete Instrumentalmusik, besonders über Symphonien', *AmZ*, 15 (1813), cols. 457–63.

the symphony. These attitudes were maintained by Mozart, Beethoven and other German masters so that the symphony is now 'the *non plus altra* of modern art, the highest and most splendid of instrumental music'. But he senses that there are three problems which will affect the future of this exalted genre. First are the demands it makes on the composer who needs to have complete mastery of musical language as well as the time, energy and strength to devote himself to a single work. Second, the symphony requires a skilled orchestra of at least twenty-eight to thirty good players. The final difficulty is the receptivity of the public to such a developed work of art, one that increasingly requires a trained ear; even cultured audiences in Paris find the experience of listening to a symphony exhausting, he remarks.

Had Gerber been writing from a specifically Viennese perspective he would have been even more concerned. Vienna, too, had developed the perspective of the great lineage of Haydn, Mozart and Beethoven; yet it was less commonly articulated and, after the Liebhaber Concerte of 1807–8, never encountered in concerts. As regards instrumentalists there was an ample supply of skilled players in Vienna but, compared with major German cities such as Berlin, Leipzig and Mannheim, there was no continuing tradition of channelling these resources into the performance of symphonies. As for Gerber's third requirement, trained ears, the discrimination of the aristocracy and its eagerness to pursue tastes that were demanding and exclusive were real enough, as was the intention to make this a public phenomenon rather than a socially exclusive one, but political and economic factors had stifled its natural development in the period 1808–1814.

Following the defeat of Napoleon and the signing of the first Treaty of Paris in May 1814, Emperor Franz invited the heads of all the European states to a conference, the Congress of Vienna, designed to map out the future of Europe after a quarter of a century of fighting. For five months from October 1814 Vienna was home to the crowned heads of Europe and their ministers. While the real business of the congress was diplomacy, hundreds of people took part in the associated festivities, dances, hunts, military tattoos, sleighrides, banquets, *tableaux vivants*, operas and concerts.[26] For his monthly report in the December issue of the *Allgemeine musikalische Zeitung* the Viennese correspondent took the opportunity to

---

[26] For musical life during the Congress of Vienna see the following: I. Fuchs, 'The Glorious Moment – Beethoven and the Congress of Vienna', *Denmark and the Dancing Congress of Vienna. Playing for Denmark's Future* (Copenhagen, 2002), pp. 182–96; O. Biba, 'The Congress of Vienna and Music', ibid., pp. 200–214; M. Landenburger, 'Der Wiener Kongreß im Spiegel der Musik', *Beethoven. Zwischen Revolution und Restauration*, ed. H. Lühning and S. Brandenburg (Bonn, 1989), pp. 275–306.

reflect on his experience of musical life in the city, covering twenty years, and his hopes for the future.[27] Although he would have read Gerber's essay from two years earlier, his outlook is rather different and his tone is certainly more forlorn. His hero, again, is Joseph Haydn, 'this ornament of his nation'; he is coupled with Mozart to form the first period of musical greatness in Vienna. Since their time, musical life in Vienna has deteriorated immeasurably. Beethoven's name is not even mentioned, not out of malice but because the narrative of Haydn to Mozart to Beethoven, glimpsed in the Liebhaber Concerte of 1807–8, was not yet a secure one in Vienna, and in the symphony wholly absent in the Vienna of 1814. The view of the correspondent is that a great age had come to an end with Haydn and Mozart, a new one had not yet broken out, and he is wearily ambivalent about the future rather than optimistic. He notes that many concerts given by native and foreign musicians during the Congress of Vienna were playing to half-empty houses and that the music of Haydn and Mozart was neglected. For him the only ray of hope is the Gesellschaft der Musikfreunde, 'a grand splendid institution' that might lead Vienna into a second period of musical greatness.

SCHUBERT'S EARLY SYMPHONIES: THE PAST RECREATED IN PRIVATE

Between 1813 and 1818 Schubert completed six symphonies, a noticeably large number for any composer in Vienna and, it might be thought, an output that bucks the general trend. But the circumstances of their composition and performance are so peculiar to Schubert as not to link in with any broader development. The performances were all private ones, the works were never published and no public performances took place until after his death; indeed in the case of Symphonies Nos. 1 and 3 the first public performances took place in London, in 1881.[28] While the symphonies reflect many of Schubert's youthful musical enthusiasms, they also ignore certain characteristics of the genre that had evolved in the first years of the nineteenth century.

Schubert was sixteen when he completed his first symphony in October 1813. It was written for the orchestra of the Stadtkonvikt, the boarding school in the centre of Vienna which he had first attended as a choirboy in

---

[27] *AmZ*, 16 (1814), cols. 826–31.
[28] For surveys of Schubert's symphonies see B. Newbould, *Schubert and the Symphony. A New Perspective* (Surbiton, 1992) and W. Steinbeck, '"Und über das Ganze eine Romantik ausgegossen." Die Sinfonien', *Schubert Handbuch*, eds. W. Dürr and A. Krause (Kassel, 1997), pp. 550–669.

the Hofkapelle and was still entitled to do so even though his voice had broken the previous year. As well as singing, Schubert played the violin (later viola) and the piano. Earlier, his musical upbringing had been focused on church music and music-making at home, with no documented contact with the Viennese milieu associated with the symphony. His father was a schoolteacher, a background that would not have enabled him to mix with the first and second aristocracy that attended concerts in the Lobkowitz palace or those presented by Würth and by the Liebhaber Concerte. Schubert would have been too young to attend the notable benefit concerts given by Eberl in 1804 and 1805 and by Beethoven in 1800 and 1803, even probably the monster concert of 1808. 1808 was the year Schubert, aged eleven, entered the Stadtkonvikt where his educational and musical life revolved around the church year. The venerable Salieri was his principal teacher and instructed him in species counterpoint, fugue, canon and vocal writing.[29] His formal instruction at the Stadtkonvikt lasted until November 1813, a few days after he completed his first symphony. The combination of his age, the circumstances of his upbringing and education, and the decline of the genre, must have severely restricted opportunities for hearing performances of symphonies and Schubert's acquaintanceship with the genre was based largely, perhaps even exclusively, on the holdings of the library of the Stadtkonvikt, as the following account by his friend Josef von Spaun relates.[30]

I got to know Franz Schubert in November 1808, when, at about the age of eleven, he began his studies at the Imperial Seminary [Stadtkonvikt] as a choirboy of the Court Chapel [Hofkapelle] . . .

As he was already fairly accomplished on the violin, he was incorporated into the small orchestra, which at that time used to perform an overture and a symphony every day after supper, and frequently indeed with very laudable success, having regard to the youthfulness of its members. – I took my place as leader of the second violins and the little Schubert played from the same music, standing behind me. Very soon I became aware that the little musician far surpassed me in the sureness of his beat. My attention having been drawn to him by this, I noticed how the otherwise quiet and indifferent-looking boy surrendered himself in the most lively way to the impressions of the beautiful symphony we were playing. We possessed over thirty symphonies by Haydn and several by Mozart and Beethoven. Haydn was performed the most and also the best. – The Adagios from the Haydn symphonies moved him profoundly and of the G minor Symphony by Mozart he often said to me that it produced in him a violent emotion without his knowing exactly why. He declared the Minuet in this symphony to be enchanting and in the Trio it

[29] W. Dürr, 'Schubert in seiner Welt', *Schubert Handbuch*, pp. 10–11.
[30] O. E. Deutsch, *Schubert: Memoirs by his friends*, trans. R. Ley and J. Nowell (London, 1958), pp. 125–6.

seemed to him that the angels were singing too. With Beethoven's Symphonies in
D major and A [recte Bb] major his delight reached its climax. Later on he liked
the C minor Symphony even better . . .

At this time Krommer's symphonies were also in vogue and had a great success
among the young people on account of their gaiety. Schubert was annoyed when-
ever one of them was played and used to say repeatedly during the performance,
"O how boring". He did not understand how one could perform such stuff, as he
called it, when Haydn had written symphonies without number. Once when they
were playing a symphony by Kozeluch and a lot of people were grumbling about
the old-fashioned music he really got very excited and cried out in his childish
voice: "There is more rhyme and reason [*Hand und Fuss*] in this symphony than
in the whole of Krommer, which you are so fond of playing."

Schubert's formative experiences of the symphony, therefore, were based
on performances by a school orchestra of a repertoire that was quite
old; the Haydn, Mozart and Kozeluch symphonies were probably largely
manuscript parts, probably first purchased from Traeg in the 1780s and
1790s, supplemented by printed material for the two later composers mentioned, Beethoven and Krommer. Although Spaun's reminiscences do not
pretend to be comprehensive in detail, the names of other symphony composers from the 1790s and 1800s are noticeably absent, including Eberl,
Hoffmeister, Gyrowetz, Anton Wranitzky and Paul Wranitzky. Furthermore, the report gives precedence to Haydn and Mozart rather than to
Beethoven; the Second and Fourth Symphonies represented the limits of
his knowledge of Beethoven; the Fifth Symphony came later and Spaun
makes no mention at all of the *Eroica* or the *Pastoral*. The circumstances of
the performances – after supper – recalls the old practice of *Tafelmusik*, once
common in seminaries throughout Austria, circumstances that would not
have suited the extra-musical and public stance of many of Paul Wranitzky's
symphonies as well as the *Eroica* and the *Pastoral*.

Accounts of Schubert's life devoted to the period after he left the
Stadtkonvikt, that is from late 1813 to 1818, confirm that he was more
acquainted with the symphonic repertoire from the eighteenth century
than that from his own age. He began to train as a teacher, living at home
once more, where *Hausmusik* evenings were at the centre of his musical
experience. Leopold Sonnleithner's reports on these evenings chart their
increasingly ambitious nature and give some information on the emphasis
given to the symphony.[31] Quartet arrangements of some of Haydn's symphonies were played in Schubert's house before the eagerness of some wind
players to join in forced them to a larger venue, Franz Frischling's house in

[31] Ibid., pp. 338–41.

the Dorotheergasse, where they played 'the smaller symphonies of Pleyel, Rosetti, Haydn, Mozart and others'. Still expanding numbers forced two further changes of venue, to the house of the violinist Otto Hatwig in the Schottenhof at the end of 1815 and to his new home in the Gundelhof in 1818; 'they had become such a good ensemble that they were also able to give effective performances of the larger symphonies of Haydn, Mozart, Krommer, A. Romberg, etc. and the first two of Beethoven, together with the overtures of these masters and those of Cherubini, Spontini, Catel, Méhul, Boieldieu, Weigl, Winter and others.'

The orchestra was now a fairly consistent body of thirty-five players, almost entirely amateurs who paid a subscription to defray the costs: seven first violins, six second violins, three violas (led by Schubert), three cellos, two double basses, one flute, two oboes, three clarinets, three bassoons, two horns, two trumpets and one timpani player. It was for these evenings that Schubert wrote his next five symphonies: No. 2 in B♭ (1815), No. 3 in D (1815), No. 4 in C minor (1816), No. 5 in B♭ (1816) and No. 6 in C (1818). It was inevitable that the style and content of Schubert's symphonies should reflect the repertoire of the orchestra, a view of the symphony that was dated by some ten to fifteen years. For Schubert this was not a self-conscious exercise in historicism or a deliberate avoidance of the Beethovenian agenda, merely the product of circumstances in contemporary Vienna.

Of these six early symphonies, only No. 5 is not cast in the mould of four movements with a slow introduction, the preferred pattern of the Viennese symphony c.1800. The standard dotted figuration of the introduction to No. 1 is built round the harmonic cliché of a descending tetrachord in the bass (D, C♯, C, B, B♭, A), a compositional trick Schubert may have been taught by Salieri. But, as more than one commentator has pointed out, the unusual formal feature of this movement is the reappearance of the slow introduction at the beginning of the recapitulation b. 305, not in the original Adagio tempo but rewritten in notes of twice the value in the prevailing Allegro vivace, an arresting moment that is almost certainly modelled on the first movement of Mozart's Serenade in D ('Posthorn', K320).[32] The seven-movement serenade, composed in 1779, was more widely known as a three-movement symphony, sold in manuscript by Traeg from the 1780s onwards and published by André in 1792;[33] almost certainly the Stadtkonvikt possessed parts (manuscript or published) of this symphony. Schubert was evidently captured by the excitement of the full orchestra

[32] Steinbeck, 'Die Sinfonien', p. 560.
[33] D. Edge, 'Mozart's Viennese Copyists', pp. 791–4. Matthäus, *André*, p. 235.

working its way through the tetrachord and returns to the idea near the end of the fourth movement (b. 335 onwards).

Memories of three other symphonies by Mozart are kindled elsewhere in the work: K550 in the chromatic writing for woodwind that prepares for the recapitulation section in the first and last movements; the 'Prague' symphony in the 6/8 slow movement; and the 'Paris' symphony in the bustle of the finale. Haydn's influence is less specific but no less telling: *sforzando* accents, comparatively high and insistent writing for trumpets and horns, doubling of the melodic line at the lower octave by the bassoon in the Trio, and the recurring stamp of a three-note motif in the finale.

Of these two composers, Haydn is the stronger influence on Symphony No. 2, if only because of its sonority. In two of the London symphonies (Nos. 98 and 102), four of the late masses (Missa Sancti Bernardi, 'Theresienmesse', 'Schöpfungsmesse' and 'Harmoniemesse') and several movements in *The Creation*, Haydn had created a new sound world of B♭ major coloured by trumpets and timpani, so distinctive that it is not found in any symphony by Mozart or, indeed, other Viennese composers before the 1790s. Paul Wranitzky evoked the sonority in a symphony (P48) published by André in 1798, Anton Wranitzky added trumpets and timpani to an existing symphony in B♭ (B♭1) and Beethoven included them in his Fourth Symphony. Haydn's influence can be discerned too in the slow movement, a set of variations on an Andante theme in 2/4, the only time Schubert used variations in a symphony. Steinbeck has pointed out that the theme has the quality of a *romance* melody,[34] emphasizing the Haydn connection. But if Haydn is the undoubted source of this kind of movement, it should be remembered that by Schubert's time it was commonly encountered in the symphonies of other composers, including the despised Krommer (his F major symphony).

Apart from sonority the most striking element of Schubert's second symphony is its rethinking of tonality and formal function in sonata form, an interaction that fascinated the composer for much of his composing life. Rather than the conventional separation into two tonal areas, tonic and dominant, the first movement and the finale have sonata forms in three well-separated tonal areas, tonic, subdominant and dominant; furthermore the first movement begins the recapitulation in the subdominant rather than the tonic. The same seeking of viable alternatives to standard patterns lies behind Schubert's decision to place the minuet in C minor, rather than the

34 Steinbeck, 'Die Sinfonien', pp. 578–9.

conventional tonic of B♭. One consequence of this is that the finale has to start on a sustained dominant seventh to channel the music back to B♭.

For his third symphony Schubert returned to the key of his first, D major. The slow introduction even begins with the same harmonic plan of a descending tetrachord; the subsequent move to F major is Schubert's wholly internalized use of third-related keys in the slow introductions of several of Haydn's later London symphonies (Nos. 98, 99, 100, 102 and 103). His interest in reconfiguring the tonal pillars of sonata form is evident in both the first movement and the finale, with the first movement having a recapitulation of the second subject in the subdominant, and the finale a three-key exposition (tonic, subdominant, dominant) together with a recapitulation that begins in the dominant.

Schubert's next symphony, No. 4, was his first in the minor key. He scrupulously avoided G minor, the key of his favourite Mozart symphony – that work was to be invoked in the minuet of his next symphony – and, instead, chose C minor. This choice of that minor key has often invited commentators to compare the work with Beethoven's Fifth, an invitation that is difficult to refuse since Schubert gave his symphony the emotive title 'Tragic' ('Tragische'). Inevitably Schubert's work fails the Beethoven test, and even sympathetic commentators have been left struggling to explain its nature in a manner that does not patronize it. But, as Wolfram Steinbeck has pointed out, to approach this C minor symphony from the Beethovenian perspective leads to 'crass misinterpretation'; Schubert's epithet 'Tragische' indicates the melancholy, the plaintive and the yearning aspects of the word rather than the forceful and the epic.[35] Approaching the work from that side of the palette certainly leads to a more congenial experience, yet suppressing knowledge of Beethoven's symphony is such an artificial exercise that it begs the question whether Schubert himself was in this position when he composed the work in 1816. Did he, in fact, know Beethoven's Fifth Symphony at the time?

Spaun, it will recalled, stated quite explicitly that Schubert's admiration for Beethoven's symphony came 'later', after his time in the Stadtkonvikt, but he does not say how much later. Sonnleithner's account is concerned with the period 1813–18 and does not even mention the Fifth Symphony, making the explicit point that the orchestral society played only 'the first two' of Beethoven's symphonies. In fact, the list of players given in Sonnleithner's account would not have been sufficient to perform Beethoven's Fifth, unless one piccolo, one flute, one contrabassoon and three trombone

[35] Ibid. p. 593.

players were specially engaged. The assumption that Schubert must have heard the symphony is not a safe one, given the decline in the presence of the genre generally in the musical life of Vienna. Only three public performances of the symphony are known to have taken place after Beethoven's benefit concert in December 1808 and its repetition the following evening at Clement's benefit: at the benefit concert in the Kleiner Redoutensaal on 14 March 1811 of Heinrich Baermann (the well-known clarinettist, but on this occasion playing the bassoon);[36] on 5 May 1812 at one of the summer Augarten concerts directed by Schuppanzigh;[37] and, almost exactly a year later, on 1 May 1813, again directed by Schuppanzigh at the Augarten.[38] From 1808 to 1813 Schubert was at the Stadtkonvikt where it may have been difficult for boys to attend benefit concerts in the evening and summer concerts in the early morning, even if it was socially acceptable for youths to do so. There were no performances in 1814, 1815 and the early months of 1816, when Schubert was an independent young man. Only from 1820 onwards does the symphony begin to feature regularly in the concert life of Vienna, when the work is included in the programmes of the Gesellschaft der Musikfreunde and the Concerts Spirituels;[39] this must be the period referred to as 'later' by Spaun.

The orchestral parts had been published by Breitkopf and Härtel in 1809 and were available in Vienna, but there would seem to have been little incentive for the young Schubert to study a work that he may not have heard. Also he could have read E. T. A. Hoffmann's celebrated review of the work in the *Allgemeine musikalische Zeitung* in 1810, plus some other reviews,[40] and formed an impression of the work from them, but it was to take several years for Beethoven's expressivity in this work to become indelibly associated with the image of the composer: the teenage Schubert's view of Beethoven was quite different from that of the middle-aged Brahms over half a century later.

It is obviously impossible to prove the negative assertion that Schubert did not know Beethoven's C minor symphony when he was writing his fourth symphony. But in the absence of concrete evidence of the opposite, the hypothesis does have the virtue of reflecting the nature of musical life in Vienna.

One dominant reality of concert life in Vienna that is reflected in the symphony is Haydn's *The Creation*, a work that was difficult to avoid

---

[36] *AmZ*, 13 (1811), col. 292.   [37] *AmZ*, 14 (1812), cols. 442–3.

[38] *AmZ*, 15 (1813), col. 416.   [39] See Chapter 7, pp. 185–8.

[40] See the reviews given in W. Senner, R. Wallace and W. Meredith (eds.), *The Critical Reception of Beethoven's Compositions by His German Contemporaries* (Lincoln, Nebraska, 2001), vol. 2, pp. 92–115.

in Vienna; performances often used Hofkapelle forces and Schubert may well have sung in those given by the Tonkünstler-Societät in April 1809 and April 1811.[41] At the beginning of the symphony it is the opening of the oratorio that is evoked, the 'Representation of Chaos'. The long-held unison C, the melodic line that reaches towards the submediant before weaving itself into the texture, and the harmonic plan that incorporates the distant as well as the near all suggest a personal response to the unprecedented adventurousness of Haydn's introduction. The initial reach of the minor sixth also outlines the tonal polarity of the exposition, with the second subject area placed in A♭ rather than the conventional E♭ or G minor. Schubert's incorporation of E major and C major along the way do much to undermine the lure of C minor and when, at the equivalent point in the recapitulation, C major is heard for the first time, the music then stays in that key. A♭ major returns for the slow movement, a five-part structure (ABABA) that alternates statements of a *cantabile* main theme with a more agitated section, first in F minor, then in B♭ minor.

By placing the minuet and trio in E♭ rather than the tonic major or minor, Schubert not only makes it clear that comparisons with Beethoven's Fifth are inappropriate, but that comparisons with the C minor to C major trajectory of Symphonies Nos. 78 and 95 by Haydn are also misguided. For Schubert in this work C minor is a tonal colour, not a participant in a tonal drama that has its moment of catharsis when C major finally triumphs. Nowhere is this more clear than in the finale, at the point when the music turns to C major for the recapitulation, a moment of considered understatement rather than transformation.

If the most historically sympathetic approach to Schubert's fourth symphony is to regard it as a very individual enhancement of an eighteenth-century court symphony, then Schubert's next symphony is even more of an exercise in what might be termed, rather casually, neo-classicism. Completed within six months of the C minor symphony, the B♭ symphony is the shortest of Schubert's symphonies and is scored for the smallest orchestra, one flute, two oboes, two bassoons, two horns and strings; there are no clarinets, trumpets or timpani. Also absent is a portentous slow introduction; after some held woodwind chords the movement launches immediately into the first subject, *pianissimo*; the music does not reach a *forte* until b. 41. There is nothing in the history of the symphony in Vienna from the 1790s onwards that comes close to the transparency and lightness of the orchestral textures of this work. Rather, it is closer to the 1770s and 1780s in this

⁴¹ Morrow, *Concert Life*, p. 354; Pohl, *Tonkünstler-Societät*, p. 68.

respect and helps explain why Schubert argued a preference for Kozeluch over Krommer as a symphonist.

In the sixth symphony Schubert turned to a familiar type in the Viennese symphony, a C major work with trumpets and timpani. But again Schubert explores the more reserved side of this tradition rather than the extravagantly theatrical one displayed in the many examples by Paul Wranitzky in particular. Only the slow movement, with its general approach of a tuneful main section interrupted by a noisy section with trumpets and timpani, reflects newer trends.

This was the last symphony that Schubert composed for the private orchestral society. Sonnleithner's account indicates that from 1818 onwards it increasingly featured works for soloist and orchestra and even performances of oratorios,[42] two aspects of music making that brought it closer to the conventions of contemporary public concert life. The society now met in the large apartment of a Hungarian businessman named Anton Pettenkofer. When he won first prize in a lottery and moved to a large country estate the society folded and Schubert's highly individual career as a composer of symphonies came to a temporary close.

CZERNY AND THE SYMPHONY: THE PRESENT CONFRONTED IN PRIVATE

Born in the Leopoldstadt district of Vienna on 21 February 1791, Carl Czerny was six years older than Schubert and his upbringing was even more sheltered. His father, Wenzel Czerny, was a piano teacher who secured a basic living in the city, well-regarded yet without ambition and revealing a contentment that was to characterize the career of his only child too. Prodigiously gifted, Carl Czerny was taught by his father; a period of lessons with Beethoven was terminated because he could not afford the time to take the young boy. His general education was similarly unstructured, even casual. The family language was Czech and Carl Czerny relied on some of his father's pupils to teach him French and German in lieu of payment. At the piano Czerny astonished everyone with his sight reading, musical memory and wide repertoire including works by Bach, Scarlatti and every single piano piece by Beethoven. A career as a travelling virtuoso beckoned but his family circumstances and inherited diffidence combined to ensure a more private existence.[43]

---

[42] Deutsch, *Schubert: Memoirs*, pp. 340–41.

[43] C. Czerny, 'Recollections from my life', trans. E. Saunders, *Musical Quarterly*, 42 (1956), p. 311.

. . . since I evinced the necessary talents at an early age I occasionally took over my father's place as teacher even before I was fourteen. The pupils expressed satisfaction. To take advantage of my playing, my parents would have had to take me on tours, and for that they were already too old, quite apart from the fact that the warlike conditions of the time made it impossible to plan such undertakings anyway. And although I was, considering my age, quite proficient as a pianist, as a sight-reader, and in the arts of improvisation, my playing lacked that type of brilliant, calculated charlatanry that is usually part of a travelling virtuoso's essential equipment.

Beethoven remained a steadfast admirer, and Czerny along with Schuppanzigh and Krumpholz became a permanent part of the composer's inner circle of musical friends. Czerny was regularly employed as a proof-reader by Beethoven and later as a piano teacher for his nephew, Karl. For his part, Czerny admired Beethoven for much more than his piano music and expressive piano playing. His reminiscences mention Beethoven's 1803 benefit concert as a formative experience.[44]

I was especially interested in the symphonies [Nos. 1 and 2] and I was so curious to find out how such orchestral works are written that I conceived the notion of making my own scores of these works from the parts, so that pretty early in my life I got a fairly correct concept of instrumentation. I enjoyed this type of work so much that I applied the same procedure to several Haydn and Mozart symphonies (something far more useful for the student than to study a ready-made score). At the same time this activity endowed me with great skill in speedy writing of musical notation, a skill that came in very handy later on.

'Speedy writing of musical notation' came into its own from 1818 onwards when, by accident rather than design, Czerny began composing piano music of all kinds for a market that was to prove insatiable; by his death he had written over 600 piano pieces, supplemented by editions of older music, transcriptions and several treatises. This was the public face of Czerny. The private man remained the same, teaching and living at home with his parents, and acquiring the sizeable fortune that had eluded them. There was another aspect to the private man, his interest in composing large-scale works. Another passage in his reminiscences alludes to this interest: 'Notwithstanding this strenuous daily activity [of teaching] I nonetheless composed every free moment I had, especially in the evening, and experimented with most types of compositions.'[45] 'Most types of composition' included concertos, overtures and several symphonies.

---

[44] Ibid., p. 308.   [45] Ibid., p. 313.

Example 6.1 Czerny, Symphony in D, third movement, bb. 1–17.

For six months in 1814 Czerny laboured on the score of a symphony in D major, each movement of the autograph score meticulously outlining its progress: the first movement was begun on 21 April and completed on 11 May; the slow movement took from 14 May to 23 July; the scherzo was composed comparatively quickly, from 23 July to 11 August; then, after

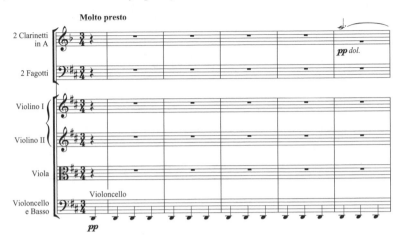

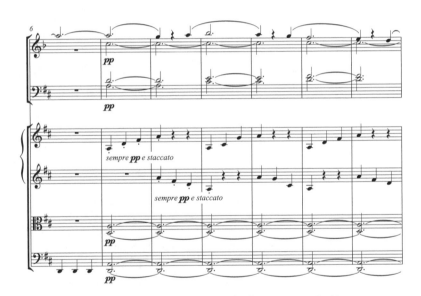

Example 6.2 Czerny, Symphony in D, third movement, trio, bb. 1–19.

a break of a few weeks, the finale was begun on 7 September 1814 and completed on 9 October, 'at 9.30 in the evening'.[46] This long period was not merely a consequence of a busy lifestyle but the ambitious scale of the

[46] Autograph manuscript, Gesellschaft der Musikfreunde, Vienna.

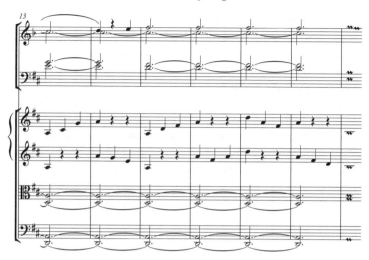

Example 6.2 (*cont.*)

work. A cautious estimate of the duration would be fifty minutes, longer than the *Eroica* symphony and therefore much longer than any symphony to date in the Viennese tradition. Scored for an orchestra of double woodwind (including clarinets), two horns, two trumpets, timpani and strings, some of the energy and expressive reach of the work is evident from the following list of movement headings, keys and time signatures.

1. Allegro molto quasi presto, D major, 12/8
2. Adagio quasi Andante, F major, 2/4
3. *Scherzo*: Molto presto, D minor, 3/4
4. *Finale*: Allegro molto, D major, 2/4

Unlike Schubert, Czerny responded fully to the challenge of Beethoven's symphonies, works that he obviously knew well as a privileged friend of the composer. The unusual compound metre of the first movement produces a similar momentum to the first allegro of Beethoven's Seventh Symphony but even more impressive is the composer's careful placing of dramatic events through deft control of long-term harmonic tension. The coda of the first movement of the *Eroica* had momentously heralded its departure with a step down from E♭ to D♭; Czerny begins his coda with a semitone rise from D to E♭ to embark on a similarly lengthy coda, amounting to over a quarter of the movement. Equally Beethovenian is the third movement, a one-in-a-bar scherzo that begins in a *piano* dynamic. Ex. 6.1. Like the D-minor scherzo in Beethoven's Ninth the trio turns to the tonic major and to the pastoral. Ex. 6.2.

Along with the rest of his substantial library, the autograph score of Czerny's symphony was bequeathed to the Gesellschaft der Musikfreunde on the composer's death in 1857. There is no titlepage, dedication or any indication of the circumstances of composition. Since 1814 saw the end of the Napoleonic Wars and the summoning of the Congress of Vienna, it is possible that Czerny anticipated a public performance in the winter of 1814–15 but there is no record of any. It was not to figure in the newly invigorated concert life of postwar Vienna and was never published. A product of commanding musicianship, it seems to have been the victim of Czerny's own lack of worldly ambition.

CHAPTER 7

Beethoven and the decline of the symphony

LOSING A WAY OF LIFE AND DECIDING A CAREER

When Beethoven arrived in Vienna in November 1792 it was for a specific purpose, to receive lessons from Haydn. The two had first met nearly two years previously when Haydn stayed at the electoral court in Bonn *en route* to his first visit to London. On the return journey in the summer of 1792 he again called at the court when it was agreed that Beethoven should follow Haydn back to Vienna as soon as practicable; his position as second organist in the musical retinue at Bonn was to be kept open and his stipend was maintained. The intention was that Beethoven should return to Bonn a more proficient and experienced composer, ready to assume a central role and, when the opportunity arose, perhaps even the post of Kapellmeister. The court orchestra of forty players, in which Beethoven occasionally played the viola, was a large one by contemporary standards, and performed in church services and the opera as well as private concerts at court. Part of the Holy Roman Empire, the electorate was essentially a Habsburg court since the elector, Maximilian Franz, was the brother of Joseph II, and in culture as well as politics it took its lead from Vienna. Indeed in musical matters it could fairly be said to be more active than the imperial court in Vienna, with a repertoire of Catholic church music, contemporary operas (including those of Mozart) and instrumental music of all kinds. The symphony was central, as is suggested by a surviving inventory that lists over 650 works, including ones by Dittersdorf, Haydn, Kozeluch, Mozart, Pichl, Pleyel, Vanhal and Paul Wranitzky.[1]

As a fledgling composer Beethoven began two symphonies in Bonn, one in C major and one in C minor. The 111 bars of the latter, on a two-stave score, reveals the composer's acquaintance with the nervously energetic *Sturm und Drang* idiom including the customary use of Neapolitan

---

[1] J. Riepe, 'Eine neue Quelle zum Repertoire der Bonner Hofkapelle im späten 18. Jahrhundert', *Archiv für Musikwissenschaft*, 60 (2003), p. 100, p. 104, p. 108.

harmony at the cadence; more individual is Beethoven's ability to create tension through varied phrase patterns.[2] Although these two symphonies, and perhaps others for which there is no surviving evidence, were never completed, it was only a matter of time before the Bonn composer would have completed a symphony for the court orchestra.

Studying with Haydn in Vienna would have given the composer the added confidence to complete a symphony for Bonn, particularly as Beethoven was able to witness Haydn working on his latest symphonies, Nos. 99–101, destined for London. At the same time Beethoven would have been struck by the fewer opportunities that Vienna seemed to offer a composer of symphonies. Haydn was still the Esterházy Kapellmeister but, unlike Bonn, there was no court orchestra. Public concerts would have been a comparatively unfamiliar phenomenon to the young Beethoven and in 1793 he almost certainly attended Haydn's own benefit concert in the Kleiner Redoutensaal on 15 March, including three recent symphonies, and one of the traditional two concerts of the Tonkünstler-Societät in December, the programme of which again included three symphonies by Haydn.[3] He would have visited the music dealer Johann Traeg in the Singerstrasse, noted the large stock of symphonies that was available and perhaps wondered where he could hear these works. The obvious answer was that the Bonn court was more likely than Vienna.

The formal part of Haydn's instruction consisted of the customary systematic march through species counterpoint. Beethoven also completed some original compositions in 1793 under Haydn's tutelage, a quintet for oboe, three horns and bassoon (Hess 19), a wind octet (op. 103), an oboe concerto (lost), a set of variations for violin and piano on 'Se vuol ballare' (WoO 40), but no symphony. The number of works that involve wind instruments may well be a reflection of the availability of an Harmonie ensemble at the Esterházy court where Beethoven and Haydn spent the summer months; perhaps if Haydn still had an orchestra at his disposal then Beethoven would, as a matter of course, have written a symphony in 1793.

Haydn had committed himself to making a second visit to London in 1794. He obviously felt that Beethoven's period of instruction was not complete and entrusted him to Albrechtsberger, the leading teacher of theory and composition in Vienna. As before, theoretical study was combined

[2] J. Kerman (ed.), *Ludwig van Beethoven. Autograph Miscellany from circa 1786 to 1799. British Museum Additional Manuscript 29801, ff. 39–162 (The 'Kafka' Sketchbook)* (London, 1970), vol. 2, pp. 175–6. See also discussion in Cooper, *Beethoven*, pp. 22–4.
[3] Morrow, *Concert Life*, pp. 282–3.

with lessons in free composition; in particular Albrechtsberger's interest in the string trio – his op. 9 was published in 1796 – seems to have sparked Beethoven's own interest in the medium. Three decades earlier Albrechtsberger had composed eight symphonies but during his subsequent career as a church composer no further works in the genre were written;[4] unlike Haydn, therefore, he was not a teacher who could be expected to nurture any interest in the genre. For Beethoven 1794 was a year that saw increasing assurance as a composer and widening recognition in Vienna; it was also the year when he was compelled to realize that his future lay in that city rather than Bonn. As late as August 1794, in a letter to Simrock,[5] he expressed his intention to return to Bonn but the course of the French Revolution, as it spilled beyond France, was to dictate otherwise. As the brother of the guillotined Marie Antoinette, Elector Maximilian Franz feared for the safety of the Bonn electorate and placed the court on a war-footing, one small consequence of which was that Beethoven's stipend was stopped in March 1794. By the autumn the court had left Bonn, never to be re-established.

Having lost the security of a court position in Bonn, Beethoven was faced with the problem of how to secure a livelihood in Vienna. The equivalent post of a player-cum-composer at an aristocratic court was largely a thing of the past in the Austrian territories, with Anton Wranitzky's position at the Lobkowitz court being the exception that proved the rule; Beethoven's contact with opera houses in Vienna was non-existent; and although Albrechtsberger could have set him on his way as a church musician, this career was a rather lacklustre one for a young musician, particularly following Joseph II's reforms in the 1780s. Beethoven alighted on a career in Vienna that focused on his talents as a piano player, performing, teaching and composing music that featured the instrument, and assuming an active presence in what Mozart had excitedly termed 'Clavierland'.[6] Such an existence sought to exploit the active salon culture of Vienna and the practices of its music publishers and, in this respect, Beethoven was no different from Gelinek (1758–1825), Kozeluch (1747–1818), Wölfl (1773–1812) and many others. The symphony did not figure in this existence.

This career was formally launched in the summer of 1795 with the publication of the composer's op. 1, three piano trios. Issued by Artaria, the most prestigious music publisher in Vienna, the venture was supported by an

---

[4] R. N. Freeman (ed.), *Austrian Cloister Symphonists. The Symphony 1720–1840*, ed. in chief, B. S. Brook, B/VI (New York, 1982), pp. xxii–xxxiii.

[5] Brandenburg (ed.), *Briefwechsel* (Munich, 1996–8), vol. 1, pp. 25–6.

[6] Letter to his father, 2 June 1781. W. A. Bauer, O. E. Deutsch and J. H. Eibl (eds.), *Mozart. Briefe und Aufzeichnungen* (Kassel, 1962–75), vol. 3, p. 125.

unprecedentedly large list of subscribers, 126 in number, gathered together by Beethoven's principal benefactor, Prince Lichnowsky. As more than one commentator has remarked, this remarkable list is powerful testimony to the social allure of music in the city.[7] Many of these 126 names were to feature on further dedication pages of published music by Beethoven in the next few years, a network of patronage that engendered admiration and ensured a livelihood. But if one scans the list looking for patrons who could support performances of symphonies rather than piano trios, the result is equally revealing about the nature of musical patronage in Vienna in the mid 1790s: only one subscriber, Count Haugwitz, had a court orchestra; Prince Lobkowitz had not yet set up his small retinue of musicians; and there are a number of individuals who employed the fashionable Harmonie ensemble, Baron Braun, Prince Liechtenstein and Prince Schwarzenberg.[8]

At the same time as Beethoven was preparing for the publication of his op. 1, he began working on a symphony, a project that occupied him intermittently for three years before eventually being abandoned.[9] Traditionally this would-be first symphony has been viewed as evidence of Beethoven's eagerness to grapple with one of the most challenging forms of the time, an ambitious and idealistic outlook that also helps to explain why it was not completed. It would be mulish to deny that Beethoven in the 1790s already had that desire, matched in living composers only by Haydn, to fashion individuality out of a common language, yet that view needs to be tempered with a broader appreciation of the standing of the symphony in the 1790s. Without it, it is all to easy to impose later outlooks – on Beethoven, the symphony and Vienna as a musical centre – in a way that distorts the history of the genre in that decade. Beethoven was not yet the colossus he was to become; the symphony was not central to musical life in Vienna; and the compelling narrative of the Classical School, Haydn, Mozart, to Beethoven, had not been conceived.

Why did Beethoven embark on the composition of a symphony in 1795? Clearly performance at a private court was not a realistic prospect. Public concert life, however, offered some hope. In March of that year Beethoven had made his public debut as a pianist in Vienna at the first of the two Easter concerts of the Tonkünstler-Societät, playing the B♭ piano concerto. Haydn's symphonies and Wranitzky's symphonies were played in the concerts of the society in the 1790s and, having made an impact as a pianist,

[7] The subscription list is reproduced in H. C. Robbins Landon (ed.), *Beethoven. A Documentary Study* (London, 1970), pp. 64–5.
[8] Moore, 'Beethoven and musical economics', p. 574, p. 566, pp. 576–7, p. 587.
[9] Cooper, *Beethoven*, p. 61, p. 64, pp. 67–70.

Beethoven may well have thought that a symphony would be welcome. A more immediate focus, however, was the journey he undertook to Prague, Dresden, Leipzig and Berlin between February and July 1796. Two of these cities, in particular, Prague and Leipzig, would have furnished opportunities for performance, and the symphony may have been intended for this journey, however expectantly. Perhaps what Beethoven really needed was a realistic deadline that would have compelled him to work quickly. By the end of the trip extensive sketches for the first three movements and some brief ideas for a finale existed.

In comparison with other first essays in a particular genre, especially the piano trios (op. 1) and the piano sonatas (op. 2), this first symphony is rather cautious.[10] The key, C major, could not be more conservative, chosen not because it was the key of Mozart's last symphony or one of the latest symphonies by Haydn that he would have known, No. 97 (1792), but because it enabled the symphony to take its place amongst any number of C major works with trumpets and timpani composed in the eighteenth century; other recent examples include two by Gyrowetz (C1 and C4), one by Hoffmeister (C2), three by Pleyel (B128, B131 and B143), four by Paul Wranitzky (P2, P5, P8 and P14), and two by Anton Wranitzky (C1 and C2). Beethoven's first thoughts for the opening of the symphony are similarly cautious, a slow introduction of eight bars rather similar in scope to the earliest symphonies of Paul Wranitzky. Later sketches yield a longer introduction with an arresting rising motif of tonic, mediant to submediant, coincidentally also used by Wranitzky at the beginning of a C major symphony, P5 (the one performed in Frankfurt in 1792) and, before that, by Mozart in the 'Linz' symphony (K425). Equally striking is the slow movement which, at first, was placed in E major, part of a fascination that Beethoven and Haydn shared in the 1790s for third-related keys; subsequently Beethoven pushed the movement up a semitone to F, a more conventional key for a slow movement of a symphony in C. The likely reason for this change lay in the structure of the movement, a straightforward sectional design of ABACA (possibly ABA); the tonal goal of one of the contrasting sections was the relative minor; D minor was a much more convenient key for orchestra than the C♯ minor that would have resulted from leaving the movement in E major.

One of the regrettable gaps in modern knowledge of Beethoven's life in the 1790s is the composer's relationship with Paul Wranitzky, a key figure in musical life generally and someone who was notably successful as

---

[10] Kerman (ed.), *The 'Kafka' Sketchbook*, vol. 2, pp. 166–74, pp. 176–7.

a composer of symphonies. He was already secretary of the Tonkünstler-Societät when Beethoven made his debut as a pianist in 1795 at one of their concerts, and the two were clearly on good terms because Wranitzky ensured that Beethoven was made an honorary member of the society in 1797;[11] for his part, Beethoven made certain that Wranitzky directed the orchestra at his first benefit concert in the Burgtheater in April 1800. More than any aristocratic patron in the 1790s, Wranitzky would have been in a position to encourage Beethoven to compose a symphony. Not only could he place a performance on the programmes of the Tonkünstler-Societät but, equally if not more attractively, he could have used his position as André's agent in Vienna to recommend the work to that publisher, where it would have joined similar works by Gyrowetz, Haydn, Krommer, Mozart and Paul Wranitzky himself. Strangely, no music by Beethoven, of any kind, was ever issued in an authorized edition by that firm.

Paul Wranitzky would also have been a natural ally in any attempt by Beethoven to secure a benefit concert at the Burgtheater, one that would have capitalized on the younger composer's growing reputation as a performer and, more unusually, allowed him to be presented as a composer too. The manager of the court theatres, Baron Peter Braun, typically sanctioned no more than two individual benefit concerts in Lent in addition to the traditional pair presented by the Tonkünstler-Societät. His wife, Josephine, was an accomplished pianist to whom Beethoven dedicated his op. 14 sonatas when they appeared in December 1799, an emollient gesture that may have encouraged Braun to grant a benefit evening the following April, Beethoven's first opportunity to present a symphony. Five days earlier, on 28 March, Anton Weidinger, inventor of the 'organized trumpet', held a benefit concert that included the first public performance of Haydn's trumpet concerto, an aria by Süssmayr, a sextet by Kauer, two vocal numbers by Mozart and three symphonies by Haydn.[12] Beethoven's programme was similarly eclectic, though without the eccentric appeal of Weidinger's instrument: Beethoven the performer was represented by a performance of the C major piano concerto and an improvisation; there was a chamber work, the septet (op. 20); two numbers from *The Creation* provided the vocal items (Haydn's oratorio was the featured work in the forthcoming concerts of the Tonkünstler-Societät and the soloists were the same); a symphony by Mozart opened the evening, a work that the Burgtheater orchestra and Wranitzky presumably already knew; finally, Beethoven's First Symphony concluded the concert.

[11] Albrecht (ed.), *Letters*, vol. 1, pp. 46–7.   [12] Morrow, *Concert Life*, pp. 303–4.

Prompted by the names of the three composers represented on this programme – Haydn, Mozart and Beethoven – commentators have seized on this concert as a defining moment in the history of the symphony: Beethoven was finally able, after several years of preparation, to rise to the challenge of Haydn and Mozart. No-one would wish to deny the striking craftsmanship and energy of the First Symphony, even more so the composer's ability to play consequences with the language of music. Yet, there were elements of circumspection too.

As in the earlier, aborted symphony Beethoven gives his audience an approachable work, firmly in the tradition of C major symphonies with trumpets and timpani. As in many symphonies by Paul Wranitzky, as well as Haydn, these instruments interrupt the progress of an appealingly tuneful slow movement. When the concert was reviewed in the *Allgemeine musikalische Zeitung*, the symphony was favourably received though the critic thought the wind instruments were too prominent; 'it was more Harmoniemusik than orchestral music.'[13] Since the critic is unlikely to have objected to any moments of delicacy in the handling of wind instruments, this remark must be interpreted as a comment on overscoring. Loud sonorities, even abrasive and relentless ones, are commonplace in the symphonies of Wranitzky and it is difficult to imagine that the scoring of Beethoven's symphony would have been found offensive. Much of the report in the *Allgemeine musikalische Zeitung* is given over to a trenchant criticism of the standard of performance and the attitude of the players; the apparent misuse of wind instruments may have been down to unruly execution.

Within a few years it was the very opening of the symphony that captured the attention of commentators;[14] and it continues to do so. Rather than beginning with a tonic chord, Beethoven famously begins off-key, with the dominant seventh of F. This was a rather neat distortion of a standard opening phrase that went from the tonic through some form of harmonic occlusion before moving to a cadence. The opening of Haydn's Symphony No. 97 and Krommer's Symphony in F (see Ex. 5.1, p. 101) are good examples. Beethoven simply omits the first element, the tonic chord, and begins with the second, the harmonic ambiguity. Perhaps it would have taken Paul Wranitzky, the director of the performance, to appreciate this sleight of hand; he certainly would have recognized the cliché that begins the following Allegro: four-bar theme, link, followed by repetition of the

---

[13] *AmZ*, 3 (1800–01), col. 49. English translation: Senner, Wallace and Meredith (eds.), *The Critical Reception*, vol. 1, pp. 162–3.

[14] See the reports given in Senner, Wallace and Meredith (eds.), *The Critical Reception*, vol. 1, p. 167, p. 169, pp. 170–71.

theme up a tone, very similar to the first subject of his symphony in C (P8) quoted in Ex. 4. 2 (pp. 87–9).

MONEY, PRESTIGE AND THE SYMPHONY

While the *Allgemeine musikalische Zeitung* reported that Beethoven's first benefit concert had been 'the most interesting concert for a long time' nothing is known about the financial success or otherwise of the evening. The pattern of presenting a new symphony alongside a new piano concerto appealed to Beethoven and already in the autumn of 1800 he began work on the Second Symphony. At this stage Beethoven seems to have been content with the very limited financial reward that was associated with composing a symphony. There was no commission fee; moreover, Beethoven had to pay for the parts to be copied. His principal publisher was Artaria, who had long avoided the financial risk of printing symphonies in favour of piano music and small-scale chamber works. The sole income generated was that associated with any benefit concert that could be arranged. That Beethoven was content with the situation is suggested by the continued absence of any approach to André and by his attitude when, quite unexpectedly, Hoffmeister approached him seeking new compositions for his latest business venture.

In 1800 Hoffmeister had teamed up with Ambrosius Kühnel to establish the new firm of Bureau de Musique, based in Leipzig. Beethoven was keen to help his fellow composer and offered a number of works. In a letter written in January 1801 he listed the items, each with a suggested price.[15]

. . . for the time being I am offering you the following compositions: a septet [op. 20] (about which I have already told you, and which could be arranged for the pianoforte also, with a view to its wider distribution and to our greater profit) 20 ducats – a symphony 20 ducats – a concerto [op. 19] 10 ducats – grand solo sonata [op. 22] (Allegro, Adagio, Minuetto, Rondo) 20 ducats. (This sonata is a first-rate composition, most beloved and worthy brother). Now for a fuller elucidation. Perhaps you will be surprised that in this case I make no distinction between sonata, septet and symphony. The reason is that I find that a septet or a symphony does not sell as well as a sonata. That is the reason why I do this, although a symphony should undoubtedly be worth more.

Two motives lay behind Beethoven's willingness to sell the symphony for the same price as a piano sonata, a genuine desire to help Hoffmeister and

---

[15] Brandenburg (ed.), *Briefwechsel*, vol. 1, pp. 63–4. Translation from Anderson (ed.), *Letters*, vol. 1, pp. 47–8.

the seizing of an unexpected opportunity to have his music distributed in Germany. At the same time the last couple of sentences are a brutal indication of the musical market in Vienna at the turn of the century. Hoffmeister's edition was published in December 1801.

The enterprise of the Bureau de Musique in Leipzig together with an awareness of Beethoven's growing reputation as reported in the *Allgemeine musikalische Zeitung* seem to have prompted Breitkopf and Härtel (the publisher of the journal) to contact Beethoven, the beginning of a fifteen-year relationship between composer and publisher. From the outset Beethoven used his plans with other publishers to drive more lucrative deals with Breitkopf, often in a deceitful manner. In the early years the Second Symphony was an integral part of this manoeuvring, which now sought to relate musical worth to a financial return.

Most of the correspondence was entrusted to Beethoven's brother, Carl, a civil servant who acted as the composer's secretary. He first replied to a general enquiry from Breitkopf and Härtel in March 1802, suggesting that the firm made an offer for the next concerto (No. 3) and symphony;[16] none was forthcoming until June when the firm offered 200 Bankozettel for each,[17] that is c.44 ducats, more than twice the money that Beethoven had received from Hoffmeister for the First Symphony. Carl could afford to wait before making a reply since neither work was yet complete. Meanwhile, quite unexpectedly an exploratory letter from André of Offenbach was received – it is not known if it was prompted by Paul Wranitzky – which asked whether the firm could publish any new music by the composer. Carl Beethoven replied that there was indeed a symphony and a concerto, and asked for 300 florins each, that is c. 67 ducats, substantially more than Breitkopf and Härtel had offered.[18] The following January Breitkopf and Härtel offered 500 florins (c. 111 ducats) for the two works[19] but, once again, Carl Beethoven prevaricated, this time because a third publisher, the Bureau des Arts et d' Industrie in Vienna, had entered the picture; it offered 700 florins for both works, that is c.77 ducats each.[20] The symphony was published by the Viennese firm in March 1804.

Therefore, in just over two years, the period that separated the publication of the First and the Second Symphony, wily negotiation had resulted

[16] Brandenburg (ed.), *Briefwechsel*, vol. 1, pp. 102–03.
[17] Ibid., vol. 1, p. 113. In the following discussion three currency denominations are encountered: Bankozettel (a paper note), florin (a coin) and ducat (a coin). To aid comprehension the various sums are all given in ducats also, using the standard value of 4.5 florins per ducat. See the comprehensive currency tables in Senner, Wallace and Meredith (eds.), *The Critical Reception*, vol. 1, pp. xv–xviii.
[18] Brandenburg (ed.), *Briefwechsel*, vol. 1, p. 134.　　[19] Ibid., vol. 1, p. 152.
[20] Carl Beethoven to Breitkopf and Härtel, ibid., vol. 1, p. 156.

in a fee for a Beethoven symphony rising from 20 ducats to c.77 ducats. If André's entry into the fray was unaccountably late, then the generous deal for a symphony that was concluded with a Viennese firm, the Bureau des Arts et d'Industrie, is strikingly irregular, going against the norms of publishing practice in the city at the time.

It was a new firm, established in May 1801 by a group of four people, Joseph Sonnleithner, Joseph Schreyvogel, Jakob Hohler and Johann Siegmund Rizy.[21] Also known in its German formulation Kunst- und Industrie-Comptoir, the firm published art engravings and maps as well as music, with the success of the 'Industrie' being used to support the 'Kunst'. The driving force behind the firm was Joseph Sonnleithner (1766–1835), a trained lawyer who worked in the imperial treasury. A keen musician, he developed a penchant for the history of music and began to organize a historical anthology of music, *Geschichte der Musik in Denkmälern*, with Haydn, Albrechtsberger and Salieri as volume editors. After the plates of the first volume were seized by invading French troops in 1805 and used for munitions, the project was abandoned. In 1804 he became the secretary of the two court theatres plus the Theater an der Wien, and was the librettist of Beethoven's *Leonore*. Later, he was to be the first secretary of the Gesellschaft der Musikfreunde. This combination of artistic highmindedness and patriotism can be sensed in the publication practices of the Bureau.

As in the catalogues of Artaria, Mollo, Traeg and other publishers in Vienna, dances, piano music and chamber music dominated, with the names of Eberl, Gyrowetz, Hummel and Krommer featuring extensively; Sonnleithner's interest in older music is revealed in the publications of music by C. P. E. Bach, J. S. Bach, Handel and Scarlatti, as well as some music by his father, Christoph Sonnleithner. Between 1801 and 1814, when Josef Riedl took over the firm, forty-four publications of music by Beethoven were issued, mainly sonatas, chamber music and songs but also three symphonies (Nos. 2, 3 and 4), the Third Piano Concerto and the Violin Concerto. Large-scale items of this nature are very rare in the catalogue of the Bureau and the three symphonies by Beethoven are unique; there are no symphonies by other composers. As always there was no commercial incentive for publishing symphonies in Vienna, with its limited opportunities for performance. When the firm was founded there was an intention that it should have an office in Leipzig too,[22] which would have extended the potential market to Germany and Scandinavia, but nothing came of

---

[21] A. Weinmann, 'Vollständiges Verlagsverzeichnis der Musikalien des Kunst- und Industrie Comptoirs in Wien 1801–1819', *Studien zur Musikwissenschaft*, 22 (1955), pp. 217–52.

[22] Biba (ed.), *"Eben komme ich von Haydn . . .",* p. 130.

this. For Sonnleithner, supporting Beethoven in this way was a novel form of patronage, to be set alongside the sundry fees and gifts the composer received from the aristocracy. The generous fee of c.77 ducats for the Second Symphony was a welcome largesse. The fee received for the *Eroica* symphony is not known but the Bureau paid the equivalent of c. 56 ducats for the Fourth Symphony, published in 1807.[23] By this time inflation had begun seriously to eat into the purchasing power of all income but as an act of patronage it was still notable, even more so given that the raw costs of engraving and printing too had risen.

The generous support of the Bureau des Arts et d'Industrie was only one strand in a web of patronage that allowed Beethoven to compose symphonies in the first years of the nineteenth century. As a house composer at the Theater an der Wien from 1803 and with the particular support of Sonnleithner, he was able to secure the evening of 5 April for a benefit concert in which the Second Symphony received its first performance. Prince Lichnowsky, who had supported Beethoven from his earliest days in Vienna, now provided an annual allowance of 600 gulden. When the customary rehearsal on the day of the concert became fraught, the prince ordered hampers of food and wine to placate the performers. His commitment and generosity were rewarded with the formal dedication of the symphony when it was published by the Bureau – 'composée et dediée à son Altesse Monseigneur le Prince CHARLES DE LICHNOWSKY par Louis van Beethoven' – which, in turn, was very likely rewarded with a further gift, either in money or in kind. Plate 7.1.

Inherently precarious, this pattern of support had continually to be renegotiated and reassembled for Beethoven to maintain a presence as a composer of symphonies. Nevertheless the receipts from the second benefit concert were encouraging, 1800 gulden (400 ducats), and Beethoven, along with his patrons, Sonnleithner and Lichnowsky, would have been equally gratified by the wondrous tone of the review of the published edition that appeared in the *Allgemeine musikalische Zeitung* just over a year later.[24]

It cannot be a matter of indifference to any society of musicians and friends of art that at last a second symphony by Beethoven has just now appeared (engraved in Vienna, in the Kunst- und Industrie-Comptoir). It is a noteworthy, colossal work, of a depth, power, and artistic knowledge like *very few*. It has a level of difficulty,

---

[23] The symphony was sold for 1500 gulden as part of a package of six major items. See Brandenburg (ed.), *Briefwechsel*, vol. 1, pp. 317–18.

[24] *AmZ*, 6 (1803–4), cols. 542–3. English translation from Senner, Wallace and Meredith (eds.), *The Critical Reception*, vol. 1, p. 196.

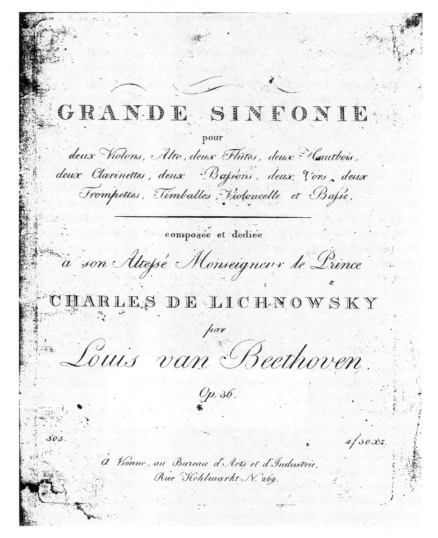

Plate 7.1 Title page of Beethoven, Symphony in D major, op. 36 (Bureau des Arts et d'Industrie, 1804).

both from the point of view of the composer and in regard to its performance by a large orchestra (which it certainly demands), quite certainly unlike *any* symphony that has ever been made known. It demands to be played again and yet again by even the most accomplished orchestra, until the astonishing number of original and sometimes very strangely arranged ideas become closely enough connected, rounded out, and emerge like a great unity, just as the composer had in mind. It must also be heard again and yet again before the listener, even a knowledgeable one, is in a position to follow the details in the entire piece and the entire piece in the details and to enjoy it with enthusiasm in the necessary repose.

By the time this review appeared Beethoven had completed a third symphony, the *Eroica*. Carl and Ludwig van Beethoven were realistic enough to realize that exactly the same pattern of financial support could be not be maintained. A third benefit concert to present, once more, a new symphony and a new piano concerto never materialized, though not for want of trying. As for publication they dangled the symphony in front of no fewer than four firms, Breitkopf and Härtel, Clementi (London), Simrock (Bonn) and George Thomson (Edinburgh), and at one stage Breitkopf and Härtel even began work on printing the symphony; it was finally published by the Bureau des Arts et d' Industrie in Vienna in 1806. But there were new elements of patronage that were accommodated along the way, ones that again provided material support as well as nurturing the exclusive nature of the genre: the interest of Prince Lobkowitz in Beethoven's music and the two series of concerts organized by Joseph Würth and the Liebhaber Concerte.

Prince Lobkowitz had supported Beethoven's career from at least 1795, when he subscribed to six copies of the op. 1 piano trios.[25] Although there is no direct evidence that he attended Beethoven's two benefit concerts in 1800 and 1803 it is very likely that he did. From 1803 to 1808, that is the period covering the *Eroica* Symphony to the *Pastoral* Symphony, he played a decisive part in allowing Beethoven to develop his career as a symphonist. Unlike Lichnowsky he was able to supply direct musical assistance. In the early summer of 1804 he subsidized two rehearsals of the *Eroica* symphony in the Lobkowitz palace that allowed Beethoven to alter the score; a performance of the symphony was given in the Lobkowitz palace in Eisenberg in August, possibly followed by one in October in the family palace in Raudnitz.[26] Back in Vienna in January, Lobkowitz allowed the symphony to be played in Würth's series on 20 January and at his own palace three days later. The fact that these performances were determined by Lobkowitz rather than Beethoven, and that the composer was not even present at the private performances in Bohemia, is explained by the common practice of ceding temporary ownership of a work to a patron in exchange for a fee. In Beethoven's case this process had been

---

[25] See Volek and Macek, 'Beethoven und Fürst Lobkowitz', pp. 203–17.
[26] Brauneis, "'. . . composta per festeggiare'", pp. 59–66, pp. 69–70.

clearly explained by his brother, Carl, in a letter to Breitkopf and Härtel in December 1802.[27]

> ... I shall acquaint you with the manner in which my brother sells his works. We already have 34 works and about 18 [opus] numbers in print. These pieces were mostly commissioned by music lovers, and with the following agreement: he who wants a piece pays a specified sum for its exclusive possession for a half or a whole year, or even longer, and binds himself not to give the manuscript to *anybody*; after this period the author is free to do as he wishes with the piece.

The *Eroica* symphony was subject to this process in 1804–5 for which Beethoven was paid a fee of 700 gulden (c. 156 ducats) by the prince, and circumstantial evidence suggests that the Fifth and Sixth Symphonies were likewise temporarily owned by Lobkowitz in 1808;[28] protocol demanded that all three symphonies were dedicated to the prince when they were published and Beethoven duly obliged. The *Eroica* never featured in a Beethoven benefit concert; its first public performance was given in a benefit concert for the violinist, Franz Clement, at the Theater an der Wien in April 1805. The Fifth and Sixth Symphonies were given their first public performances at Beethoven's third benefit concert, in December 1808, once more alongside a new piano concerto (No. 4).

Beethoven's correspondence in the period during which he composed his first six symphonies repeatedly demonstrates how difficult it was to be a composer of such works in Vienna. At the same time his sketchbooks reveal the musical will to succeed, from initial impulses to protracted reworking. Whereas most composers avoided the genre, Beethoven wrote symphonies despite the prevailing circumstances, an act of defiance that was integral to the composer's artistic outlook. But even Beethoven became tired of the constant manoeuvring, the seeking of performances, publishers and adequate recompense in a period of increasing economic uncertainty, and this largely explains the petition in December 1807 to the court authorities to become an opera composer. There is no doubt that his interest in a potential career in the theatre was borne of real musical enthusiasm; if that enthusiasm could be matched by the expectation of new commissioned works for the stage, regularly supplied and adequately performed, and all for a steady income, then that was an attractively secure existence.

It was at this very moment when Beethoven was seeking a new career that the Liebhaber Concerte began their series. There were no new works by Beethoven but the whole enterprise, with its emphasis on the works of Haydn, Mozart and Beethoven, articulated impulses increasingly apparent

---

[27] Albrecht (ed.), *Letters*, vol. I, p. 86.
[28] See D. W. Jones, *Beethoven. Pastoral Symphony* (Cambridge, 1995). pp. 41–2.

over the previous few years: three great composers, high art, a Viennese tradition and the centrality of the symphony. Had the Liebhaber Concerte moved into a second series, in 1808–9, they would no doubt have featured performances of Beethoven's most recent symphonies, Nos. 5 and 6, as well as repeat performances of earlier symphonies and if, from there, the concerts had become a permanent feature of musical life, they would have provided an unprecendently stable and supportive environment for the composition of symphonies by the composer. Instead, having completed six symphonies in nine years, Beethoven did not return to the genre for nearly four years, composing the Seventh Symphony in the winter of 1811–12 and the Eighth Symphony later in 1812. Lobkowitz was no longer in a position to sponsor private rehearsals and performances, a function that Archduke Rudolph was able in part to fulfil when he paid for a run-through of the two symphonies in his apartments in the Hofburg in April 1813; but the archduke was not able to sponsor private concerts to make sure that the works became more widely known.

Beethoven's attempts to secure an evening for a benefit concert were equally dispiriting. His contempt for the musical scene in Vienna was vented in a letter to Breitkopf and Härtel in May 1812: 'I am composing three new symphonies, one of which is finished . . . But in the sewer [*Kloacke*] in which I here find myself all that work is as good as lost.'[29] Without a performance, publication by Breitkopf and Härtel or anybody else could not be entertained and for a few months in 1813 it seemed that the Seventh and Eighth Symphonies were destined to be the most exclusive of Beethoven's career, savoured by the composer as works of art and heard only by a handful of people in the imperial apartment of an archduke. A very different kind of work, *Wellington's Victory*, led to several performances in the months leading up to the end of the Napoleonic Wars and during the Congress of Vienna. Repeated performances of *Wellington's Victory* first paved the way for the successful revival of *Fidelio* and to Beethoven writing a whole series of patriotic works: a chorus 'Germania, Germania wie stehst du jetzt im Glanze da' for a singspiel called *Die gute Nachricht*; a chorus to welcome the heads of state to the Congress of Vienna, 'Ihr weisen Gründer glücklicher Staaten'; and a cantata, *Der glorreiche Augenblick*. For the first time in his career Beethoven was at the very centre of musical life in Vienna and he was able to present no fewer than five benefit concerts in 1814, on 2 January, 27 February, 29 November, 2 December and 25 December. Lured by the topical fervour of *Wellington's Victory*, audiences were given also

---

[29] 'Three new symphonies' includes preliminary sketches for No. 9. Brandenburg (ed.), *Briefwechsel*, p. 263; English translation from Anderson, *Letters*, vol. 1, p. 372.

the Seventh and Eighth Symphonies; while the relentless jubilation of the former suited the mood of the times, the Eighth Symphony was less well received. Beethoven made a considerable amount of money in 1814 but in the process a good deal of the accumulated prestige attached to the genre was lost too. The symphony had been drowned out by other music.

BEETHOVEN AND EBERL: A FORGOTTEN RIVALRY

Prestige and individuality of utterance in Beethoven's first eight symphonies may be seen as the product of a creative friction between the musical environment in Vienna and the towering musical genius of the composer. The nineteenth century often detached Beethoven from this environment, while Vienna itself invented a hazy musical past that hallowed the composer. A crucial element in this construction was the 'Viennese Classical School' which presented the city as a continuing beneficial force that had developed and promoted the talents of Haydn, Mozart and Beethoven. For Beethoven the symphonist it became a fundamental truth that he built on the musical accomplishment of only these composers, viewpoints that were already nascent in the first years of the century.[30] Even while he was still active as a composer of symphonies, Paul Wranitzky was being excluded from this historical agenda and was completely forgotten as a symphony composer within a few years of his death in 1808. A more intriguing figure in this historical process was Anton Eberl, who composed symphonies at the same time as Beethoven, presented them alongside those of Beethoven in several concerts, and provoked comparison that was not always to the benefit of Beethoven. This was a very different relationship to the one between Beethoven and Haydn, or between Beethoven and Mozart; here was a contemporary who had his own ideas on how the symphony might develop. It was the only time in Beethoven's life that he had a rival. Table 7.1 summarizes their careers as composers of symphonies between 1803 and 1806.

Anton Eberl's name is absent from most modern biographies of Beethoven, largely a consequence, one imagines, of the fact that it does not crop up in any correspondence associated with the composer or figure to any extent in the rich anecdotal heritage. The only known contemporaneous biographical remark that links the two occurs in the diaries of Joseph Carl

---

[30] For a broader consideration of the origins of these outlooks see O. Biba '"Grundsäulen der Tonkunst" – Von der Enstehung des Bildes der klassischen Trias', *Wiener Klassik. Ein musikgeschichtlicher Begriff in Diskussion*, ed. G. Gruber (Vienna, 2002), pp. 53–63; and R. Flotzinger, 'Herkunft und Bedeutung des Ausdrucks "(Wiener) Klassik"', ibid., pp. 41–52.

Table 7.1. *The symphonic careers of Beethoven and Eberl, 1803–6*

Beethoven	Eberl
1803 c. June–October, *Eroica* symphony composed	1803 private performance(s) of E♭ symphony in Lobkowitz palace(s)?
1804 May–August/October, private rehearsal and performances of *Eroica* in Lobkowitz's palaces in Vienna and Bohemia	1804 6 January, performance of E♭ symphony at Eberl's benefit concert, Jahnscher Saal Summer, performance of E♭ symphony at Augarten concerts
1805 20 January, performance of *Eroica* at Würth's concert, Vienna 23 January, performance of *Eroica* in Lobkowitz palace, Vienna 7 April, public performance of *Eroica*, Theater an der Wien	1805 25 January, first performance of D minor symphony at Eberl's benefit concert, Jahnscher Saal 27 January, performance of E♭ symphony at Würth's concert 1 May, performance of D minor symphony at Augarten concert
1805–6	1805–6 Both symphonies published in Leipzig: E♭ (Kühnel), D minor (Breitkopf and Härtel)
1806 October, *Eroica* published by Bureau des Arts et d' Industrie, Vienna Symphony No. 4 composed	

Rosenbaum who, after attending Beethoven's second benefit concert in the Theater an der Wien on 5 April 1803, wrote the following.[31]

At the Lusthaus [in the Prater], I talked with Willmann [a cellist] about Beethoven's academy; he spoke highly of it, although I heard just the opposite from everyone else. – Eberl told me that Beethoven did not measure up to the public's expectations at his academy yesterday; nothing was entirely worthy of a great master.

At the time of the first performance of the Second Symphony Eberl was completing his symphony in E♭ and if, as is likely, the eventual dedication to Lobkowitz implies that he was able to give private performances in the period before the public one in January 1804, then there is the tantalizing possibility that Beethoven may have heard the work as he was working on his symphony in E♭. The appearance of a march in C minor for the slow movement of Eberl's work, instead of the more traditional approach of a

[31] E. Radant, 'The Diaries of Joseph Carl Rosenbaum 1770–1829', *Haydn Yearbook*, 5 (1968), p. 107.

tuneful movement in B♭ (as in Haydn Nos. 76, 84 and 91, Paul Wranitzky P32 and Anton Wranitzky E♭1), is the only direct point of correspondence, but a striking one; it is not difficult to imagine Beethoven taking the idea of a C minor march that turned to C major, and transforming it into the emotive drama of the *Marcia funebre*.

When these two symphonies in E♭ were performed in successive weeks in Würth's concerts in January 1805 they prompted a comparison that was very much to the detriment of Beethoven's symphony: Eberl's symphony seemed to offer a more satisfactory development of the genre forward from Beethoven's First Symphony (played on 13 January), the *Eroica* was a step too far.[32] After a few months of reflection and having heard the *Eroica* once more, at Clement's benefit concert in the Theater an der Wien, the same critic expanded a little on his concerns.[33]

To be sure, this new work of B. has great and daring ideas, and, as one can expect from the genius of this composer, great power in the way it is worked out; but the symphony would improve immeasurably (it lasts an entire hour) if B. could bring himself to shorten it, and to bring more light, clarity, and unity into the whole. These are qualities that are in Mozart's Symphonies in G minor and C major, Beethoven's in C and D, and Eberl's in E♭ and D which, with all their wealth of ideas, all their interweaving of the instruments, and all their interchange of surprising modulations, are never lost at any point.

The same critic also attended the performance of Eberl's D minor symphony at the Augarten on 1 May after which he once again mentions the composer alongside Haydn, Mozart and Beethoven.[34]

. . . a mighty, daring poem, in which the strength of this composer and the fire of his soul freely and audaciously breaks forth. Great vigour lies in the last fugal movement, and an entirely splendid instrumental effect in the beautiful march. Since the symphonies of Mozart, Haydn and Beethoven virtually nothing in this genre has appeared to date that can be regarded so honourably.

---

[32] See pp. 121–2. Anton Schindler quoted the remarks on the *Eroica* in his biography of the composer, before adding a couple of disdainful sentences. 'There follows in contrast a eulogy of a new symphony by Eberl. Our master was thus given to understand that he would do better to write in a similar style.' In a footnote Schindler gives some information on Eberl, ending with the dismissive comment 'None of his works have survived.' D. W. Macardle (ed.), *Beethoven as I knew him. A Biography by Anton Felix Schindler* (London, 1966), p. 117.

Indicative of the way modern Beethoven scholarship has continued to sideline Eberl is the reproduction of the criticism in the following two volumes, where the sentences on Beethoven First Symphony and the *Eroica* are included but not the favourable remarks on Eberl's symphony. Senner, Wallace and Meredith (eds.), *The Critical Reception*, vol. 1, pp. 167–8; and S. Kunze (ed.), *Die Werke im Spiegel seiner Zeit. Gesammelte Konzertberichte und Rezensionen bis 1830* (Laaber, 1996), p. 50.

[33] *AmZ*, 7 (1804–5), cols. 501–2; English translation from Senner, Wallace and Meredith (eds.), *The Critical Reception*, vol. 2. p. 17.

[34] *AmZ*, 7 (1804–5), col. 536.

It is highly likely that Beethoven knew these two symphonies by Eberl, equally likely that he read the criticism in the *Allgemeine musikalische Zeitung*. Nothing is known about Beethoven's views on Eberl and his symphonies, views that almost certainly would have helped to sharpen perception of Beethoven's own outlook as a composer of symphonies at this crucial time. The critic of the *Allgemeine musikalische Zeitung* repeatedly mentions length and complexity as attributes that separate Beethoven from Eberl, but another characteristic, the programmatic impulse of the *Eroica* symphony is noticeable by its absence from these observations. There was a simple reason for this: Beethoven's symphony did not have a title at this stage. Between the summer and autumn of the previous year Beethoven had famously changed his mind about calling the work 'Bonaparte'[35] and there is no mention of Napoleon in any of the reviews that appeared in the *Allgemeine musikalische Zeitung* in 1805; the work is habitually and simply referred to as a Symphony in E♭. Unfortunately, the parts prepared for Lobkowitz and used in Würth's concert in January and, very likely, Clement's benefit in March have not survived and whether they were similarly headed cannot be determined.[36] By the time the symphony was published in October 1806 by the local firm of Bureau des Arts et d'Industrie, the composer had decided to aid performance and comprehension in two ways: there was now a title, *Sinfonia Eroica*, and a suggestion that the work be placed at or near the beginning of the concert to avoid tiring the listener. These accommodating measures were a considered response to the criticism in the *Allgemeine musikalische Zeitung* in 1805, but since that criticism was usually coupled with complimentary comments on Eberl's two symphonies they can also be read as tacit acknowledgement by Beethoven of Eberl's success.

It is a measure of Eberl's confidence and imagination as a composer of symphonies that the new work he produced at his second benefit concert, in January 1805, was quite different from the E♭ symphony. Eberl was striving to create an individual identity for each new symphony and these two symphonies are as contrasted as any pair by Beethoven. While it is impossible to state whether Eberl had heard the *Eroica* before embarking on the D minor symphony – the likelihood is that he had not – he was confident enough to find his own way forward as an innovative composer, using some of the same means to stretch the emotional range of the genre that appealed to Beethoven, namely a march (first movement) and a fugue (finale).

[35] T. Sipe, *Beethoven. Eroica Symphony* (Cambridge, 1998), pp. 50–51.

[36] For a list of surviving manuscript and published sources of Beethoven's music in the Lobkowitz library see Fojtíková and Volek, 'Die Beethoveniana der Lobkowitz-Musiksammlung', pp. 221–3.

The view that Beethoven's First Symphony was a considered response to the symphonies of Haydn and Mozart, and that the Second and, especially, the *Eroica* were the symphonies that staked out the composer's independence are ingrained in perception and understanding, covenanted truths even. It has already been suggested that the stylistic background to the First Symphony needs to be expanded to include other composers like Paul Wranitzky and Krommer. For that work this wider repertoire provided the common language from which Beethoven fashioned a personal response. Knowledge of Eberl's symphonies from the period 1803–5 invites a similar broadening outlook on the course of Beethoven's career as a symphonist, and at a particularly decisive time. Similar, but not identical, since Eberl's and Beethoven's symphonies from 1803 onwards are not part of a wider lingua franca, but resolutely progressive and individual statements. Beethoven is incontestably the greater composer; but Eberl deserves better than whitewash.

BEETHOVEN AND THE PROGRAMME SYMPHONY

Beethoven's three programme symphonies are spread evenly across his symphonic output from 1799 to 1813, the *Eroica* in 1803, the *Pastoral* Symphony five years later in 1808, and *Wellington's Victory* a further five years later in 1813. Their subject matter, individual and universal heroism, followed by the escapist, partly secular, partly sacred world of the pastoral, and, finally, the graphic evocation of battle and victory were familiar ones to Beethoven's audiences and, as Richard Will has demonstrated, constitute a continuation and a culmination of practices in the classical symphony that go back several decades.[37] Within the Viennese tradition at the turn of the century there were some figures, notably Eberl and Krommer, who did not compose any programme symphonies, and the emerging image of Mozart the symphonist in the early 1800s, as projected by the handful of late symphonies that constituted the repertoire at the time, was also of a composer who did not write programme symphonies. Haydn's situation was more ambiguous; none of the London symphonies has a declared programme but the 'Military' symphony (No. 100) enjoyed particular popularity at the time because of the topicality of the slow movement, a march that runs the full gamut of mood, from the daintily ceremonial to the gruesome.

In the 1790s and early 1800s it was the symphonies of the Wranitzky brothers that most frequently provided the context for Beethoven's three

---

[37] Will, *The Characteristic Symphony*.

programme symphonies. At one stage Beethoven wanted to give the title 'Bonaparte' to the third symphony and dedicate it to the eponymous hero, an outlook that was in keeping with the mood of contemporary politics in Austria; Beethoven's well-known change of mind coincided with a shift in the diplomatic position of Austria, when it entered into a defensive alliance with Russia against France.[38] Symphonies for and about temporal leaders had been written by Anton Wranitzky (the 1796 birthday symphony for Prince Lobkowitz) and, especially, Paul Wranitzky (symphonies concerning the Hungarian diplomacy of Joseph II and Leopold II, the election of Franz II as Holy Roman Emperor, and the marriages of Archduke Joseph and of Count Nicolaus Esterházy). Whereas the subject matter of Anton Wranitzky's symphony produced a work that was intimately bound up with its subject matter, the programmatic content of Paul Wranitzky's symphonies was conveniently imprecise in each case to allow the music to stand on its own feet, in particular to take its part in the familiar tradition of jubilant works in C and D major. For his musical tribute, Beethoven steered a different course from Anton and Paul Wranitzky, choosing the more unusual key of E♭ major for such a work. As already mentioned the perplexed reception that the symphony received when it was performed in private and public in Vienna in 1805 was due to its length and complexity. By suppressing a title and not writing a work in C or D, Beethoven had also made it difficult for his audience to relate the work to a local tradition.

Paul Wranitzky's most celebrated programme symphony had been the *Grand Characteristic Symphony for the Peace with the French Republic*, composed in 1797. Given its French subject matter and the inclusion of a funeral march in C minor it is tempting to link the work with the *Eroica*, but these points of contact are precisely that, and nothing more.[39] The detailed programme of the work alters the internal structure of the symphony to such an extent that Wranitzky's symphony cannot be appreciated without it. Its journey from 'The Revolution' in C minor to 'Jubilation at the Restoration of the Peace' in C major has parallels with the emotional course of Beethoven's Fifth Symphony but, again, claiming particular significance for Wranitzky's work would be inappropriate. The sources of both Beethoven's C minor style and of the C minor to C major trajectory within one work are much wider than the symphonic tradition, never mind one work within that tradition. As an orchestral work Wranitzky's *Grand Characteristic Symphony* has much more in common with Beethoven's *Wellington's Victory*

[38] Sipe, *Eroica Symphony*, pp. 39–51.
[39] For an alternative view see Will, *Characteristic Symphony*, pp. 209–10.

which similarly collapses the tautness of a standard four-movement struc-ture in favour of a series of vivid contrasts held together by a narrative.

Between them, the *Eroica* symphony and *Wellington's Victory* denote the range of musical experience covered by the term programme symphony, from a work that takes the extra-musical as a point of departure in order to explore it in heightened abstraction to a work in which the extra-musical controls rather than liberates the composition. Moving in the most beguil-ing way between these two opposites is the *Pastoral* Symphony, a highly sophisticated exploration of these tensions, summarized in the composer's cautionary injunction 'More the expression of feeling than painting' ('Mehr Ausdruck der Empfindung als Malerei').[40] Although the pastoral as a local musical topic features from time to time in Viennese symphonies composed in the 1790s and early 1800s, whole works devoted to its resonant imagery are few in number. Ditterdorf's Ovid symphonies, composed in the 1780s, were forgotten works by 1800; Hoffmeister composed a symphony in F major in 1793 to which he gave the title *La primavera*, but no detailed programme. Anton Wranitzky's symphony, *Aphrodite*, is a rare, probably unique example from Beethoven's time. As a private tribute that belonged to the exclusive world of the Lobkowitz court, the symphony may not have been performed after 1792 and Beethoven may never have heard it, but, once more, the composer's reach in the *Pastoral* Symphony was wider than one earlier work in the same tradition.

PRIVATE AND PUBLIC AUDIENCES FOR BEETHOVEN'S SYMPHONIES

As well as the distinct decline in the popularity of the symphony that occurred in Vienna between c.1790 and c.1815, there was the associated move of the symphony from the private surroundings of the court to the public arena of the concert hall: from numerous works written for a small audience to fewer works written for a large audience. But this broad brush view of the audience for the symphony is replete with problems and con-tradictions. Even in the eighteenth century the division had never been a hard and fast one, with works performed in private also being performed in public and with the locus of a church service often acting as a kind of public concert. The notion of a concert hall is itself also difficult. In many aristocratic palaces there was a designated music room associated with

---

[40] See Jones, *Pastoral Symphony*, pp. 25–80; Will, *Characteristic Symphony*, pp. 156–87; and R. Will, 'The Nature of the Pastoral Symphony', *Beethoven Forum*, 9 (2002), pp. 205–15.

performances; in the city of Vienna, on the other hand, there was no purpose built public concert hall until 1831 when one was opened in the Tuch-
lauben by the Gesellschaft der Musikfreunde[41] and, instead, symphonies
were performed in theatres and multi-purpose halls such as the Jahnscher
Saal, the Mehlgrube, the Kleiner and Grosser Redoutensaal, and the hall
of the university.[42] Peculiar to the city were performances of symphonies
for a clientele that was neither totally private nor totally public, such as
the audience that attended the Liebhaber Concerte in its one and only season in 1807–08. If one then extends the definition of an audience beyond
merely the people who sat (or stood) listening to a performance to embrace
a broader ambience of critical debate and evaluation that influenced the
reception of the symphony then this, too, is complex in Vienna. There is
ample anecdotal and circumstantial evidence that music was a subject of
constant debate, casual and informed, but discussion in print was, to all
intents and purposes, non-existent. Unlike Leipzig, London and Paris, in
particular, writing about music was not a constant and determining part
of the culture until after the Napoleonic Wars. Before that the only regular
source of comment and debate are the reports submitted to the *Allgemeine
musikalische Zeitung* in Leipzig, reports which by definition become less
Viennese and more *Allgemeine*, 'universal', in import.

For the most part, Haydn's symphonic output can be accommodated
under the division of private and public, court and concert hall, without too
much distortion. Most of his symphonies were written for the aristocratic
courts of the Morzin and Esterházy families; the London symphonies, on
the other hand, are perfect examples of a successful symbiotic relationship
between the composer and the wider public sustained over a number of
years. Only the Paris symphonies (Nos. 82–87), to which could be added
Nos. 88–92 also destined for the city, do not fit into this neat division
of private and public: written at Eszterháza, were they composed with
Parisian orchestras, concert halls and audiences in mind, an environment
that Haydn never experienced, or do they represent a natural enhancement
of the Esterházy court symphonies?

Beethoven was never to experience the stable environments, the equivalent of the Esterházy court or the London concert halls, that enabled
Haydn to produce his symphonies, and the concept of the intended audience for Beethoven's symphonies is an equivocal one. In this Beethoven was

[41] Hanslick, *Geschichte des Concertwesens*, vol. 1, pp. 289–90.
[42] For a survey of concert locations in the period see Biba, 'Concert Life in Beethoven's Vienna', pp. 77–
93; and H. Ullrich, 'Aus vormärzlichen Konzertsälen Wiens', *Jahrbuch des Vereins für Geschichte der
Stadt Wien*, 28 (1972), pp. 106–30.

not alone since similar shifting circumstances governed the symphonies of other composers, particularly Anton Eberl and Paul Wranitzky.

As a youth Beethoven's entire experience of the symphony was as a private work performed at court, in Bonn, and had the French Revolution not taken its course he would have returned to this environment in the 1790s. The First and Second Symphonies were always intended for public performance, staple works in the benefit concerts at the Burgtheater in 1800 and the Theater an der Wien in 1803. The *Eroica*, Fifth and Sixth Symphonies were also ultimately destined for public performance but were first performed in private at the Lobkowitz court. Meanwhile, following a visit to the estate of Count Franz Joachim Oppersdorff in Oberglogau (Głogów), Silesia, Beethoven was commissioned to write a symphony for the count's orchestra, No. 4, subsequently dedicated to him. Nos. 7 and 8 were again first performed as public works, in the hall of the university in 1813 and in the Grosser Redoutensaal in 1814 respectively; there were no preliminary performances in private. Whether initially performed in private or public, many of these symphonies soon appeared in the opposite milieu as when Beethoven on arriving in Oberglogau was greeted by the court orchestra of servants playing his Second Symphony.

If the history of the venues associated with early performances of Beethoven's symphonies suggests that a division into private and public is not a helpful one, then the evidence of performance practice relating to the size of orchestras indicates, rather surprisingly, that there was no longer a meaningful difference between a court orchestra and a public orchestra. Beethoven's First Symphony was played at the Burgtheater using the theatre orchestra, a total of thirty-six players with a string section of twelve violins (probably six firsts, six seconds), four violas, three cellos and four double basses.[43] The orchestra of the Theater an der Wien was of a similar size, about thirty-six players.[44] The performing forces at the charity concerts of the Tonkünstler-Societät were typically very large for oratorios and other choral works but in 1792, when a Haydn symphony was on the programme, the orchestra was reduced to thirty-three, a practice that may have existed in other years.[45] An orchestra of about thirty-five players with a similar disposition of strings is the one suggested by surviving manuscript sources for symphonies in the Lobkowitz library, as well as by surviving documents.[46]

[43] Schönfeld, *Jahrbuch* pp. 92–3. Theodore Albrecht has shown that Schönfeld's lists of players in the various theatres reflect payrolls from 1794; T. Albrecht, 'Anton Dreyssig: Mozart's and Beethoven's *Zauberflötist*', *Words About Mozart. Essays in Honour of Stanley Sadie*, ed. D. Link and J. Nagley (Woodbridge, 2005), p. 184.

[44] Albrecht, 'Anton Dreyssig', p. 187.   [45] Biba, 'Concert Life', p. 88.

[46] See discussion in Chapter 3, p. 44, p. 46.

Although the size of the orchestra, about thirty-five, was similar whether the performance was in private at a Lobkowitz palace or in public in a theatre, the impact that the music made must have been very different, clangorous and sometimes overpowering in the 120 square metres of the Lobkowitz music room in the Vienna palace,[47] more agreeable, though probably rather unfocused in the theatres. The Burgtheater held an audience of 1300 in comfort, a few hundred more in discomfort; the Theater an der Wien was a larger theatre, capable of holding in excess of 2000. The music room in the Lobkowitz palace is known to have had eighteen benches with back support for the listeners;[48] and it probably held no more than about thirty in comfort. The Liebhaber Concerte, playing to an audience of 1000 in the hall of the university, a rather resonant room with a high ceiling, could call on a orchestra of fifty-five players, larger than the norm. The difference was entirely due to the number of strings, thirteen first violins, twelve second violins, seven violas, six cellos and four double basses, and a reflection of the number of amateur players who wished to participate in the series.[49] That Beethoven himself was not averse to large-scale performances of his symphonies if the venue was a suitable one is suggested by the size of the orchestra that took part in his benefit concert in the Grosser Redoutensaal on 27 February 1814. The room held between 600 and 1000 people[50] and the Seventh and Eighth Symphonies, plus *Wellington's Victory*, were given by an orchestra of over 120 with double wind; Beethoven gleefully recorded in his *Tagebuch* that 'at my last concert in the Grosser Redoutensaal there were 18 first violins, 18 second violins, 14 violas, 12 violoncellos, 7 contrabasses, 2 contrabassoons'.[51] When *Wellington's Victory* was published by Steiner in 1816, it included a preface signed by the composer that offered advice on performance, including the succinct statement, 'the larger the room, the greater the forces',[52] a remark particularly suited to the work in question but which Beethoven may well have regarded as a general principle for his symphonies.

Although the history of Beethoven's symphonies up to 1814 suggests a collapsing of the distinction between a court symphony and a public symphony in terms of intended venue and performance practice, it would be a mistake to dismiss private patronage as a formative force in the developing

---

[47] For a full description of the room see Brauneis, '". . . composta per festeggiare', pp. 72–3.

[48] Volek and Macek, 'Beethoven und Fürst Lobkowitz', p. 208.

[49] Biba, 'Beethoven und die "Liebhaber Concerte"', pp. 87–92.   [50] Biba, 'Concert Life', p. 84.

[51] M. Solomon, 'Beethoven's Tagebuch of 1812–1818', *Beethoven Studies 3*, ed. A Tyson (Cambridge, 1982), p. 222. Albrecht (ed.), *Letters*, vol. 2, pp. 26–7, pp. 30–33.

[52] *Beethoven Werke II/I. Ouvertüren und Wellingtons Sieg*, ed. H.-W. Küthen (Munich, 1974), p. 124.

CHAPTER 8

The reformulation of the symphony and Beethoven

WAITING FOR A TRADITION, 1815–19

For Beethoven, the years immediately after the end of the Napoleonic Wars were uncharacteristically fallow ones. Between 1815 and 1819 only three major works were completed, the 'Hammerklavier' sonata and the two cello sonatas of op. 102. For a while in 1818 he worked intermittently on the first movement of a new symphony (No. 9) but put it aside the following year in favour of the more urgent task of composing the Missa Solemnis. Other major works, including a piano concerto and a piano trio, were begun in this period but were destined never to be completed. For later commentators this hiatus in composition provided a convenient point of demarcation between the composer's middle and late periods, and for the composer's symphonies an appropriate period of contemplation before the epochal Ninth could be brought to fruition.

For the symphony in general in Vienna the years between 1815 and 1819 constituted a period of renewed activity, measured in progress but not one that suddenly thrust the genre into prominence. The Gesellschaft der Musikfreunde presented four concerts each season in the Grosser Redouten-saal that deliberately espoused a range of music, orchestral, virtuoso, oper-atic and choral, with new fashionable composers like Paer, Rossini and Voříšek heard along the venerable Cherubini, Handel and Mozart. The symphonic repertoire belonged firmly to the venerable category. With one exception, a symphony in Eb by the German composer Friedrich Fesca per-formed in 1818, all the repertoire consisted of old works, by Haydn, Mozart and Beethoven.[1]

Outside the concerts of the Gesellschaft der Musikfreunde the symphony was rarely encountered. The bi-annual concerts of the Tonkünstler-Societät remained a highlight of the musical calendar, presenting large-scale perfor-mances of choral works, especially by Handel and Haydn. The featured

---

[1] Hanslick, *Geschichte*, vol. 1, pp. 156–7. Fesca symphony identified in *AmZ*, 20 (1818), col. 389.

work in the two Lenten concerts in 1817 was Beethoven's *Christus am Oelberge*, a comparatively short work that, unusually, allowed the society to present two instrumental works, Beethoven's Seventh Symphony and a polonaise for flute and orchestra by an unidentified composer.[2] Encouraged by political stability and increasing economic confidence, one-off benefit concerts increased noticeably in number in the years immediately after the end of the Napoleonic Wars, to the point that the regular reports of the Viennese correspondent of the *Allgemeine musikalische Zeitung* increasingly resembled a calendar of events rather than an account of two or three musical evenings. In the issue of 30 April 1817 he enthusiastically reported on the activities that had taken place the previous February: 'the 25th was one of the most musically rich days in the history of Vienna, with no fewer than five public concerts, as well as several private music events.' 'Musically rich' did not, however, mean that the symphony was central. At midday there was the fourth concert of the Gesellschaft der Musikfreunde which included Haydn's 'Drumroll' symphony (No. 103) alongside an aria by Simon Mayr (1763–1845), a Phantasy and Polonaise for piano by Nicolaus Krufft (1779–1818) played by Hohenadel, and a cantata, *Frühlingsfeier*, by Maximilian Stadler (1748–1833). In the evening there were three benefit concerts in three different theatres: at the Theater an der Wien for the benefit of the Barmherzige Brüder there was a mixed programme of overtures, vocal numbers, chamber music, two tableaux and two readings; at the Leopoldstadt Theatre a benefit for an actor named Einweg offered a concert of instrumental and vocal music plus recitations and a mime, all framed by the first and last movement of a symphony by Krommer; while at the Josephstadt Theatre the music director, Merk, had his benefit, sixteen miscellaneous items beginning with the first movement of a symphony in C by Mozart. Also in Leopoldstadt, at the Saal zum Sperl, a regimental Kapellmeister named Martin Scholl presented a concert.[3]

Beethoven's Seventh Symphony had enjoyed considerable popular success in 1813–14 and for a few years afterwards it was the most frequently performed of all symphonies in Vienna; in addition to the performances presented by the Gesellschaft der Musikfreunde and the Tonkünstler-Societät, it was performed at a charity concert in December 1816 for the Bürgerspital[4] and at another charity concert for the Austrian army in April 1818;[5] the popular slow movement was performed at a charity concert for the widows of lawyers given in the university in July 1817.[6] A comparatively new

---

[2] Pohl, *Tonkünstler-Societät*, p. 70.   [3] *AmZ*, 19 (1817), cols. 304–6.
[4] *AmZ*, 19 (1817), col. 65.   [5] *AmZ*, 20 (1818), col. 387.   [6] *AmZ*, 19 (1817), col. 584.

publishing force in Vienna, S. A. Steiner & Comp., played a part in promoting the popularity of this work. As part of the contract it signed with the composer in April 1815, the firm agreed to publish the Seventh and Eighth Symphonies and a number of other works over the next few years. The two symphonies appeared in 1816–17 in several formats, including score, parts, and arrangements for Harmonie, string quintet, piano trio, piano duet, two pianos and solo piano; the arrangements were clearly meant to subsidize the sale of scores and parts.[7] Later, in the 1820s, Steiner acquired the stock of the Bureau des Arts et d'Industrie, including the parts for Beethoven's Symphonies Nos. 2, 3 and 4.[8] As had been the case with the Bureau des Arts et d'Industrie, these five symphonies were the only ones issued by the firm.

Even if only fitfully demonstrated in the years immediately after the end of the Napoleonic wars Beethoven's position as a composer of symphonies was recognized and was already casting a shadow over the development of the genre. One of his longest acquaintances was the viola player Franz Weiss (1778–1830), a member of Schuppanzigh's quartet from the mid-1790s. He was also a competent composer who at a benefit concert in the Grosser Redoutensaal on 5 March 1818 presented the first performance of a symphony in C he had composed. The review in the *Allgemeine musikalische Zeitung* was scathing.[9] The correspondent did not doubt that the composition had cost him a good deal of effort but the result was a mongrel species ('Bastarden-Geschlecht') that brought the composer no honour. Rather more sympathetically, yet at the same time very evocatively, he then outlines the challenge facing any young composer of symphonies.

Should, then, Beethoven always be the only model for our artistic youth, and the reef on which the lighter vessel of many an otherwise not unskilled seaman is smashed? Is it just not that Beethoven's individuality is so complete that it suits him alone, and can find favour, also the most skilled imitation, in no-one?

As a genre the symphony was in an awkward position, venerated and vulnerable at the same time. While composers of operas, concertos, quartets, piano music and songs could pursue careers in a musical environment that encouraged their composition and did not subject them to comparison with past achievements, composers of symphonies who did manage to overcome the practical obstacles and write new symphonies would almost certainly be found wanting. Over the next few years, instead of making

---

[7] A. Weinmann, *Vollständiges Verlagsverzeichnis Senefelder, Steiner, Haslinger. Band 1: A. Senefelder, Chemische Druckerey, S. A. Steiner, S. Steiner & Comp. (Wien 1803–1826)* (Munich, 1979), pp. 143–4.
[8] Ibid., pp. 215–6.   [9] *AmZ*, 20 (1818), col. 294–5.

the musical environment more conducive to the composition of new symphonies, Vienna did the opposite, cementing musical values that were to govern the perception of the genre for ever.

From 1819 onwards musical life in Vienna acquired a public concert life that was at last characterized by stability and durability. The Gesellschaft der Musikfreunde was proving to be an institution of permanence, dependent not on the impresario-like initiative of one individual but on a web of committees and procedures that ensured a continued presence even if it sometimes also emasculated musical judgement and initiative. Within ten years of its founding, it was already an institution of real consequence. Its archive was growing, notably boosted by the acquisition of most of Gerber's library in 1819, the training of young musicians in the conservatoire was already yielding dividends, a regular series of chamber music concerts (Musikalische Abendunterhaltung) was well established, as was the annual pattern of four vocal and orchestral concerts across the winter season. Held in the Grosser Redoutensaal for up to 1000 members of the society, the last-mentioned always included a symphony. Table 8.1 lists the symphonies performed in the ten-year period, 1819–28.

Beethoven's presence as a symphonist is overwhelming, twenty performances, almost half the total number, with Nos. 2, 3 and 5 the most frequently performed; the least frequently performed was the *Pastoral* Symphony, an indication of the increasing insensitivity of the new age to this work. Mozart's symphonies, including the last three, were performed on seven occasions while Krommer, now in his sixties, saw an unexpected renewal of his symphonic career with five performances. Before considering further implications of this symphonic repertoire the activities of a second concert organization in Vienna need to be presented.

One of the most industrious committee members of the Gesellschaft der Musikfreunde was Franz Xaver Gebauer (1784–1822), Kapellmeister at the Augustinerkirche. Born in Eckersdorf (Kłodzko), he moved to Vienna in 1810 where he soon earned a reputation as a piano teacher. In 1816 he was made Kapellmeister at the Augustinerkirche where he set about improving the quality of the liturgical music, both in repertoire and standard of performance. Unlike most church musicians in Vienna, Gebauer was anxious to be involved with music elsewhere in the city. In 1819 he changed his weekly rehearsal of liturgical music into a 'practice-concert'

Table 8.1. *Symphonies performed at the concerts of the Gesellschaft der Musikfreunde, 1819–28*

Year	Haydn	Mozart	Beethoven	Others
1819	–	–	Nos. 2, 3	Fesca in E♭
1820	–	C	Nos. 3, 5, 8	Krommer in C minor
1821	–	–	Nos. 4, 7	Lannoy in E, Krommer
1822	–	K551	Nos. 1, 5	Romberg in E♭
1823	–	–	No. 2	Voříšek in D, Krommer in C minor, Krommer in D
1824	No. 101	K551	No. 8	–
1825		K543	Nos. 3, 4	Ries in D
1826		D, K550	Nos. 2, 7	–
1827	–	–	Nos. 1, 6, 9 (mts. 1 and 2)	Krommer in C minor
1828	–	K551	Nos. 5, 8	Schubert No. 6 (D589)

The information is taken from the following sources: C. F. Pohl, *Die Gesellschaft der Musik-freunde des österreichischen Kaiserstaates und ihr Conservatorium* (Vienna, 1871), pp. 73–83; and E. Hanslick, *Geschichte des Concertwesens in Wien* (Vienna, 1869), vol. 1, pp. 157–60. In both sources the information is presented according to calendar year rather than concert season (autumn to spring). Supplementary information has been taken from the *Allgemeine musikalische Zeitung*. Individual works have been identified only where there is no doubt.

(*Übungs-Konzert*). On payment of a subscription, singers and instrumentalists were invited to attend a rehearsal every other Thursday or Friday in the Mehlgrube between four and six. Alongside liturgical works for the Augustinerkirche, the evening included a run-through of a symphony. Interested observers could purchase an entrance ticket for the entire season of eighteen concerts. By the second season, 1820–21, the evenings were known as the Concerts Spirituels and had caught the imagination of all high-minded musicians in Vienna. Plate 8.1 shows the handbill for the first concert of the 1821–22 season with the indication that the mass (Beethoven's Mass in C) will be given as part of the service at the Augustinerkirche on the following Sunday. The critic of the *Allgemeine musikalische Zeitung* indicated his approval by quoting an unidentified local newspaper.[10]

... all bravura singing, even all arias and instrumental concertos are excluded from their productions, and only old and new church music, the best choruses in a high style and symphonies are included. This precept appropriately indicates the serious

---

[10] *AmZ*, 23 (1821), col. 456.

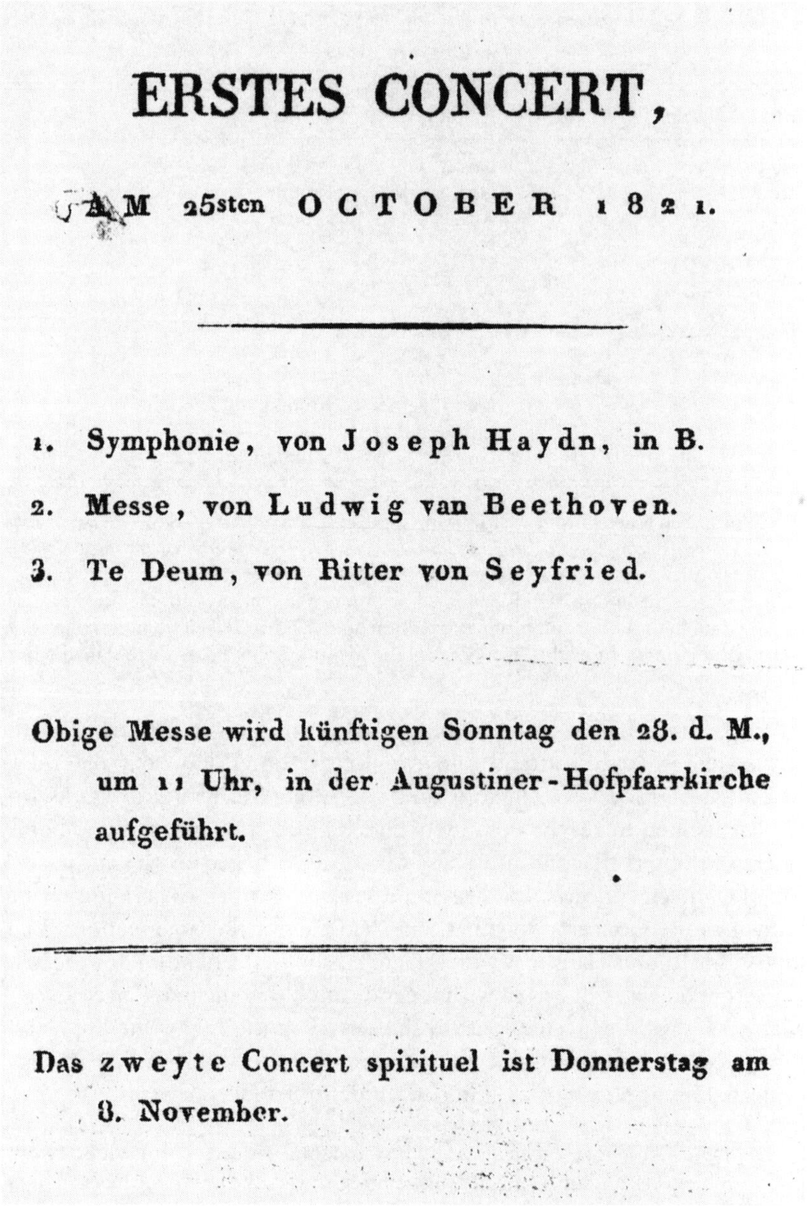

ERSTES CONCERT,

AM 25sten OCTOBER 1821.

1. Symphonie, von Joseph Haydn, in B.

2. Messe, von Ludwig van Beethoven.

3. Te Deum, von Ritter von Seyfried.

Obige Messe wird künftigen Sonntag den 28. d. M., um 11 Uhr, in der Augustiner-Hofpfarrkirche aufgeführt.

Das zweyte Concert spirituel ist Donnerstag am 8. November.

Plate 8.1 Handbill for the first concert of the 1821–22 season of the Concerts Spirituels.

character affirmed by the institute; and annual experience proves the unflinching vigilance with which Herr Gebauer and his assembled friends implacably keep to their plan. It is appropriate, therefore, to regard this unity as a dam for true art, built with ever more zealous and worthy conviction; a bulwark set against the universal and prevailing pressures of decorated and contorted taste behind which the friend of beauty can flee, and for two hours be certain that nothing of trios and caprices, pauses and staccatos, sforzandos and ritardandos, polonaises and bagatelles, cadenzas and reminiscences will figure.

In the following season the Concerts Spirituels moved to the Landständischer Saal, a larger room capable of holding up to 300 people and with good acoustics. In December 1822 Gebauer died and no series was held that winter. Just over a year later the Concerts Spirituels were revived under the direction of Ferdinand Piringer (1780–1829), Gebauer's former assistant, and Johann Geissler, at the time also the secretary of the Gesellschaft der Musikfreunde. In a reorganization that suggests collaboration with the Gesellschaft the concerts were now limited to four in number and were held in Lent, overlapping with the third or fourth of the Gesellschaft concerts; the programmes now regularly included overtures and secular choruses as well as symphonies and sacred music, though the proscription of operatic arias and concerto-like works was maintained; it is likely too that the rather ad hoc arrangements of the early practice-concerts were replaced by a more formal rehearsal and performance, and that the link between concert and subsequent liturgical performance at the Augustiner-kirche was loosened. Firmly established as a major presence alongside the concerts of the Gesellschaft der Musikfreunde, the Concerts Spirituels were to remain active until 1848.[11] Table 8.2 lists the symphonies presented at the concerts between 1819 and 1828.

As in the concerts of the Gesellschaft der Musikfreunde, the symphonies of Beethoven feature very strongly, twenty-two performances in ten years. In the first two years, there was a complete cycle of Beethoven's symphonies to date; in 1821–22 Gebauer seems to have embarked on a second cycle before his death interrupted the series and then encouraged its reorganization. In 1827 the Ninth Symphony was given whole on 15 March, preceded by an overture by Vogler and movements from Mozart's *Davidde penitente* (K469); just over a month later, on 19 April, a performance of the first movement was followed by Cherubini's Mass in D minor.[12]

[11] Hanslick, *Geschichte*, vol. 1, pp. 185–90, pp. 307–313; Handlos, 'Die Wiener *Concerts spirituels*', pp. 283–99.

[12] M. Handlos, 'Studien zum Wiener Konzertleben im Vormärz' (PhD diss., University of Vienna, 1985), p. 177.

Table 8.2. *Symphonies performed at the Concerts Spirituels, 1819–1828*

Season/Year	Haydn	Mozart	Beethoven	Other
1819–20	E♭, C, D,	D, C, D, K550,	Nos. 1, 2, 3,	Krommer, Schneider,
		E♭	4, 6	Spohr, Fesca, Romberg
1820–21	3 works E♭, D, and one other		Nos. 5, 7, 8	Ries in D, Spohr in D minor, Fesca, Leidesdorf, Pixis in C, Romberg in C, Krommer in C minor
1821–22	B♭, G, E♭	C, K550, D	Nos. 1, 2, 3, 6	Spohr in D minor, Lannoy in C, Krommer in C minor, Fesca, André in E♭, Krommer in E♭
1824	Nos. 103, 100	K550	No. 6	–
1825	–	K543	Nos. 3, 5, 7	–
1826	–	K550	Nos. 1, 4	–
1827	–	C	No. 6, 9 (whole) 9 (1st mvt)	–
1828	–	K550	No. 4	–

The following sources were used in the denoted periods. 1819–21: E. Hanslick, *Geschichte des Concertwesens in Wien* (Vienna, 1869), pp. 189–90, supplemented by *Allgemeine musikalische Zeitung*. 1821–2: *Allgemeine musikalische Zeitung*. 1824–8: M. Handlos, 'Studien zum Wiener Konzertleben im Vormärz' (PhD diss. University of Vienna, 1985), pp. 173–8, supplemented by *Allgemeine musikalische Zeitung*. Individual works have been identified only where there is no doubt.

Beethoven's domination of the series is not as total as that in the Gesellschaft der Musikfreunde. There were thirteen performances of symphonies by Mozart, predominantly of the four last symphonies (assuming that at least some of the C major works were K551 and some of the D major works were K504). Haydn is much better represented in the concerts of the Concerts Spirituels, a total of eleven performances, probably of the London symphonies, compared with only one by the Gesellschaft der Musikfreunde in the same period. From 1825, however, Haydn's symphonies are entirely absent from the programmes of both organizations, part of the continuing readjustment of his appeal that had begun in the early years of the nineteenth century. Formerly his symphonies had constituted the benchmark for others, Beethoven included; now, while his commanding position in Viennese music was still celebrated, much more emphasis was placed on

The Creation, The Seasons and the choral version of *The Seven Last Words*, allowing Beethoven to occupy centre stage as a symphonist.

In comparison with the programmes of the Liebhaber Concerte in 1807–8, which had propagated the view that the symphonies of Haydn, Mozart and Beethoven were more estimable than symphonies by Eberl, Gyrowetz, Krommer and Wranitzky, the concerts of the Gesellschaft der Musikfreunde and Concert Spirituels present a more complex outlook.

As the institution dedicated to raising musical standards in general in Vienna, the Gesellschaft der Musikfreunde was wholly ineffectual in one area, stimulating new compositions. While its conservatoire offered the customary training in figured bass and, more unusual, compulsory instruction in the Italian language, it did not train composers; likewise its concert committees seem not to have commissioned works on a regular basis. As a society it was clearly anxious to promote the symphony as a genre but it laid greater emphasis on the past than on the future. Apart from Beethoven only three living Viennese composers figured in the concerts of the society. One, Krommer, was able to reactivate his career in the 1820s with five performances. The fortunes of two other composers resident in Vienna, Voříšek and Schubert, were pitiful: Voříšek's symphony was played in February 1823, twenty months before his death at the age of thirty-four; and Schubert's Symphony No. 6 in C was first performed in December 1828, a few weeks after his death at the age of thirty-one. Had both composers lived longer it is possible that they might have consolidated their careers as symphonists and together with Beethoven and Krommer formed a new grouping of composers to supplant the venerated one of Haydn, Mozart and Beethoven. Both, however, would have had to contend with the fact that the impetus for symphonic composition had to come from the composer himself, rather than be a response to a commission, whether by an institution or an individual.

One further local composer of symphonies who figures on the programmes of the Gesellschaft der Musikfreunde is the interesting figure of Baron Eduard Lannoy (1787–1853). Born in Brussels, where his father was part of the imperial civil service in the Austrian Netherlands, he was educated in Graz, Brussels and Paris. Between 1806 and 1809 he lived alternately in Graz and Vienna, deepening his love of poetry and music, interests that were to flourish during his adulthood in Vienna. He was an early member of the Gesellschaft der Musikfreunde, involved himself in the organization of the Concerts Spirituels, translated Rossini's *Tancredi* into German, composed a one-act opera, *Margarethe oder die Räuber* that was performed in Graz (1814) and Vienna (1819), and was an early collector of national songs and dances. In 1830 he assumed the position of Director of the Vienna Conservatoire.[13] Here, apparently, was a Lobkowitz for a new era: socially well connected, a capable musician and a tireless promoter of musical discrimination in the imperial capital. Yet he seems never to have commissioned a symphony or facilitated a rehearsal or performance. Instead, he composed three symphonies of his own, in E, B♭ and C. The autograph score of the B♭ symphony is written in the meticulous hand of a gifted amateur;[14] the music itself reveals a bland competence, with rather four-square phrase patterns and a limited harmonic palette.

The role played by symphony composers other than Haydn, Mozart and Beethoven in the programmes of the Concerts Spirituels is noticeably different. When Piringer reactivated the series in 1824 the symphonies of those three composers only were played, a marked change of direction from when Gebauer was in charge. As well as promoting local composers like Krommer and Lannoy, Gebauer had, in addition, purchased symphonies published in Germany, enabling the Viennese tradition to be set alongside a broader German one. Johann Anton André (1775–1842) was the composer of eight symphonies published by his own firm in Offenbach; Friedrich Ernst Fesca (1789–1826) was a central figure in the musical life of Karlsruhe, two of whose symphonies were published in Leipzig; Ferdinand Ries (1784–1838) lived in London between 1813 and 1824 where he composed all but three of his eight symphonies, mainly published by Simrock (Bonn) and Breitkopf and Härtel; and Bernhard Heinrich Romberg (1767–1841), for four years between 1815 and 1819 a Kapellmeister in Berlin, also composed several symphonies subsequently published in Leipzig. Natural curiosity about the wider musical world was Gebauer's undoubted musical motivation but it draws to attention to two further aspects of the standing of the symphony in Vienna in 1820. First, already hinted at, was the dearth of local composers who were anxious to compose symphonies, a complete change from the situation that had existed forty years earlier. The second aspect is the complex relationship between the symphony in Vienna and the symphony in Germany.

From the 1790s onwards many composers of symphonies who lived and worked in Vienna had sought distribution of their works in Germany, principally through the publishing firms of André, Breitkopf and Härtel, and the Bureau de Musik; Beethoven, Eberl and Paul Wranitzky in particular had gained a wider German reputation in this way. The publishing

[13] C. Wurzbach, *Biographisches Lexikon des Kaiserthums Oesterreich* (Vienna, 1856–91), vol. 14, pp. 142–4.
[14] Gesellschaft der Musikfreunde, Vienna.

houses of Germany promoted these composers of symphonies alongside many others from the German territories as part of a symphonic tradition that fed the active public concert life of major cities such as Frankfurt, Leipzig and Mannheim; it was given further impetus and status through the review columns of the *Allgemeine musikalische Zeitung* and other journals such as the *Journal des Luxus und der Moden*, published in Weimar, and the *Zeitung für die elegante Welt*, published in Leipzig. This flourishing tradition of composition, performance and debate contrasted starkly with the chronic insecurities associated with composing symphonies in Vienna. Indeed, it could be fairly said that the symphony as a genre prospered in civic Germany at a time when it might have disappeared completely in Vienna.

There is nothing in the statutes of the Gesellschaft der Musikfreunde that openly acknowledges the superior musical culture of these German cities, but everything that they did was designed to bring Vienna up to date. There were wider political currents at work too. During and after the Congress of Vienna Metternich was anxious to assume a leading role for Austria in pan-German politics, particularly in the newly established German Confederation.[15] In music, Vienna held the trump card, or rather several trump cards. It was the city in which Haydn, Mozart and Beethoven worked, and its belated promotion of these composers and of the local symphonic tradition was a powerful demonstration of cultural standing. In the 1820s, therefore, a tension between two intertwining traditions began, a Viennese musical tradition and a German musical tradition, a tension that was to figure in music history for over a century, most obviously in the reception of Beethoven and his music, and which is still evident today.

BEETHOVEN IN HIS OWN TRADITION

With so many performances of symphonies by Beethoven it was almost inevitable that the composer would add to what was already a canon of works. Paradoxically the impulse for the Ninth Symphony did not come from Vienna, but from the Philharmonic Society in London in 1817, before concert life in Vienna had established its impetus and energy. Through the intermediary of Ferdinand Ries, Beethoven's former pupil, the society coupled the commission with an invitation to visit London. Perhaps struck by the thought that he could emulate Haydn's achievement in the 1790s, Beethoven responded enthusiastically to the idea and began sketching the

[15] Ingrao, *The Habsburg Monarchy*, p. 241.

first movement. A combination of ill health and preoccupation with the legal battle over the guardianship of his nephew Karl fuelled Beethoven's chronic nervousness about travel, and the symphony was put to one side. Instead, the next few years were devoted to the last four piano sonatas (op. 106, op. 109, op. 110 and op. 111), the 'Diabelli' variations and the Missa Solemnis. In 1823 the project was revived and Beethoven worked enthusiastically on the work, prompted by a commission fee of £50 from the Philharmonic Society and, once again, apparent enthusiasm about travelling to London. Although Beethoven was an ardent Anglophile, he must have realized during the composition of the Ninth Symphony that there had never been a more encouraging environment in Vienna to present a new symphony; at the very least this realization would have provided him with another excuse not to travel to London.

Already in the autumn of 1823 Beethoven began contemplating a concert to present the new symphony and the Missa Solemnis. Benefit concerts for composers rather than for performers were still very unusual in Vienna. The last one had been on 14 March 1822 at the Kleiner Redoutensaal for Carl Maria von Weber when, to maximize takings, he presented himself as the soloist in two concertante works for piano and orchestra; neither of his two symphonies, composed in 1806–7, was included in the programme.[16] To avoid the stresses and strains of organizing a benefit concert and, more positively, to associate himself directly with the major force in Viennese concert life, Beethoven sounded out the Gesellschaft der Musikfreunde about presenting a special concert. There was another motive at work here. Beethoven was meant to be composing an oratorio for the society but for nearly nine years had prevaricated and dissembled about its progress; proposing a concert with the symphony and the Missa Solemnis, the latter regarded as a substitute for the promised oratorio, would have conveniently discharged his obligations. The Gesellschaft discussed the suggestion at a meeting in January 1824 but rejected it on the grounds that the costs of preparing the performing material and other expenses were too onerous.[17] A whole series of other venues was then considered: the composer's favourite Theater an der Wien, the Landständischer Saal (the home of the Concerts Spirituels), the Grosser Redoutensaal (the venue of the Gesellschaft concerts) and the Kärntnertortheater.

Rumours had been circulating for a while that Beethoven had completed a new symphony. Prompted by a particular rumour that it was going to be given its first performance in Berlin, an open letter was published in two

[16] *AmZ*, 24 (1822), col. 306–7.   [17] Brandenburg (ed.), *Briefwechsel*, vol. 5, pp. 261–2.

local journals, the *Allgemeine Theaterzeitung* and the *Wiener Allgemeine musikalische Zeitung*, urging Beethoven to present his music in Vienna. Signed by thirty leading members of the musical community in Vienna, including Count Moriz von Dietrichstein (director of the court theatres), Count Ferdinand Palffy (proprietor of the Theater an der Wien), Raphael Georg Kiesewetter (Vice president of the Gesellschaft der Musikfreunde), Vinzenz Hauschka (treasurer of the Gesellschaft), Leopold Sonnleithner (member of the concerts committee of the Gesellschaft), the music publishers Artaria and Steiner, the composers Czerny and Maximilian Stadler, plus several bankers and court officials, the letter is an extraordinary act of possession couched in nine paragraphs of convoluted, orotund prose.[18]

Out of the wide circle of reverent admirers that surrounds your genius in this your second native city, a small number of disciples and lovers of art approach you today to express long-felt wishes, and timidly to proffer a long-suppressed request . . .

Above all, the wishes of those of our countrymen who venerate art are those that we desire to express here; for although Beethoven's name and his creations belong to all contemporaneous humanity and every country that opens a sensitive heart to art, it is Austria that is best entitled to claim him as her own. Among her inhabitants, appreciation for the great and immortal works that Mozart and Haydn created for all time within the lap of their home has not died, and [these inhabitants] are conscious with joyous pride that the sacred triad, in which these names and yours glow as the symbol of the highest within the spiritual realm of tones, sprang from the soil of the fatherland . . .

Do not withhold any longer from the popular enjoyment, do not keep any longer from the oppressed sense of that which is great and perfect, the performance of the latest masterworks of your hand. We know that a grand sacred composition has joined the first one [Mass in C] in which you immortalized the emotions of a soul, penetrated and transfigured by the power of faith and superterrestrial light. We know that a new flower grows in the garland of your glorious, still unequalled symphonies. For years, ever since the thunders of the *Victory at Vittoria* [*Wellington's Victory*] ceased to reverberate, we have waited and hoped to see you distribute new gifts from the fullness of your riches to the circle of your friends. Do not disappoint the general expectations any longer! Heighten the effect of your newest creations by giving us the joy of becoming first acquainted with them through you yourself! Do not allow these, your latest offspring, to appear some day, perhaps as foreigners in their place of birth, perhaps introduced by persons who are also strangers to you and your spirit. Appear soon among your friends, your admirers, your venerators! This is our first and foremost prayer.

The exalted status of Haydn, Mozart and Beethoven, the 'sacred triad' of the open letter, was grandly laid out in the four concerts of the Concerts

---

[18] Ibid., vol. 5, pp. 273–7; translation from Albrecht (ed.), *Letters*, vol. 3, pp. 4–6.

Spirituels that season. The first concert, on 4 March, was devoted to Haydn, Symphony No. 103 followed by the oratorio *Seven Last Words*; on 18 March the concert was devoted to Mozart, the G minor symphony (K550), the 'Dies irae' from the Requiem, the Fantasy in C minor for orchestra (that is the arrangement by Seyfried of the Fantasy and Sonata in C minor for piano, K475 and K457) and 'Heiliger, sieh gnädig' (a contrafactum using the Kyrie from the Litaniae de venerabili altaris sacramento, K125); on 1 April it was Beethoven's turn, the *Pastoral* Symphony followed by the Credo from the Mass in C, the overture to *Coriolan* and part of the oratorio *Christus am Oelberge*. A week later, on 8 April all three composers were featured together: Haydn's Symphony No. 100 ('Military'), the last movement of the Mass in C by Beethoven, the first finale from *Ahasverus* (a recent opera by Seyfried based on music by Mozart), Beethoven's overture *Egmont*, the storm chorus from Haydn's *Il ritorno di Tobia* and the fugue from Mozart's 'Heiliger, sieh gnädig', a contrafactum of 'Pignus futurae' from the Litaniae de venerabili altaris sacramento.[19]

Given this unprecedented enthusiasm for Beethoven and his music it is not surprising that he took the unusual step of presenting two benefit concerts. The first was held in the Kärntnertortheater on 7 May when the programme resembled that of a Concerts Spirituels concert: the overture to the *Consecration of the House*, the Kyrie, Credo and Agnus Dei from the Missa Solemnis, and the Ninth Symphony. The second concert was held just over a fortnight later in the Grosser Redoutensaal, the venue associated with the Gesellschaft der Musikfreunde, a factor that might have encouraged Beethoven to replace the Credo and Agnus Dei with two secular vocal items, the trio 'Tremate, empi, tremate' (op. 116) and an aria from Rossini's *Tancredi*, 'Di tanti palpiti'. The first concert, in particular, was an artistic success, but the expenses that had been incurred and the disappointing attendance at the second concert in the Redoutensaal – it was a beautifully sunny day – meant that the total proceeds were negligible. Nevertheless, the sense that Vienna had witnessed an epochal musical event is palpable in the review of the two concerts that appeared in the *Wiener Allgemeine musikalische Zeitung*, an essay of some 5,500 words written by Friedrich August Kanne, one-time composer, now an ardent, if occasionally eccentric, champion of Beethoven.[20]

---

[19] Handlos, 'Studien', p. 174.

[20] Kunze (ed.), *Die Werke im Spiegel seiner Zeit*, pp. 477; translation from D. Levy, *Beethoven. The Ninth Symphony* (New York, 1995), p. 138. For a discussion of Kanne's review see ibid., pp. 138–41 and R. Wallace, *Beethoven's Critics. Aesthetic dilemmas and resolutions during the composer's lifetime* (Cambridge, 1986), pp. 74–7.

The first *Allegro* in D minor, which ought to be designated a colossal fantasy for orchestra if one wishes to describe it precisely, likewise offers again the power of instruments decided opportunity for shining moments of effect. Like a volcano, Beethoven's power of imagination makes the earth, which tries to impede the rage of his fire, burst, and with an often wonderful persistence, develops figures whose peculiar formation, at first glance, not seldom expresses an almost bizarre character, but which become transformed under the artful master's skilled hand into a stream of graceful elaborations that refuse to end, swinging upward step by step, into an ever more brilliant loftiness.

These few months had represented a heady coming together of genre, composer and place, the symphony, Beethoven and Vienna. Though its origins can be traced back to the Liebhaber Concerte of 1807–8, perhaps even earlier to the private concerts of Würth and Lobkowitz, it was now both commanding and unequivocal in its authority, and it would have been a travesty for the Ninth Symphony to have been given its premiere in London or Berlin.

The sense that the symphony belonged to Vienna is also apparent in the music itself. Commentators have often drawn attention to the retro-spective aspects of the symphony, a work that celebrates the Beethovenian tradition: four movements in the heroic mould, a tonal trajectory from minor to major, the setting of a fervent text, the culmination of several decades of dialectical thinking in the standard forms of sonata, scherzo and variations, and the ability, as in the finale of the *Eroica* symphony, to create a movement that drew on a number of formal principles to create a unique entity. The vocal finale, too, may be seen as traditional, the perfectly natural consequence of a local concert life that featured vocal music, both sacred and secular, solo and choral, alongside orchestral music. It was the one movement about which Beethoven had doubts, telling Czerny that he wished to write a wholly new finale for instruments alone.[21] Here, too, was a worry that was the product of its time and place: the Viennese had elevated Beethoven and the instrumental symphony to a new plane; was it appropriate that his latest symphony should court popularity by having voices?

While working on the Ninth Symphony Beethoven had already noted some sketches for a tenth symphony, in E♭ major. In 1824 and 1825 he worked a little further on the work before putting it aside in favour of the C♯ minor quartet (op. 131) and, then, the F major quartet (op. 135).[22] It is

[21] E. Forbes (ed.), *Thayer's Life of Beethoven* (Princeton, 1964), pp. 895–6.
[22] Cooper, *Beethoven*, pp. 386–7; B. Cooper, 'Newly Identified Sketches for Beethoven's Tenth Symphony', *Music and Letters*, 66 (1985), pp. 9–18.

impossible to know whether Beethoven would have completed the work had he lived beyond March 1827. Perhaps the composer's usual high standards of self-criticism would have prevented completion; perhaps too Beethoven was already conscious, in a way that he had never before experienced, of public expectations. What is certain, however, is that Vienna would have embraced a new symphony wholeheartedly.

KROMMER AS A COMPOSER OF SYMPHONIES FROM 1820 TO 1830

The most productive composer of symphonies in Vienna in the 1820s was Franz Krommer, now in his sixties and something of an establishment figure. After years of hankering after a position in the Hofkapelle, in June 1815 he was given the post of Doorkeeper of the Antechamber (Antekammer-Türhüter), complete with salary, living expenses and a uniform. This was an old-fashioned administrative convenience that allowed Krommer to became a favoured musician at the court of Emperor Franz, accompanying him on foreign journeys and participating in performances of chamber music; he was even given permission to dedicate a set of three string quintets, op. 100, to the emperor. After Leopold Kozeluch's death in 1818, Krommer was able to succeed him as Hofkomponist, a post he held until his death early in January 1831.[23] Following the death of Salieri in 1825 he assumed the mantle of a revered senior figure, enhanced when he was asked to prepare the official arrangement for imperial regimental bands of the Austrian national anthem, 'Gott erhalte Franz den Kaiser'.[24]

Krommer had always been a prolific composer, and it was this fluency together with his status in musical life in general that encouraged him to compose six symphonies between 1820 and 1830. Krommer numbered his symphonies from 1 to 9; No. 8, composed between 1824 and 1830, is lost. Symphonies Nos. 4 and 5 were published by André, reactivating the sequence that had languished in 1808, and received a number of performances in Vienna; Symphonies Nos. 6 and 7 were not published and the latter, in particular, was not well received; there is no evidence that No. 9 was ever performed and it survives only as an autograph manuscript. The performance and publication history of the extant symphonies in the period 1820–30 are summarized in Table 8.3.

---

[23] Padrta, *Franz Krommer*, pp. 33–7, pp. 159–61.
[24] O. Biba, *Gott erhalte! Joseph Haydns Kaiserhymne* (Vienna, 1982), pp. 7–8.

Table 8.3. *Krommer's symphonies, 1820–30*

Symphony No. 4 in C minor
Composed: 1819–20
Published: André, op. 102, 1820
Performances: April 1820, Gesellschaft der Musikfreunde; 1822, Concerts Spirituels; 16 February 1823, Gesellschaft der Musikfreunde; 11 March 1827, Gesellschaft der Musikfreunde; 22 February 1828, charity concert for the Bürgerspital.
Symphony No. 5 in E♭
Composed: 1821
Published: André, op. 105, 1822–3
Performances: October 1821, Gesellschaft der Musikfreunde; 1822, Concerts Spirituels; 25 December 1822, charity concert for the Bürgerspital.
Symphony No. 6 in D
Composed: 1823
Performances: 16 November 1823, Gesellschaft der Musikfreunde; 25 December 1823, charity concert for the Bürgerspital.
Symphony No. 7 in G minor
Composed: 1824
Performance: 8 May 1828, concert for members of the Kirchen- and Musikverein of the parish of Sankt Laurenz.
Symphony No. 9 in C
Composed: 1830

Dates of composition are taken from K. Padrta, *Franz Krommer (1759–1831). Thematischer Katalog seiner musikalischen Werke* (Prague, 1997); performance dates are taken from *Allgemeine musikalische Zeitung* and *Wiener Allgemeine musikalische Zeitung*.

It is clear that Krommer was well connected with the Gesellschaft der Musikfreunde, who presented three new symphonies in the space of four years. The first of these, in C minor, was given in April 1820; the following concert in the series including Beethoven's Fifth Symphony,[25] the beginning of the real performance history of that work in Vienna. Like Schubert in his fourth symphony, Krommer may well have composed his C minor symphony with no sense that he was emulating Beethoven. As in all his symphonies, early and late, he follows the standard pattern of slow introduction, sonata form, slow movement, minuet and finale, and there is little feeling of a stirring tussle between minor and major; the first movement turns to C major when the second subject is recapitulated; C major is heard in the trio as a contrast to the C minor of the minuet; and the finale begins and ends in the major key.

[25] Hanslick, *Geschichte*, vol. 1, p. 158.

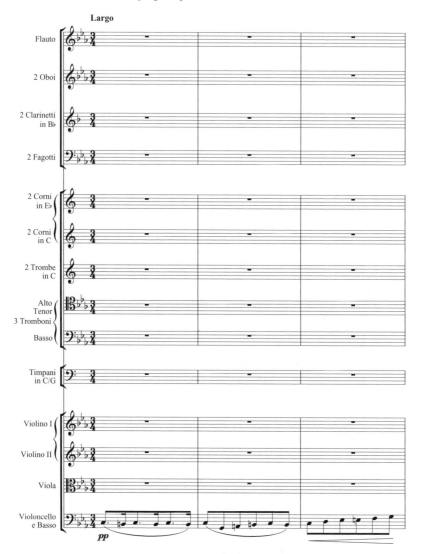

Example 8.1 Krommer, Symphony in C minor, op. 102, first movement, bb. 1–12.

The opening of Krommer's work presents a new sonority in the history
of the symphony in Vienna. A *legato* quaver line in cellos and basses twice
leads to a full tutti response: Krommer's orchestra now has four horns and
three trombones (alto, tenor and bass) that combine to give a portentous
weight, a low centre of gravity, to the tutti sound. Ex. 8.1. All Krommer's

Example 8.1 (*cont.*)

Example 8.1 (*cont.*)

late symphonies have four horns and three trombones, and the resulting orchestral sound is constantly reminiscent of that in Schubert's Eighth and Ninth Symphonies; occasionally, as towards the end of the exposition of the first movement of the C minor symphony and in the slow movement of the D major symphony, Krommer gives thematic leads to trombones, also characteristic of Schubert's last two symphonies.

Following the first performance of the sixth symphony in 1823 the Viennese critic of the *Allgemeine musikalische Zeitung* described the work, with some condescension, as 'clear and understandable',[26] qualities most obviously associated with the composer's habitually uncomplicated structures which never feature the unexpected. Krommer tends to think in blocks of about thirty bars at a time, which are then either repeated or followed by another similar sized paragraph; melodic ideas are attractive but never memorable; and the harmonic language fails to capitalize on the occasional arresting gesture. The fast movements of the symphonies – minuets as well as sonata forms – always have a good deal of surface energy and when combined with a slow-moving harmonic rhythm the result, again, recalls Schubert.

The G minor symphony is a shorter work and much the weakest of Krommer's eight extant symphonies. Krommer once more has a slow introduction in the minor key, and follows with an Allegro vivace whose first theme is blatantly modelled on the opening of Haydn's Symphony No. 83 ('La Poule'), a work Krommer would have remembered from his youth but which was now entirely forgotten. The finale, in turn, resorts to a stolid fugue for its first subject, repeated more or less exactly at the beginning of the recapitulation. This symphony was never taken up by the Gesellschaft der Musikfreunde.

Krommer's final symphony was completed only four months before his death and is a much more ambitious and resourceful work, especially in its use of tonality. The home key is C major, but A minor figures repeatedly in the course of the four movements: as the key of the slow introduction, the point of departure for the development in the same movement, as an unexpected loud chord in the trio, and the key of the first subject area in the finale. From A minor the finale then moves through C major (transition) to G major for the second subject. The repetition of this tonal pattern down a fifth in the recapitulation, D minor, F major to C, suggests that Krommer had been studying similar procedures in sonata form movements by Schubert. More generally, the thematic and harmonic gait of this

---

[26] *AmZ*, 25 (1823), col. 865.

large-scale symphony in C indicates that Krommer had, at the very least, heard Schubert's 'Great C major' symphony (D944) when it was rehearsed by students of the conservatory of the Gesellschaft der Musikfreunde sometime in 1827–8.

VOŘÍŠEK'S SINGLE SYMPHONY

Voříšek was a generation younger than Beethoven and Krommer. Born in Wamberg (Vamberck) in northeast Bohemia in 1791 he received his first musical training from his father, headmaster of the local school and a capable musician. At the age of fifteen he went to study piano, theory and composition with Václav Tomášek in Prague, later enrolling as a law student in the university. In 1813 he moved to Vienna where he was taught for a while by Hummel. His university background and his gifts as a pianist made him a natural member of those social circles that were beginning to mould the musical scene in Vienna. Active in the Gesellschaft der Musikfreunde, in 1818 he was commissioned to write an oratorio by the society, a request he turned down because of the lack of experience; at the same time he recommended that the idea of commissioning an oratorio from Beethoven should be resurrected.[27] He became interested in the private concerts devoted to old music organized by Raphael Georg Kiesewetter, and succeeded Gebauer in 1820 as their conductor. Earning a living as a salon pianist, composer of piano music and occasional conductor was a precarious business and Voříšek sought security by becoming a clerk in the imperial war council (Hofkriegsrat). In 1822 he was appointed second organist in the Hofkapelle, becoming first organist in the following year. His piano music and songs were regularly published in Vienna and his appointment at court enabled him to produce an increasing number of church compositions. He contracted tuberculosis and, despite medical treatment in Vienna, Graz and Karlsbad, died in November 1825 at the age of only thirty-four.

A potentially significant expansion of Voříšek's career had occurred in 1823. On 21 January, as the autograph manuscript notes, he completed a symphony in D major.[28] He had secured the promise of the Gesellschaft der Musikfreunde that it would be included in a forthcoming concert, and the society were to bear the costs of preparing the parts. That process took a few weeks, and the symphony was given for the first time on 23 February

---

[27] Brandenburg (ed.), *Briefwechsel*, vol. 4, p. 191.
[28] Modern edition (with biography and editorial note) by F. Bartoš, Musica Antiqua Bohemica 34 (Prague, 1974).

1823 when it shared the programme with Beethoven's oratorio, *Christus am Oelberge.*[29] This might have initiated a symphonic career for Voříšek akin to that of Krommer in the 1820s, but with one difference: Voříšek was much the more imaginative composer.

Voříšek does away with a slow introduction favoured by Krommer and immediately presents a descending scalic motif in unison that is to reappear during the course of the movement in different guises and with different consequences. Within a compact, regular sonata form of 215 bars Voříšek's thematic invention never wanes and his control of harmonic tension is unfailingly secure. The descending opening motif had come to rest on the submediant (B) and it is to the relative minor, B minor, that the slow movement turns, an unusual relationship for slow movements in Viennese symphonies, and a rare key in its own right. A four-bar introduction features the same descending motif to bring the music to rest on an expectant dominant. The following principal theme is played by cellos and again cleverly incorporates the same downward scalic pattern. In full sonata form the recapitulation is placed in B major, shortened and colourfully scored.

The following movement is equally memorable. Instead of a minuet and trio in the tonic, D major, Voříšek presents a scherzo in D minor and in 9/8, a novel contrast in all respects. The momentum is maintained for the trio in B♭, a lyrical movement led by woodwind and horns. When the Viennese correspondent of the *Allgemeine musikalische Zeitung* wrote briefly about the premiere of the symphony, he was especially enthusiastic about the first and second movements but thought that the unusual metre of the scherzo was not successful and felt the finale was disappointing.[30] The last movement, a regular sonata form, does not have the novel features of the first three movements, though the energy of the Allegro con brio in 2/4 is skilfully maintained through to the end.

SCHUBERT AND THE SYMPHONY, 1820–28: 'STRIVINGS AFTER THE HIGHEST IN ART'

After the demise in 1820 of the private orchestra that had prompted the composition of five of Schubert's six symphonies to date, the composer's career as a symphonist in Vienna up to his death in 1828 can only be described as an abject one if measured in terms of completed works, public performance and publication. Only one work was completed, the 'Great' C major (D944) and four others exist in incomplete form, the two movements

---

[29] Hanslick, *Geschichte*, vol. 1, p. 158.   [30] *AmZ*, 25 (1823), cols. 209–10.

that form the 'Unfinished' symphony (D759), a draft score for a symphony in E (D729) and sketches for two symphonies in D major (D708A and D936A).[31] None of these symphonies was performed in public and none was published. Biographers of the composer have sought to explain this dispiriting tale as a consequence of Schubert's diffidence, particularly in the face of the awesome presence of Beethoven, and as such it plays its part in the seductive trope of the young composer who died with so much unfulfilled.[32]

But there were other, less personal circumstances at work. Composing symphonies and having them performed was a fickle business in Vienna in the 1820s. Some pointers can be seen in the careers of Krommer and Voříšek. Krommer was a senior figure in the musical life of the city, well-connected at court and with the new establishment of bankers, government officials and aristocrats who ran the Gesellschaft der Musikfreunde; for over twenty years his music had been published in Germany, principally by André of Offenbach, as well as in Vienna. Because of his legal training and subsequent career as a government official, Voříšek likewise moved naturally in those circles that could ensure performances of symphonies. Even though he was only six years younger than Voříšek, Schubert had none of these social and musical advantages.

From the end of 1818 onwards Schubert worked regularly in the theatres in Vienna, composing a singspiel, *Die Zwillingsbrüder*, for the Kärntnertortheater (1820), a melodrama, *Die Zauberharfe*, for the Theater an der Wien (1820), two items for Hérold's opera *Das Zauberglöckchen* performed at the Kärntnertortheater (1821), incidental music for the play *Rosamunde, Fürstin von Zypern* given at the Theater an der Wien (1823), as well as a good deal of music that for one reason and another was never performed; in 1821 Schubert even worked as a repetiteur at the Kärntnertortheater for a while.[33] This contact with the theatres led to his music featuring fairly frequently in benefit concerts. Since the repertoire of such concerts hardly ever included symphonies, it is not surprising that none by the composer was ever performed; instead these concerts promoted Schubert as a composer of songs and partsongs. For instance a charity concert at the Kärntnertortheater on 7 March 1821 presented a typical miscellany of music, readings and tableaux. Alongside an overture by Boieldieu,

---

[31] Steinbeck, 'Die Sinfonien', p. 669.

[32] See C. H. Gibbs, '"Poor Schubert": Images and Legends of the Composer', *Cambridge Companion to Schubert*, ed. C. H. Gibbs (Cambridge, 1997), pp. 36–55.

[33] For a survey of Schubert's stage works see U. Schreiber, 'Glücklose Liebe zum Theater. Die Bühnenwerke', *Schubert Handbuch*, pp. 304–44.

an Adagio and Rondo for cello by Romberg, the first movement of a violin concerto by Spohr, a set of variations for two pianos by Voříšek and an aria by Mozart, three items by Schubert were given: a partsong for four voices, 'Das Dörfchen' (D598), the song 'Der Erlkönig' (D328) and a partsong for eight voices, 'Der Gesang der Geister über den Wassern' (D714).[34]

One of the mysteries of Schubert's life is that he seems never to have become professionally involved with the Concerts Spirituels until the last few weeks of his life. Schubert's own tally of liturgical music includes over thirty items, encompassing masses, Marian antiphons, several settings of the Salve Regina and Tantum ergo, and some works in the German language, but none of this music found its way into the repertoire of the Concerts Spirituels; had it done so it might well have paved the way for performances of Schubert's symphonies. It was only in 1829, a few months after the death of the composer, that his music was included for the first time, the Hymnus an den heiligen Geist (D964), written specifically for the Concerts Spirituels, on 5 March, and the Sixth Symphony on 12 March.[35]

Schubert's relationship with the Gesellschaft der Musikfreunde was a determining one in his career as a composer of songs, piano music and chamber music; with a little bit more entrepreneurial flair and less bureaucratic plodding, the society might have done the same for the composer's symphonies.[36] Schubert first applied for membership of the Gesellschaft der Musikfreunde in 1818 as a piano accompanist, when he was turned down because he was not an amateur. From 1821 his music was regularly included in the programmes of the evening concerts devoted to small-scale music, becoming in a short time one of the best represented composers in these concerts. The large-scale concerts, in which symphonies were regularly programmed, included Schubert's Overture in E minor in its programme on 18 November 1821. Sometime during the same year Schubert had been accepted as a member, apparently admitted as a viola player and a pianist, and it is possible that he might have played in subsequent performances of symphonies by Beethoven, Krommer, Voříšek and others promoted by the society. While there is no evidence that either Schubert or the Gesellschaft sought to present the composer's existing symphonies his broadening experience as a listener and, perhaps, player would have stimulated his desire to compose new symphonies. It cannot be a coincidence that in the same

[34] T. G. Waidelich (ed.), *Franz Schubert. Dokumente 1817–1830* (Tutzing, 1998), pp. 62–3.
[35] Ibid., p. 497, p. 500, p. 502.
[36] The relationship was documented for the first time by O. Biba, 'Franz Schubert und die Gesellschaft der Musikfreunde in Wien', *Schubert-Kongreß Wien 1978. Bericht*, ed. O. Brusatti (Graz, 1979), pp. 23–36.

year, 1821, he began a symphony in D (D708A) and completed a draft of
another, in E major; a year later he began the composition of the 'Unfinished' symphony.

Reflecting Schubert's growing reputation in musical circles in Vienna,
members of the Gesellschaft voted him and Voříšek on to the committee of the society in September 1825. Among other rights and duties the
committee recommended works for the public concerts. That very summer Schubert had begun the composition of another new symphony, in
C major. Stimulated by the very real prospect of a performance sponsored
by the Gesellschaft, Schubert finished the work early in the following year,
his first completed symphony since 1818. In the autumn he presented the
work to the Gesellschaft. While Voříšek's symphony had been performed
just over a month after its delivery to the society, no room for Schubert's
symphony could be found in the 1826–7 season. Nevertheless, in the usual
way, the Gesellschaft paid for the orchestral parts to be prepared from the
score in order to facilitate a performance in the future.

In February 1828 Schubert received two letters from publishers in
Germany, Probst of Leipzig and Schott of Mainz, enquiring whether the
composer would like to nominate any compositions for publication. For
symphonies, Schott was the more suitable publisher; as was explained in the
exploratory letter to Schubert, the firm had issued 'many a bulky *opus*' by
Beethoven, including the Ninth Symphony.[37] Schubert replied promptly,
listing ten items of chamber music, plus piano music, songs and partsongs.
Underneath the list he wrote, almost as an afterthought, 'This is the list of
my finished compositions, excepting three operas, a Mass and a symphony.
These last compositions I mention only in order to make you acquainted
with my strivings after the highest in art.'[38] Whether this reluctance to
promote the C major symphony reflected longstanding nervousness about
writing a symphony or worries about the continuing delay in establishing
a date of performance cannot be established. At some point in 1827–8 the
Gesellschaft der Musikfreunde organized a run-through of the symphony
by the students of the conservatoire when, according to a later report, it
was adjudged too long and too difficult. On 14 December, a few weeks after
the composer's death, the Gesellschaft performed Schubert's early C major
symphony (No. 6), the first symphony by him to be given by the society.
The premiere of the work that had been presented to them did not take
place until December 1839.

---

[37] O. E. Deutsch, *Schubert. A Documentary Biography*, trans. E. Blom (London, 1946), p. 737.
[38] Ibid., pp. 739–40.

CONTRADICTIONS AND CONTINUITIES

One of the highlights of the social and musical calendar in Vienna was the beginning of the summer concerts in the Augarten, on May Day every year. Since his return from Russia in 1823 Schuppanzigh had resumed the direction of the series and for the first concert of the 1824 season the following programme was put together:[39]

1. Symphony in C minor, Beethoven; Allegro and Andante
2. Aria and chorus from Rossini's *L'italiana in Algeri*, sung by Fräulein Clari
3. Piano concerto in E major by Moscheles, played by Fräulein Rzehaczeck
4. Variations for cello on a Russian theme, by Bernhard Romberg, played by Herr Gross
5. Cavatina from Rossini's *Sigismondo*, sung by Fräulein Clari
6. Concertante variations for piano and physharmonica, composed and played by Herr Lickel with Fräulein Rzehaczeck
7. Vocal quartet, 'Die Nachtigall', Schubert
8. Finale from Symphony in C minor, Beethoven

One of Beethoven's most popular symphonies is presented in two parts, at the beginning and end of the concert, a frame for an assortment of items: two operatic numbers by the most popular composer of the day, Rossini, three works focusing on instrumental virtuosity, including a curiosity instrument, the physharmonica (a small reed organ), and a partsong by Schubert. The contrast between successive items, especially the last three, could not be more disconcerting. If contemporary performances of Beethoven's symphonies by the Gesellschaft der Musikfreunde and Concerts Spirituels were designed to promote the integrity of works as four-movement entities, performances such as this one completely destroyed that ambition. Scherzo movements were often omitted from performances of Beethoven's symphonies in benefit concerts and it is likely that the word 'Finale' here does mean the fourth movement and not the third and fourth together, in which case Beethoven's mighty resolution of C minor to C major would not have been experienced in this concert; instead the fourth movement was reduced to a genre piece, an exhilarating march to signal the end of the entertainment, before listeners departed for their *déjeuner à la fourchette* in Jahn's nearby restaurant.[40]

As developed by the Gesellschaft der Musikfreunde and the Concerts Spirituels and nurtured by an intellectual elite, the grand symphonic tradition, aspirational and with Beethoven at its centre, was well under

---

[39] Waidelich (ed.), *Schubert Dokumente*, p. 218.   [40] As reported in *AmZ*, 23 (1821), col. 455.

way in Vienna in the 1820s. Yet it would be a mistake to state that this constituted the only, even the prime characteristic of musical life in the city. As
the programme of this Augarten concert indicates, the appeal of the virtuoso performer playing his own music was a constant, irresistible feature of
musical life in Vienna. Moscheles vied with Hummel, Weber, Kalkbren-
ner and others for the attention of the piano-loving public while the long
tradition of virtuoso performances on the violin by Clement, Spohr, Rode,
Polledro and others was to reach a new level when Paganini visited the city
in 1828.[41] The appeal of the performer rather than of the composer was
apparent too in the operatic repertoire that featured in benefit concerts,
and it permeated even the concerts of the Gesellschaft der Musikfreunde.
While there had been a time when the symphony had sat very easily in private and public concerts alongside all kinds of music, across four decades in
Vienna from the 1790s to the 1820s it had accrued a seriousness of purpose
that jarred with the continuing conventions of much of Viennese concert
life.

As it began to stand apart in this respect from the overture, the concerto
and Harmoniemusik, the symphony took on some of the high-minded
attributes hitherto associated with oratorio and sacred music in Vienna,
whether in the large-scale performances of the former by the Tonkünstler-
Societät and the Gesellschaft der Musikfreunde or the very systematic association of the symphony with sacred music that occured in the programmes
of the Concerts Spirituels. But, as often in the complex history of the symphony in Vienna, there was a paradox here: the symphony did not embrace
a programmatic dimension. Instead the deepening significance that the
genre acquired over the decades continued to be paralleled by the demise
of the programme symphony. In the 1790s Paul and Anton Wranitzky had
written several such symphonies, and in the following decades it fell to
Beethoven to write the very last examples in the Viennese tradition, the
Eroica symphony, the *Pastoral* symphony and the 'Battle' symphony. In
the 1820s the abstract expressive power of the genre was continually celebrated in the repetitive repertoire of the Gesellschaft der Musikfreunde and
the Concerts Spirituels in which the *Battle* Symphony was entirely absent
and the *Pastoral* nearly so; only the *Eroica* symphony, which did not have
the encumbrance of a permeating programme, was regularly performed.
Krommer, Voříšek and, most surprisingly of all, Schubert readily accepted
the precept that one of the inviolable qualities of the symphony in the 1820s
was its intrinsic, expressive power, something that eschewed a programme

---

[41] Hanslick, *Geschichte*, vol, I, pp. 208–44.

or a text. In the most fundamental way Beethoven in his Ninth Symphony questioned this precept, one that had been fashioned in his own image.

One wonders whether Beethoven ever compared the authority he exerted over the symphony in the 1820s with the one that his former teacher, Haydn, had exerted in the 1790s. There were many differences. Haydn's mastery was seen by other composers as a stimulus to contribute to a continuing expansion of a repertoire that was largely contemporary, Beethoven's own outlook when he embarked on his first symphony. A quarter of a century later, the repertoire had shrunk enormously, was predominantly an old one, and composers like Voříšek and Schubert did not take Beethoven's symphonies as their stylistic starting point, however much they admired the composer. At one and the same time Beethoven's individuality crushed would-be imitators and nurtured the originality of a few.

The symphony in Vienna had certainly been reformulated in the decade after the end of the Napoleonic Wars, a reformulation that was made possible by its near extinction in the previous few years. However much it was engineered by cultural forces in Vienna, it was not a wholly new beginning. Public rather than private, discriminating rather than meretricious, Viennese rather than German, and surreptitiously canonic rather than self-renewing, it drew on earlier manifestations of these characteristics to produce a thoroughly modern image. Soon the modern image came to control the narrative of the preceding decades, smoothing over the diversity, the contradictions and, above all, the difficulties of those years, the very circumstances that had fashioned the destiny of the symphony.

Sources, thematic catalogues and modern editions

The following checklist has three functions: to indicate the primary musical sources (manuscript and published parts, some manuscript scores) that were studied for the symphonies discussed in the text; to provide a convenient listing of relevant thematic catalogues that will direct the reader to further bibliographical information; and to list modern editions of symphonies. The symphonies of Haydn, Mozart, Beethoven and Schubert are excluded from this checklist, as are symphonies mentioned only in passing.

ABBREVIATIONS

PRINTED MATERIAL

The Symphony: B. S. Brook (ed. in chief), *The Symphony 1720–1840. A comprehensive collection of full scores in sixty volumes* (New York, 1979–86).

The Symphony Reference Volume: B. S. Brook (ed. in chief), *The Symphony 1720– 1840. Reference Volume: Contents of the Set and Collected Thematic Indexes* (New York, 1986).

RISM LIBRARY SIGLA

A-Wgm: Gesellschaft der Musikfreunde, Vienna.
A-Wn: Österreichische Nationalbibliothek, Vienna.
A-Wst: Stadt- und Landesbibliothek, Vienna.
CZ-Nlobkowicz: Roudnice Lobkowicz Library, Nelahozeves.
CZ-Pk: Archive and Library, Prague Conservatoire.
F-Pn: Bibliothèque Nationale, Paris.
GB-Lbl: British Library, London.
GB-Mp: Henry Watson Music Library, Public Library, Manchester.

CARL CZERNY (1791–1857)

D, autograph score, A-Wgm.

ANTON EBERL (1765–1807)

C. Modern edn.: N. Negrotti as Mozart, Sinfonia in do maggiore (Milan, 1944)
Eb, op. 33, manuscript parts, CZ-Nlobkowicz. Modern edn.: B. Coeyman and
S. C. Fisher, *The Symphony*, B/IX (New York, 1983), pp. 243–317.
D minor, op. 35, published parts (Breitkopf and Härtel) with manuscript score,
CZ-Pk.
Thematic catalogue: *The Symphony Reference Volume*, B. Coeyman and S. C. Fisher,
p. 207.

FRANZ HOFFMEISTER (1754–1812)

D (D1). Modern edn.: R. Hickman, *The Symphony*, B/V (New York, 1984), pp. 1–
49.
G (G5), *La festa della pace 1791*. Modern edn.: R. Hickman, *The Symphony*, B/V
(New York, 1984), pp. 51–121.
Thematic catalogue: *The Symphony Reference Volume*, R. Hickman, pp. 309–15.

FRANZ KROMMER (1759–1831)

F, op. 12, manuscript score, A-Wgm.
D, op. 40, published parts (André), A-Wn
D, op. 62, published parts (André) with manuscript score, GB-Lbl.
C minor, op. 102, manuscript score, A-Wgm.
Eb, op. 105, manuscript score, A-Wgm.
D ('No. 6'), manuscript score, A-Wgm.
G minor ('No. 7'), autograph score, CZ-Pk.
C ('No. 9'), autograph score, A-Wn.
Thematic catalogue: K. Padrta, *Franz Krommer (1759–1831). Thematischer Katalog
seiner musikalischen Werke* (Prague, 1997).

EDUARD LANNOY (1787–1853)

Bb, autograph score, A-Wgm.

ANTOINE REICHA (1770–1836)

G, autograph score, F-Pn.
F, autograph score, F-Pn. Modern edn., S. C. Fisher, *The Symphony*, B/IX (1983),
pp. 177–242.
Thematic catalogue: O. Šotolová, *Antonín Rejcha. A Biography and Thematic Catalogue* (Prague, 1990).

JOSEPH RÖSSLER (1771–1813)

C, manuscript parts, CZ-Nlobkowicz.
D, manuscript parts, CZ-Nlobkowicz.
E♭, manuscript parts, CZ-Nlobkowicz.

JAN VÁCLAV VOŘÍŠEK (1791–1825)

D. Modern edn., F. Bartoš, Musica Antiqua Bohemica 34 (Prague, 1974)

ANTON WRANITZKY (1761–1820)

C (C1), *Aphrodite*, manuscript parts and score, CZ-Nlobkowicz.
C (C2), manuscript parts, CZ-Nlobkowicz.
C (C3), manuscript parts, CZ-Nlobkowicz.
C minor (C4), manuscript parts, CZ-Nlobkowicz. Modern edn., E. Hennigová-Dubová, *The Symphony*, B/XII (New York, 1984), pp. 233–329.
D (D1), manuscript parts and score, CZ-Nlobkowicz.
D (D2), manuscript parts, CZ-Nlobkowicz.
D (D3), manuscript parts, CZ-Nlobkowicz.
D (D4), manuscript parts, CZ-Nlobkowicz.
D (D5), manuscript parts, CZ-Nlobkowicz.
E♭ (E♭1), manuscript parts, CZ-Nlobkowicz.
E♭ (E♭2), manuscript parts, CZ-Nlobkowicz.
F (F1), manuscript parts, CZ-Nlobkowicz.
G (G1), manuscript parts, CZ-Nlobkowicz.
A (A1), manuscript parts, CZ-Nlobkowicz.
B♭ (B♭1), manuscript parts, CZ-Nlobkowicz.
Thematic catalogue: *The Symphony Reference Volume*, E. Hennigová-Dubová, pp. 558–9.

PAUL WRANITZKY (1756–1808)

C (P1), published parts (André), GB-Mp.
C (P2), published parts (Bossler), A-Wgm.
C (P5), published parts (André), GB-Mp.
C (P7), published parts (André), GB-Mp.
C (P8), published parts (André), GB-Mp. Modern edn., F. Bonis (Budapest, 1978).
C (P9), manuscript parts, A-Wn.
C minor (P11). Modern edn., E. Hradecký (Prague, 1958).
C minor (P12), *Grand Characteristic Symphony for the Peace with the French Republic*, manuscript parts, CZ-Nlobkowicz, printed parts (Gombart), GB-Lbl. Modern edn., J. Wagner (Vienna, 1997).
C (P14), published parts (André), A-Wgm.
D (P18), printed parts (André), GB-Mp.

D (P20), manuscript parts, A-Wn.
D (P21), manuscript parts. CZ-Nlobkowicz. Modern edn., E. Hradecký (Prague, 1957).
D (P23), published parts (André), GB-Mp.
D (P24), published parts (André), A-Wgm.
D (P25), published parts (André), GB-Mp.
E♭ (P32), published parts (André), GB-Mp.
F (P34), published parts (André), GB-Mp.
G (P38), manuscript parts, A-Wn.
G (P39), published parts (André), CZ-Nlobkowicz.
G (P40), published parts (André), GB-Mp.
G minor (P43), manuscript parts, A-Wn.
A (P44), published parts (André), CZ-Nlobkowicz.
A (P46), published parts (André), A-Wgm.
A (P47), published parts (André), A-Wst.
A(P48), published parts (André), GB-Mp.
Thematic catalogue: M. Poštolka, 'Thematisches Verzeichnis der Sinfonien Pavel Vranickýs', *Miscellanea musicologica*, 20 (1967), pp. 101–27.

Bibliography

Albrecht, Theodore. 'Anton Dreyssig (c1753/4–1820): Mozart's and Beethoven's Zauberflötist', *Words About Mozart. Essays in honour of Stanley Sadie*, ed. Dorothea Link and Judith Nagley (Woodbridge, Suffolk, 2005), pp. 179–92

Letters to Beethoven and Other Correspondence, 3 vols (Lincoln, Nebraska, 1996)

Allgemeine musikalische Zeitung, 1–30 (1798–1830)

Anderson, Emily (ed.). *The Letters of Beethoven*, 3 vols. (London, 1961)

Antonicek, Theophil. 'Biedermeierzeit und Vormärz', *Vom Barock zum Vormärz*, ed. Gernot Gruber, 2nd edn., Musikgeschichte Österreichs, vol. 2 (Vienna, 1995)

'Musiker aus den böhmischen Ländern in Wien zu Beethovens Zeit', *Beethoven und Böhmen*, ed. Sieghard Brandenburg and Martella Gutiérrez-Denhoff (Bonn, 1988), pp. 43–61

Musik im Festsaal der Österreichischen Akademie der Wissenschaften, Veröffentlichungen der Komission für Musikforschung, ed. Erich Schenk (Vienna, 1972)

Beer, Axel. *Musik zwischen Komponist, Verlag und Publikum: Die Rahmenbedingungen des Musikschaffens in Deutschland im ersten Drittel des 19. Jahrhunderts* (Tutzing, 2000)

Bein, Werner. 'Carl Ditters von Dittersdorf (1739–1799). Stationen seines Lebens zwischen Wien und Schlesien', *Carl Ditters von Dittersdorf 1739–1799. Mozarts Rivale in der Oper*, ed. Hubert Unverricht and Werner Bein (Würzburg, 1989), pp. 13–24

Benton, Rita. *Ignace Pleyel. A Thematic Catalogue of his Compositions* (New York, 1977)

Biba, Otto. 'Beethoven und die "Liebhaber Concerte" in Wien im Winter 1807/08', *Beiträge '76–78: Beethoven Kolloquium 1977: Dokumentation und Aufführungspraxis*, ed. Rudolf Klein (Kassel, 1978), pp. 82–93

'Beobachtungen zur Österreichischen Musikszene des 18. Jahrhunderts', *Österreichische Musik – Musik in Österreich. Beiträge zur Musikgeschichte Mitteleuropas*, ed. Elisabeth Theresia Hilscher, Wiener Veröffentlichungen zur Musikwissenschaft, 34 (Tutzing, 1998), pp. 213–30

'Concert Life in Beethoven's Vienna', *Beethoven, Performers, and Critics*, ed. Robert Winter and Bruce Carr (Detroit, 1980), pp. 77–93

'The Congress of Vienna and Music', *Denmark and the Dancing Congress of Vienna. Playing for Denmark's Future* (Copenhagen, 2002), pp. 200–214

'Die adelige und bürgerliche Musikkultur. Das Konzertwesen', *Joseph Haydn in seiner Zeit*, eds. Gerda Mraz, Gottfried Mraz and Gerald Schlag (Eisenstadt, 1982), pp. 255–63

"Eben komme ich von Haydn . . .". Georg August Griesingers Korrespondenz mit Joseph Haydns Verleger Breitkopf & Härtel 1799–1819 (Zurich, 1987)

'Franz Schubert und die Gesellschaft der Musikfreunde in Wien', *Schubert Kongreß Wien 1978. Bericht*, ed. Otto Brusatti (Graz, 1979), pp. 23–36

Gott erhalte! Joseph Haydns Kaiserhymne (Vienna, 1982)

'"Grundsäulen der Tonkunst" – Von der Enstehung des Bildes der klassischen Trias', *Wiener Klassik. Ein musikgeschichtlicher Begriff in Diskussion*, ed. Gernot Gruber. Wiener Musikwissenschaftliche Beiträge, 21 (Vienna, 2002), pp. 53–63

'Nachrichten zur Musikpflege in der gräflichen Familie Harrach', *Haydn Yearbook*, 10 (1978), pp. 36–44

'Schubert's Position in Viennese Musical Life', *19th-Century Music*, 3 (1979), pp. 106–13

Boženek, Karel, 'Beethoven und das Adelsgeschlecht Lichnowsky', *Ludwig van Beethoven im Herzen Europas*, eds. Oldřich Pulkert and Hans-Werner Küthen (Prague, 2000), pp. 119–70

Brandenburg, Sieghard. *Ludwig van Beethoven. Briefwechselausgabe*, 7 vols. (Munich, 1996–8)

Brauneis, Walther. '" . . . composta per festeggiare il sovvenire di un grand uomo." Beethovens "Eroica" als Hommage des Fürsten Franz Joseph Maximilian von Lobkowitz für Louis Ferdinand von Preußen', *Jahrbuch des Vereins für Geschichte der Stadt Wien*, 52–3 (1996–7), pp. 53–88

Brook, Barry S. (ed. in chief). *The Symphony 1720–1840. Reference Volume: Contents of the Set and Collected Thematic Indexes* (New York, 1986)

Brown, A. Peter. 'The trumpet overture and sinfonia in Vienna (1715- 1822): rise, decline and reformulation', *Music in Eighteenth-Century Austria*, ed. David Wyn Jones (Cambridge, 1996), pp. 13–69

Brown, Clive. *Louis Spohr. A Critical Biography* (Cambridge, 1984)

Bryan, Paul. *Johann Wanhal, Viennese Symphonist. His Life and His Musical Environment* (Stuyvesant, NY, 1997)

Constapel, Britta. *Der Musikverlag Johann André in Offenbach am Main: Studien zur Verlagstätigkeit von Johann Anton André und Verzeichnis der Musikalien von 1800 bis 1840* (Tutzing, 1998)

Cooper, Barry. *Beethoven* (Oxford, 2000)

Beethoven and the Creative Process (Oxford, 1990)

The Beethoven Compendium. A Guide to Beethoven's Life and Music (London, 1991)

'Newly Identified Sketches for Beethoven's Tenth Symphony', *Music and Letters*, 66 (1985), pp. 9–18

Czerny, Carl, 'Recollections from my life', trans. Ernest Saunders, *Musical Quarterly*, 42 (1956), p. 302–17

DeNora, Tia. *Beethoven and the Construction of Genius: Musical Politics in Vienna 1792–1803* (Berkeley, 1995)

Deutsch, Otto Erich. *Schubert. A Documentary Biography*, trans. Eric Blom (London, 1946)

Schubert: Memoirs by his friends, trans. Rosamund Ley and John Nowell (London, 1958)

Dittersdorf, Carl Ditters von. *Lebensbeschreibung. Seinem Sohne in die Feder diktirt*, ed. Norbert Miller (Munich, 1967); translation by A. D. Coleridge, *The Autobiography of Karl von Dittersdorf, Dictated to His Son* (London, 1896)

Dürr, Walther, 'Schubert in seiner Welt', *Schubert Handbuch*, eds. Walther Dürr and Andreas Krause (Kassel, 1997), pp. 1–76

Edge, Dexter. 'Mozart's Viennese Copyists', (PhD diss., University of Southern California, 2001)

Review of Mary Sue Morrow, *Concert Life in Haydn's Vienna: Aspects of a Developing Musical and Social Institution* (Stuyvesant, NY, 1989), *Haydn Yearbook*, 16 (1992), pp. 108–66

Einstein, Alfred (ed.), *Lebensläufe deutscher Musiker von ihnen selbst erzählt. 3/4 Adalbert Gyrowetz (1763–1850)* (Leipzig, 1915)

Eybl, Martin. 'Franz Bernhard Ritter von Keeß – Sammler, Mäzen und Organisator', *Österreichische Musik – Musik in Österreich. Beiträge zur Musikgeschichte Mitteleuropas*, ed. Elisabeth Theresia Hilscher, Wiener Veröffentlichungen zur Musikwissenschaft, 34 (Tutzing, 1998), pp. 239–50

Feder, Georg, 'Drei Publikationen zur Haydn-Forschung', *Die Musikforschung*, 17 (1964), pp. 62–6

Fisher, Stephen C. 'Die C-dur-Symphonie KV⁶ Anh. C11.14: ein Jugendwerk Anton Eberls', *Mitteilungen der Internationalen Stiftung Mozarteum*, 31 (1983), pp. 21–6

Flotzinger, Rudolf. 'Herkunft und Bedeutung des Ausdrucks "(Wiener) Klassik"', *Wiener Klassik. Ein musikgeschichtlicher Begriff in Diskussion*, ed. Gernot Gruber. Wiener Musikwissenschaftliche Beiträge, 21 (Vienna, 2002), pp. 41–52

Forbes, Elliot (rev. and ed.). *Thayer's Life of Beethoven* (Princeton, New Jersey, 1967)

Fojtíková, Jana, and Tomislav Volek, 'Die Beethoveniana der Lobkowitz- Musiksammlung und ihre Kopisten', *Beethoven und Böhmen*, eds. Sieghard Brandenburg and Martella Gutiérrez-Denhoff (Bonn, 1988), pp. 219–58

Forbes, Elliot (ed.). *Thayer's Life of Beethoven* (Princeton, 1964)

Freeman, Robert N. *The Practice of Music at Melk Abbey* (Vienna, 1989)

Fuchs, Ingrid. 'The Glorious Moment – Beethoven and the Congress of Vienna', *Denmark and the Dancing Congress of Vienna. Playing for Denmark's Future* (Copenhagen, 2002), pp. 182–96

Gates-Coon, Rebecca. *The Landed Estates of the Esterházy Princes. Hungary during the Reforms of Maria Theresia and Joseph II* (Baltimore, 1994)

Gerber, Ernst Ludwig. *Historisch-biographisches Lexikon der Tonkünstler* (Leipzig, 1790–92)

Gibbs, Christopher H. '"Poor Schubert": images and legends of the composer', *Cambridge Companion to Schubert*, ed. Christopher H. Gibbs (Cambridge, 1997), pp. 36–55

Hadamowsky, Franz. *Wien. Theater Geschichte von Anfängen bis zum Ende des Ersten Weltkriegs* (Vienna, 1994)

Handlos, Martha. 'Die Wiener Concerts Spirituels (1819–1848)', *Österreichische Musik – Musik in Österreich. Beiträge zur Musikgeschichte Mitteleuropas*, ed. Elisabeth Theresia Hilscher, Wiener Veröffentlichungen zur Musikwissenschaft, 34 (Tutzing, 1998), pp. 283–320

'Studien zum Wiener Konzertleben im Vormärz' (PhD diss., University of Vienna, 1985)

Hanslick, Eduard. *Geschichte des Concertwesens in Wien*, 2nd edn., 2 vols. (Vienna, 1897)

Hanson, Alice M. *Musical Life in Biedermeier Vienna* (Cambridge, 1985)

Hausner, Henry H. 'Franz Anton Hoffmeister (1754–1812): Komponist und Verleger', *Mitteilungen der Internationalen Stiftung Mozarteum*, 38 (1990), pp. 155–62

Hellyer, Roger, 'The Wind Ensembles of the Esterházy Princes, 1761–1813', *Haydn Yearbook*, 15 (1985), pp. 5–92

Heartz, Daniel. *Haydn. Mozart, and the Viennese School, 1740–1780* (New York, 1995)

Horányi, Mátyás. *The Magnificence of Eszterháza* (Budapest, 1962)

Ingrao, Charles. *The Habsburg Monarchy 1618–1815* (Cambridge, 1994)

Jones, David Wyn. *Beethoven. Pastoral Symphony* (Cambridge, 1995)

The Life of Beethoven (Cambridge, 1998)

'Why did Mozart compose his last three Symphonies? Some new Hypotheses', *Music Review*, 51 (1990), pp. 280–89

Kerman, Joseph (ed.). *Ludwig van Beethoven. Autograph Miscellany from circa 1786 to 1799. British Museum Additional Manuscript 29801, ff. 39–162 (The 'Kafka' Sketchbook)*, 2 vols. (London, 1970)

Kim, Jin-Ah. *Anton Eberls Sinfonien in ihrer Zeit. Hermeneutisch-analytische Aspekte der Sinfonik 1770–1830*, Schriften zur Musikwissenschaft aus Münster, vol. 17 (Eisenach, 2002)

Klein, Rudolf. *Beethovenstätten in Österreich* (Vienna, 1970)

'Musik im Augarten', *Österreichische Musikzeitschrift*, 26 (1973), pp. 239–48

Kunze, Stefan (ed.), *Ludwig van Beethoven: Die Werke im Spiegel seiner Zeit. Gesammelte Konzertberichte und Rezensionen bis 1830* (Laaber, 1987)

Landenburger, Michael. 'Der Wiener Kongreß im Spiegel der Musik', *Beethoven. Zwischen Revolution und Restauration*, ed. Helga Lühning and Sieghard Brandenburg (Bonn, 1989), pp. 275–306

Landon, H. C. Robbins (ed.). *Beethoven. A Documentary Study* (London, 1970)

Haydn: Chronicle and Works, 5 vols. (London, 1976–80)

Mozart. The Golden Years (London, 1989)

'Two Orchestral Works Wrongly Attributed to Mozart', *Music Review*, 17 (1956), pp. 29–34

Larsen, Jens Peter (ed.). *Three Haydn Catalogues*, 2nd edn. (New York, 1979)

LaRue, Jan. 'A "Hail and Farwell" Quodlibet Symphony', *Music and Letters*, 37 (1956), pp. 250–59

Lawson, Colin. *Mozart. Clarinet Concerto* (Cambridge, 1996)

Leux-Henschen, Irmgard. *Joseph Martin Kraus in seinen Briefen* (Stockholm, 1978)

Levy, David Benjamin. *Beethoven: The Ninth Symphony* (New York, 1995)

Link, Dorothea. *The National Court Theatre in Mozart's Vienna: sources and documents* (Oxford, 1998)

Macartney, C. A. *The House of Austria. The Later Phase 1790–1918* (Edinburgh, 1978)

Macek, Jaroslav, 'Die Musik bei den Lobkowitz', *Ludwig van Beethoven im Herzen Europas*, eds. Oldřich Pulkert and Hans-Werner Küthen (Prague, 2000), pp. 171–216

'Franz Joseph Maximilian Lobkowitz: Musikfreund und Kunstmäzen', *Beethoven und Böhmen*, ed. Sieghard Brandenburg and Martella Gutiérrez-Denhoff (Bonn, 1988), pp. 147–201

Matthäus, Wolfgang. *Johann André. Musikverlag zu Offenbach am Main. Verlagsgeschichte und Bibliographie 1772–1800* (Tutzing, 1973)

Moore, Julia. 'Beethoven and Inflation', *Beethoven Forum*, 1 (1992), pp. 191–223

'Beethoven and musical economics' (PhD diss., University of Illinois at Urbana-Champaign, 1987)

Morrow, Mary Sue. *Concert Life in Haydn's Vienna: Aspects of a Developing Musical and Social Institution* (Stuyvesant, NY, 1989)

'Making it in the Big City: Beethoven's First Decade in Vienna', *Beethoven Journal*, 10 (1995), pp. 46–52

'Of Unity and Passion: The Aesthetics of Concert Criticism in Early Nineteenth-Century Vienna', *19th-Century Music*, 13 (1990), pp. 193–206

Murray, Sterling E. *The Music of Antonio Rosetti (Anton Rösler) ca. 1750–1792. A Thematic Catalog* (Michigan, 1996)

Myslík, Antonín. 'Repertoire und Besetzung der Harmoniemusiken an den Höfen Schwarzenberg, Pachta und Clam-Gallas', *Haydn Yearbook*, 10 (1978), pp. 110–19

Newbould, Brian. *Schubert and the Symphony. A New Perspective* (Surbiton, 1992)

Padrta, Karel. *Franz Krommer (1759–1831). Thematischer Katalog seiner musikalischen Werke* (Prague, 1997)

Pandi, Marianne, and Fritz Schmidt, 'Musik zur Zeit Haydns und Beethovens in der Preßburger Zeitung', *Haydn Yearbook*, 8 (1971), pp. 165–265

Pauly, Reinhard G. 'The Reforms of Church Music under Joseph II', *Musical Quarterly*, 43 (1957), pp. 372–82

Perger, Richard von, and Robert Hirschfeld. *Geschichte der K. K. Gesellschaft der Musikfreunde in Wien. 1. Abteilung: 1812–1870* (Vienna, 1912)

Pohl, Carl Ferdinand. *Denkschrift aus Anlass des hundertjährigen Bestehens der Tonkünstler-Societät, im Jahre 1862 reorganisirt als "Haydn", Witwen- und Waisen-Versorgungs-Verein der Tonkünstler in Wien* (Vienna, 1871)

Die Gesellschaft der Musikfreunde des österreichischen Kaiserstaates und ihr Conservatorium (Vienna, 1871)

Poštolka, Milan. *Leopold Koželuch: život a dílo* (Prague, 1964)

'Thematisches Verzeichnis der Sinfonien Pavel Vranickýs', *Miscellanea musicologica*, 20 (1967), pp. 101–27

Prod'homme, J.-G. 'From the unpublished Autobiography of Antoine Reicha', *Musical Quarterly*, 22 (1936), pp. 339–53

Pulkert, Oldřich, and Hans-Werner Küthen, *Ludwig van Beethoven im Herzen Europas* (Prague, 2000)

Radant, Else. 'The Diaries of Joseph Carl Rosenbaum 1770–1829', *Haydn Yearbook*, 5 (1968), whole issue

Rasch, Rudolf, 'Basic Concepts', *Music Publishing in Europe 1600–1900. Concepts and Issues. Bibliography*, ed. Rudolf Rasch (Berlin, 2005), pp. 13–46

Reichardt, Johann Friedrich. *Vertraute Briefe geschrieben auf einer Reise nach Wien und den Österreichischen Staaten zu Ende des Jahres 1808 und zu Anfang 1809*, ed. Gustav Gugitz, 2 vols. (Munich, 1915)

Rice, John A. *Empress Marie Therese and Music at the Viennese Court 1792–1807* (Cambridge, 2003)

Ridgewell, Rupert. 'Economic Aspects: The Artaria Case', *Music Publishing in Europe 1600–1900. Concepts and Issues. Bibliography*, ed. Rudolf Rasch (Berlin, 2005), pp. 89–113

'Music Printing in Mozart's Vienna: the Artaria Press, 1778–1794', *Fontes Artis Musicae*, 48 (2001), pp. 217–36

Riedel, Friedrich W. (ed.). *Der Göttweiger Thematische Katalog von 1830*, 2 vols. (Munich, 1979)

Riepe, Juliane. 'Eine neue Quelle zum Repertoire der Bonner Hofkapelle im späten 18. Jahrhundert', *Archiv für Musikwissenschaft*, 60 (2003), pp. 97–114.

Rumph, Stephen. *Beethoven after Napoleon. Political Romanticism in the Late Works* (Berkeley, 2004)

Scholes, Percy A. *An Eighteenth-Century Musical Tour in Central Europe and the Netherlands. Dr. Burney's Musical Tours in Europe vol. 2* (London, 1959)

Schönfeld, Johann Ferdinand von. *Jahrbuch der Tonkunst von Wien und Prag* (Vienna, 1796); facsimile edn. (Munich, 1976). Partial translation in Elaine Sisman (ed.), *Haydn and His World* (Princeton, 1997), pp. 289–320

Schreiber, Ulrich. 'Glücklose Liebe zum Theater. Die Bühnenwerke', *Schubert Handbuch*, eds. Walther Dürr and Andreas Krause (Kassel, 1997), pp. 304–44

Sehnal, Jiří. 'Die adeligen Musikkapellen im 17. und 18. Jahrhundert in Mähren', *Studies in Music History presented to H. C. Robbins Landon on his seventieth birthday*, Otto Biba and David Wyn Jones (eds.) (London, 1996), pp. 195–217

'Die Musikkapelle des Olmützer Erzbischofs Anton Theodor Colloredo-Waldsee 1777–1811', *Haydn Yearbook*, 10 (1978), pp. 132–50

Seifert, Herbert. 'Die Verbindungen der Familie Erdödy zur Musik', *Haydn Yearbook*, 10 (1978), pp. 151–63

Senner, Wayne M., Robin Wallace, and William Meredith (eds.), *The Critical Reception of Beethoven's Compositions by His German Contemporaries*, 2 vols. (Lincoln, Nebraska, 1999)

Seyfried, Bettina von. *Ignaz Ritter von Seyfried. Thematisch- Bibliographisches Verzeichnis. Aspekte der Biographie und des Werkes* (Frankfurt, 1990)

Sherman, Charles H., and T. Donley Thomas. *Johann Michael Haydn (1737–1806): A Chronological Thematic Catalogue of His Works* (Stuyvesant, NY, 1993)

Sipe, Thomas. *Beethoven. Eroica Symphony* (Cambridge, 1998)

Sisman, Elaine R. 'Haydn's Theater Symphonies', *Journal of the American Musicological Society*, 43 (1990), pp. 292–352

Sisman, Elaine R. *Haydn and the Classical Variation* (Cambridge, Mass., 1993) 'Haydn's Theater Symphonies', *Journal of the American Musicological Society*, 43 (1990), 292–352

Solomon, Maynard. 'Beethoven's Tagebuch of 1812–1818', *Beethoven Studies 3*, ed. A. Tyson (Cambridge, 1982), pp. 193–288

Šotolová, Olga. *Antonín Rejcha. A Biography and Thematic Catalogue*, trans. Deryck Viney (Prague, 1990)

Spitzer, John and Neal Zaslaw. *The Birth of the Orchestra. History of an Institution, 1650–1815* (Oxford, 2004)

[Spohr, Louis.] *Louis Spohr's Autobiography. Translated from the German*, 2 vols. (London, 1865)

Statuten der Gesellschaft der Musikfreunde des österreichischen Kaiserstaates Wien (Vienna, 1814)

Steinbeck, Wolfram. '"Und über das Ganze eine Romantik ausgegossen." Die Sinfonien', *Schubert Handbuch*, ed. Walther Dürr and Andreas Krause (Kassel, 1997), pp. 550–669

Stekl, Hannes. 'Harmoniemusik und "türkische Banda" des Fürstenhauses Liechtenstein', *Haydn Yearbook*, 10 (1978), pp. 164–75

Tomek, Peter, 'Die Musik an den Wiener Vorstadttheatern 1776–1825' (PhD diss., University of Vienna, 1989)

Tyson, Alan. 'Notes on Five of Beethoven's Copyists', *Journal of the American Musicological Society*, 23 (1970), pp. 439–71

Ullrich, Hermann, 'Aus vormärzlichen Konzertsälen Wiens', *Jahrbuch des Vereins für Geschichte der Stadt Wien*, 28 (1972), pp. 106–30

Volek, Tomasek, and Jaroslav Macek, 'Beethoven und Fürst Lobkowitz', *Beethoven und Böhmen. Beiträge zu Biographie und Wirkungsgeschichte Beethovens*, eds., Sieghard Brandenburg and Martella Gutiérrez-Denhoff (Bonn, 1988), pp. 203–17

Waidelich, Till Gerrit. *Franz Schubert. Dokumente 1817–1830* (Tutzing, 1998)

Wallace, Robin. *Beethoven's Critics. Aesthetic dilemmas and resolution during the composer's lifetime* (Cambridge, 1986)

Weber, William. *Music and the Middle Class* (London, 1975)

Weinmann, Alexander. *Die Anzeigen des Kopiaturbetriebes Johann Traeg in der Wiener Zeitung zwischen 1782 und 1805*, Wiener Archivstudien, 6 (Vienna, 1981)

Die Wiener Verlagswerke von Franz Anton Hoffmeister, Beiträge zur Geschichte des Alt-Wiener Musikverlages, Reihe 2, Folge 8 (Vienna, 1964)

Johann Traeg. *Die Musikalienverzeichnisse von 1799 und 1804 (Handschrift und Sortiment)*, Beiträge zur Geschichte des Alt-Wiener Musikverlages, Reihe 2, Folge 17 (Vienna, 1973)

Verlagsverzeichnis Johann Traeg (und Sohn), 2nd ed., Beiträge zur Geschichte des Alt-Wiener Musikverlages, Reihe 2, Folge 16 (Vienna, 1973)

Verzeichnis der Musikalien aus dem K. K. Hoftheater-Musik-Verlag, Beiträge zur Geschichte des Alt-Wiener Musikverlages, Reihe 2, Folge 6 (Vienna, 1982)

Verzeichnis der Verlagswerke des Musikalischen Magazins in Wien, 1784–1802. Leopold (und Anton) Kozeluch, 2nd edn., Beiträge zur Geschichte des Alt-Wiener Musikverlages, Reihe 2, Folge 1a (Vienna, 1979)

Vollständiges Verlagsverzeichnis Artaria & Comp., Beiträge zur Geschichte des Alt-Wiener Musikverlages, Reihe 2, Folge 2 (Vienna, 1952)

'Vollständiges Verlagsverzeichnis der Musikalien des Kunst- und Industrie-Comptoirs in Wien, 1801–1819', *Studien zur Musikwissenschaft*, 22 (1955), pp. 217–252

Vollständiges Verlagsverzeichnis Senefelder, Steiner, Haslinger. Band 1: A. Senefelder, Chemische Druckerey, S. A. Steiner, S. A. Steiner & Comp. (Wien 1803–1826) (Munich, 1979)

[Wiener] Allgemeine musikalische Zeitung, 1–8 (1817–24)

Wiener Zeitung, 1790–1827

Will, Richard. *The Characteristic Symphony in the Age of Haydn and Beethoven* (Cambridge, 2002)

'The Nature of the Pastoral Symphony', *Beethoven Forum*, 9 (2002), pp. 205–15

Wimmer, Sabine Constanze. 'Die Hofmusikkapelle in Wien unter der Leitung von Antonio Salieri von 1778–1824' (MPhil diss., University of Vienna, 1998)

Woodfield, Ian, 'John Bland: London Retailer of the Music of Haydn and Mozart', *Music and Letters*, 81 (2000), pp. 210–44

Wurzbach, Constant. *Biographisches Lexikon des Kaiserthums Oesterreich*, 60 vols (Vienna, 1856–91)

Zaslaw, Neal. 'Mozart, Haydn and the *Sinfonia da Chiesa*', *Journal of Musicology*, 1 (1982), pp. 95–124

Mozart's Symphonies. Context, Performance Practice, Reception (Oxford, 1989)

Index